THE ECLIPSE OF WESTERN NATIONS

HOW MISMANAGED HUMAN AND DEMOCRATIC RIGHTS CAN DESTROY CIVILIZATIONS

RAPHAEL ISRAELI

Strategic Book Publishing and Rights Co.

Strategic Book Publishing and Rights Co., LLC
USA | Singapore
www.sbpra.net

For information about special discounts for bulk purchases, please contact Strategic Book Publishing and Rights Co., LLC Special Sales, at bookorder@sbpra.net.

ISBN: 978-1-951530-21-1

CONTENTS

This is the last part of a quartet by this author.

The Waning of Western Civilizations, comprising:

Retreating from the Mirage of Multi-Culturalism?
published in 2018

Misnomers and Cultural Choices
published in 2019

Suicidal Democracy
also published in 2019; and

The Eclipse of Western Nations
published in 2020.

FOREWORD AS ACKNOWLEDGMENT

Weren't those the days when we all dreamt of remote and romantic countries and civilizations, unique beauties and elegant princes, charming maidens strolling around green meadows pursued by amorous young officers in their resplendent navy uniforms? Our eyes sought the aesthetic sights for their delight, the unattainable goals to dream about, and pictures to depict for us what we could not see or imagine in our minds; or else we undertook to learn, or at least just read about other countries by the means of attractive story tellers, original or translated, who knew how to lure and mystify us, charm or enchant us, to make us immediate candidates for travel to other lands. The pretexts for undertaking travel, which amounted to hardship, was difficult to come by for many, since to pick up and journey to a faraway land was not a thing of routine, nor within the power of many, and to carry out an endeavor of this sort necessitated many justifications, for who would abandon the peace and routine of a tranquil life to venture into difficulty, uncertainty, adventure, absence from work or career and possibly run the risk to his or her life? There had to be decidedly some overwhelming reasons for that.

Pretexts and reasons are many when individuals or groups launch their journey, unlike states which initiate their massive march into a neighboring country for "national" purposes or to satisfy the greed or the lust for territory of their leaders. Individual motivations include: personal curiosity, business interest, cultural interaction, linguistic training, vacation, immigration, studying or working opportunities and the like. But when one lands today in downtown Stockholm or Paris, one asks oneself: where is the Scandinavia of Hans Christian Andersen that he came to visit? Where are the beauties that he had dreamt about? And where are the streets of Paris that Victor Hugo had depicted masterfully? He wonders because he had a certain idea of Scandinavia or of Paris that he came to visit, but cannot find it in view of the multitude of different faces that he encounters in the streets; because to revel in a stunning black beauty, or a Mediterranean, or an Asian –style movie celebrity, he would have gone to Togo or Nigeria, or Kuwait or Thailand. In short, when one entertains a certain image of a country or culture one by necessity feels frustration when he or she cannot materialize it. So it goes for the art, material culture, people's conduct and all other cultural traits that one seeks in other places and cultures that raise his or her curiosity. It is like someone buying a ticket for a Mozart concert, but the orchestra plays jazz and rock music. That is beautiful, harmonious and pleasant to be sure, but that was not what he or she had expected and paid for. Or, more pertinently, you want to hear Toscanini, but instead you get Fareed al-Atrash. Both are great, but your cultural taste is slightly different from what you get.

One would have noticed that non-Western artists, scholars, scientists, clerics and cultural performers are customarily adored in the mainstream West and given more prominence than their Western counterparts, in a hardly masked and condescending attempt to patronize the others in order to adopt them as the worthy "others" to be part of us in our altered multi-cultural and politically correct world. In the same vein, instead of enjoying the Paris museum-city, an occasional visitor may find himself lamenting the downgrading of the image of the local glamorous Opera House, when an immigrant is caught squatting on the sumptuous stairs of that edifice with a broken beer bottle in his hand, scaring off the luxuriously dressed visitors, and hideously demonstrating the "other" frontline of the evolving new French "Culture" which is encountered by the fans of French Civilization who came from the outside to Paris to live it, visit it and delight in it. So, while many French people have resigned to the idea that this is the new multi-cultural France, others dare to complain that they miss the old France that has been waning away, and some among them even mobilize their audacity to rebel against the political correctness of the hour, refuse to see their beloved culture vanish, even at the risk of being dubbed "racists", "Islamophobes" and what have you, arguing that just as foreign immigrants in Paris nurture their imported cultures in the name of democracy, equality and multi-culturalism, so do they erode the cultural prevalence of their own native millennial civilization on which they were brought up and which made the fame of their country, and deprive them of their equal right to preserve their cherished patrimony.

When one wanders in certain areas of Paris, and more so in Marseille, one feels in Algiers or in Marrakesh. You would say:" What is wrong with that? That makes for the human and cultural richness and diversity of the country". Yes, for sure, but what about keeping the original French atmosphere apart from the Algerian ambience, each in its natural environment where it had evolved, and where it can be viewed and enjoyed by the people who like it and appreciate it?; it is not necessary to force it down the throats of natives of other places who dislike it because it disturbs their sense of order and aesthetics, confuses their familiar smells and tastes with new intruding ones, that they do not necessarily like. This is especially so when this denies native population of any country the sense of security that they used to feel in their culture and natural environment before it was "invaded" and "polluted" by a foreign accretion that not everyone appreciates. Of course, a taste of foreign culture can always be invited in and remunerated as a one-shot injection of an imported show biz, or as part of an exhibit or fair of international cultural relations, but when a cultural operation or an entire cultural environment is permanently transplanted into another culture, that is a certain recipe for discontent, bigotry, racist explosions, crime and violence.

A century and a half have elapsed since the Civil War and the ensuing liberation from slavery had unfolded in America, but the residue of the Blacks' justified sense of discrimination has been extant, sound and kicking, costing disruption in American society and just accusations of racism and police violence that are hurled right and left despite the tremendous advances in human rights and civil equality that have been instituted in American society and political system over the years. Yes, jazz music and basketball teams have been dominated by Black Americans for many years, but that did not wipe out white supremacists nor eliminate police violence in Ferguson, Charlottesville, and their likes. When a permanent bias, prejudice, grudge or discontent is so deeply ingrained, it can be occasionally overlooked as part of our conventional manners and courtesies, so as to make believe that we are civilized, democratically and civil-right inclined, and have learned how to behave in public and to avoid unpleasant suspicions of racism and bigotry. But when the chips are down and individuals are hard pressed, there occur outbursts of rage, hatred and outright racist violence. That is human nature, abhorrent as it may be, but it is an unchanging fact. It is it that we have to address, not the lofty but impractical ideals of equality and harmony between all humans, everywhere and at all times.

The current migratory wave from the Islamic to the European world has occasioned a growing mix of peoples and cultures on a limited territory, with the concurrent rise in frictions, fears and suspicions of the native populations from the growing insecurity, crime, change of environment, cultural alienation and estrangement that make many native Europeans strangers in their own country, and many European women who had been groomed to circulate freely and fearlessly in their city, to now avoid public transportation at certain hours, or certain neighborhoods altogether. In other European cities, citizens who have been disturbed by neighboring mosques' noisy calls for prayer at odd hours, are either embarrassed to complain for fear of being ridiculed or ignored, or accused of Islamophobia. Some countries like Switzerland have banned minarets which produce the most noisy disturbance, but how many European authorities have the guts to enforce such measures in the face of the voting Muslim constituencies? For that same reason most European governments ignore the new waves of anti-Semitism in the continent that are partly triggered or supported by Muslim organizations, including the most "moderate" among them. The influx of alien cultures into Europe and their implantation into the local environment, has so much altered it that it has become a hybrid of many things, just not what it used to be.

The world cannot be permitted to become one boring place where all the ancient cultures (European, Buddhist, Chinese, Arab, Jewish etc.) are subsumed under one hybrid and amorphic amalgam of eclectic elements taken from various cultures, at the expense of the established civilizational heritage that has enriched humanity for so many centuries. It cannot be allowed either to let the frictions between cultures, with the concomitant rise in violence and crime, cause what used to be safe and agreeably habitable Europe metastize into a dangerous space pregnant with the threat of violence, crime, rape etc. I am aware that the danger of engulfing Western cultures with invading human floods from Afro-Asia is not matched by a similar reverse trend into the less developed world, since fewer, if any, people would move there from the West, who can alter its cultural patrimony, making the danger of eclipsed national cultures unilateral in the West due to the Muslim influx into Europe, accompanied by the intention to change it, and the determination not to adapt to it but the other way round. This trend in itself will facilitate the Muslim endeavor and complicate Western defense against it. For Muslims who know that their imported cultural heritage will remain intact at its source, while they are altering the West to their tune, will scoff at any attempt to resist their "innocent" inter-cultural effort to communicate "peacefully" with other nations, while Europeans will continue to watch helplessly and hopelessly, as they do now, while their glorious cultures of the past are sinkink into oblivion.

I am extremely obliged to my friend, Gisele Littman, who afforded me the opportunity to isolate myself in her resplendent *Maison du Lac* on the shore of the Lake of Geneva during this Indian Summer to launch the first reflections on this volume. The bulk of the research and writing, however, will be pursued at my home institution, The Harry Truman Research for the Promotion of Peace at the Hebrew University, Jerusalem. To it I am deeply indebted for its scholarly ambience, collegial cross-fertilization and secretarial assistance, though the entire responsibility for my errors and misjudgments will remain solely and exclusively mine.

Geneva, 1 September, 2019

INTRODUCTION

What is at Stake?

There is almost no nation on earth which does not count among its members a minority or a plurality of minorities. Where there are minorities, conflicting interests between them and the ruling majorities emerge, like in the present situation in Europe, where the over 30 million Muslim minorities experience difficulties; or even worse, when minorities rule their countries like the *Ba'ath* in Iraq under Saddam and under Assad in Syria, or in several African countries where minority tribes have emerged at the top of their society's ladder, turn the divergence of interests into a permanent conflict. The devices of democracy and human rights, which were thought to nullify these contradictions once they established equality between all people regardless of origin, gender, racial, linguistic, national, ethnic or religious differences, simply do not work for the most part, for there is almost no place in the world where minorities do not complain about the negative and humiliating discrimination prevailing against them, and more often than not they rise in defense of what they view as their rights, often resorting to violence.

Due to the open and continuous interaction between various peoples around the globe, which often ends up in associations and family ties among them, it is practically impossible to prevent the growth of minorities at all times in all cultures and countries. The problem is one of proportions: a minority, or several minorities of a negligible percentage within the general population, are digestible and will always be too insignificant as to demand group rights, short of which a minority will not rise to become a national or social problem; a noticeable minority, which is self-confident enough to insist on its distinguishing characteristics (ethnic, religious, linguistic, and especially national) and on legitimately expressing them in public, would inevitably trigger objections by the majority, and the larger it is the more threatening it may appear to the majority, who starts fearing for its hegemony and from the competition and challenge to it. When a minority combines several of those characteristics in one (ethnic and religious, linguistic and national, racial and alien, or any amalgamation of all or part of those) the frictions might be aggravated and the ensuing violence become more disruptive and frequent, especially when the racial differences carry the stigma of color, which makes the divergence inescapable and impossible to hide or to disguise.

When the demographic situation is innate, from time immemorial, like in the Americas, where the ruling white majorities had colonized the natives and prevailed upon them, the countries have no choice than, through a slow and gradual integration between the various populations, attain some sort of harmonious co-existence into one society and political system which over the generations amalgamates into one, like in Brazil, Australia or New Zealand. But when societies, like in Europe today, consciously and willingly bring upon themselves the plight of a multi-cultural society with its built-in contradictions and inevitable clashes and conflicts, countries of shelter, just because of the democratic and human penchant to grant asylum to the needy, or of a demographic calculation of future human resources needs in a dwindling pro-creative trend in Europe, invite (or allow) refugees (genuine and fake) and various persecuted peoples into their countries, they unwittingly pave the road for future clashes and disruptions into their systems and sign the death writ for their cultures. For, while small and gradual foreign accretions of people into their societies are absorbable without many cramps of indigestion, larger portions of incoming immigrants may, as they do today, cause severe stomach disruptions, especially when coming from backgrounds which seek to impose a change on the host culture rather than adapt the guest culture to its hosts. This point has been dramatically illustrated in the compared European experience with Islam to the Islamic minority in China, for example, though in the one Islam is almost native and in the other it is migratory. To wit, the larger demographically Muslim minority in Europe (an average of 6-7%, with a peak of over 10% in France, compared to less than 2% in China), the more insistent the demand of Muslims that the host countries adapt to Islamic law and to Muslim customs, like forced marriages and "honor killings" in the families. In Europe, the Islamic assault on the host culture in order to *Islamize* it, is visible and ubiquitous while in China Muslims would not even dare to attack any element of it and are well content if they are left alone in their Muslim regions, counties and localities. The fact that the prisoner rate of Muslims in European prisons is far beyond their proportion in the population demonstrates that a basic problem exists there of Muslim minorities refusing to accept state law and seeking to gain the prevalence of their own legal and customary system in the countries where they had sought refuge.

Unlike the Western idea of nation states, which organize human societies into political entities, the world of Islam is conceived of in terms of a universal *umma*, a world community whose borders stretch to whatever territory is conquered or converted into Islam, and the establishment of a new Muslim community of immigrants in an as yet non-Muslim territory is only the harbinger of Islamizing its population in the final analysis. Hence the visible clashes between the host cultures which attempt to preserve their patrimony and the Muslim guests who defy them and pose their imported Islamic culture as the desired alternative. Hence also the declarations of many of the radical leaders among them, that they came to Europe to alter it, not to be altered by it. Those statements are serious and must be taken seriously. For in the Muslim view, if there is to reign one harmonious culture to encompass all peoples, it is obvious that it must be Islam, the faith of the future, which will by necessity replace the exhausted waning Western civilization of the past. Indeed, unlike a Buddhist, an Armenian or a Jew, who immigrate to France in order to adapt to it and accept its rules, many Muslims view their move into it as a first step toward changing it to their tune. The clashes about imposing the veil and other Islamic items of dress, minarets, honor killings, public Muslim prayers in the central squares of major European cities, unlicensed selling stands in the streets, and other opportunities to defy with impunity the local culture, much to the displeasure of the native hosts, are all the by products of these contradictions, which sometimes escalate into violence.

The Western model of nation is usually upheld by specific customs, a culture, a shared history, a language, often a religion and a patriotic attachment to a land, to create a link between a nation-state and its citizens. Muslims who immigrate anywhere operate under the assumption that any territory inhabited, and especially when ruled by Muslims, is part of *terra Islamica* where the *umma* dwells, therefore they strive to turn every place where a Muslim community is established into Muslim territory. In practice, this is what has happened in Marseille, Amsterdam, Malmo and Dearborn, where strong Muslim communities are so deeply entrenched, that they impose their own ambience on the place, including their style of dress, often imported language and discourse, and where almost always alien tastes and smells and foreign language signs dominate, so much as to make some parts of those locations inaccessible, or at least unattractive, to native French, Dutch, Swedes and Americans. Those places can also send their elected representatives, taking advantage of the prevailing universal suffrage and of democratic rules, to parliament and help tilt traditional policies that were part of the national patrimony to new directions dictated by the new immigrants. One might argue that that is precisely what democracy is all about, to reflect the changing will of the voters, but this is also precisely what is argued here: that immigrants, especially of the Muslim brand can "pollute" by distorting the national will and its culture and tradition. The French and the Swede authorities knowingly and willingly capitulate to Muslim demands, thus causing right wing parties to rise and the traditionally large parties to dwindle, but the Hungarians and the Czechs refuse to yield to this outside imposition of such changes and continue to reject the massive influx of Muslims who might seek to impose such changes. Extra-Western authoritarian countries, like China and Russia, realizing the danger of such impositions from the outside, and facing themselves domestic Muslim unrest and learning from the sorry experience of the Western liberal democracies and Israel, which are paying the price of their humanism and liberalism, refuse to let in an uncontrollable influx of Muslims. And so as not to appear "Islamophobes", or "racists" (although Muslims are not a race), the entire façade of the debate has shifted to the "immigration policy" in general, not specifically to Muslims, under the same justifiable pretext of "preserving the national character" of their country, so as to demonstrate their awareness and wariness that immigration can alter the national essence of their country.

There are many Westerners in the modern era who deprecate religion. That is their right, but they cannot uphold the right of Muslim immigrants to build mosques, to spread their faith and sing its praise in public, which is one of the matter-of-course permissibles in liberal democracies, and at the same time derogate a Christian leader who wishes to keep his nation Christian, or a Jewish leader who struggles to preserve the Jewish nature of his state and legislates for that purpose accordingly. Moreover, as long as Muslim countries prohibit freedom of religion and treat Muslim renegades as heretic traitors deserving capital penalty, there is no way to make them change their minds unless their missionary efforts are curtailed in return in the West. It is only ironical that the Muslims who have historically discriminated against Christians, annihilated Christian civilizations in the process of Islamizing their conquests and deported countless thousands, should be pampered in Europe today, affording them a generous welcome into Western democracies and at times even going so much out of their way as to accommodate them, that they raise the ire of their own citizens who see them so favorized by their own governments in housing, lodging, work and social welfare as to create the backlash of bitterness that contributes to the rise and strengthening of right wing parties. That is not what the citizenry originally wanted, but it is driven to do that by the continuous gnawing at their culture that their governments allow the Muslim immigration to exercise, at the expense of the local culture and values, like religion and age -old traditions that are devalued and derogated as part of "political correctness".

The historical experience of the attempts to bend the contradictions between various religious, ethnic or national groups into sharing one state, which would have catered to John Stuart Mill's lofty ideals, did not seem to work very positively, even when all partners were Christian and European, like the Austro-Hungarian Empire, during the religious wars in France, the Yugoslavian break-up, the English-Irish conflict, and the latest Czech-Slovakian split. Die-hard nationalists may even see in the Brexit yet another proof of the failure of multi-ethnic statehood. How much more so when the skeptics of such an enterprise are aliens bent of altering the cultural system of their host country of asylum?. M. Nisan, in his seminal *Minorities in the Middle East*, notices that

> The malaise of polyethnic countries can sometimes be more than a benign illness, though not [always] terminal in its consequences. National cleavages will complicate the establishment of statewide consensus on basic values.

The role of religion may inhibit full integration or equality between groups if the state, under major-group domination, itself bears a religious identity in a formal or legal sense. More destabilizing and perhaps politically lethal can be a minority group's assertion of an "ethnic imperative" that challenges the state regime's rationale or territorial boundaries. The demand for national self-expression, not merely minority coherence, will then call for more than cultural autonomy as a sufficient and dignified solution for the numerically inferior community.[1]

So much more so when such a massive influx of aliens which breaks into Europe not always legally, imbued with a self-confident sense of superiority and intent to alter the host country to suit its taste. Indeed, Muslim religion is a key element in the incongruence between the incoming immigrants into Europe and the receiving hosts, unlike in the other cases of ethnic discrepancies in Europe, involving Catalans, Basques, Sicilians, Corsicans, Scots, Irish and the like. But the wide divergences between the very many Muslim groups in themselves is based on different sub-divisions of national, linguistic and ethnic categories such as the Turks and Syrians in Germany; North Africans in France, Belgium and Holland; Indians, Pakistanis and Bangladeshis in the U.K.; and a host of other minority groups from Afghanistan, Iran, Iraq and lately Syria and other troubled places where massive acts of war have compelled refugees to flee in the millions to Europe. In most of those cases, only the massive numbers of Muslims, who are organized on religiously-based communities grew problematic in no time, since they soon after their resettlement started to advance their demands from their host societies. Other groups of refugees or labor immigrants,

---

[1] Mordecai Nisan, *Minorities in the Middle East: A History of Struggle and Self-Expression*, McFarland & Company., Jefferson, NC. 2002

who were either non-Muslim or did not move to Europe to make their Islam prevalent, had much less difficulty to adapt and integrate and never felt the necessity to challenge their shelter country.

Jewish minorities worldwide have become a special case among all the others, not only due to their tenacity and endurance along centuries and millennia in practically all their locations of settlement, but also due to their persistent persecution that was due to their refusal to integrate into the majority cultures among which they lived, as reflected in the words of Haman to King Ahasuerus in the Book of Esther (3:8-9): "There is a certain people, dispersed among the many peoples in all the provinces in your kingdom; their laws are different from those of all other people; they do not keep your Majesty's laws. It does not befit your majesty to tolerate them. If it please your majesty, let an order be made in writing for their destruction…". What has made the Jews a special case? There have been numerous cases of ethno-linguistic and /or religio-national minorities, or even racial and tribal grouping across the globe, but they got assimilated within others and gradually waned out. Others, like the Assyrians and the Yazidis in Iraq, the Alawites in Syria, the Copts in Egypt, the Druze and the Kurds all over the Middle East, or the Berbers and the Kabyls in North Africa and the Sikhs in India, and the multitude of ethnic minorities in China and southeast Asia, may have survived into modern times, and in that regard they have shared with the Jews their lack of sovereignty over any defined territory, but all of them have been considered from time immemorial part of the native demographic make-up of the country, and thus none of them(except for the Kurds) has practically considered realizable any aspiration for independence or autonomy, let alone sovereignty.

Moreover, Jews, like other minorities have gradually adapted to their localities of settlement following many years of adopting the material cultures of their hosts, like dress, language, customs, diet, and they often even converted to the religion of the hosts, so much so that as a result many of them paved thus their way to total assimilation locally. At any rate, they have never challenged the rule of their hosts and they were happy enough to be left alone.Sometimes the new converts of Jewish origin became so enthusiastic about their new faith as to grow into some of its prominent scholars and zealous practitioners. But there is no parallel to the survival of Jewish solidarity and uniformity of ritual in the same ancient holy tongue (Hebrew) which though dead as a practical language for everyday use, was preserved along the centuries as a *lingua franca* for religious essays and theological dissertations throughout the Jewish dispersion. There also is no precedent in human history that a ethno-religious group that had been forcibly expelled from its land, should maintain its yearning for its land and succeed in modern times to implement it, through regaining sovereignty, reviving its language and culture and gathering its dispersed people in more than a hundred lands into its original homeland. There may be many reasons for that, which perhaps did not exist in other extant cultures or tribal groupings, and therefore it may be said that the establishment of modern Israel in 1948, after half a century of active Zionism, surely qualifies for the greatest miraculous political and constructive event of the 20th Century. Granted, of course, that the other great global events of that century, like the two World Wars, the rise and fall of fascism and communism and the ascendance of China into the world scene, cannot be labeled as necessarily "constructive".

The revival of Israel has nonetheless put the half of world Jewry which has remained in the Diaspora for now(about 7 out of 14 million in *toto)* in a new light, unlike the Copts, Scots, Kurds, Assyrians or the Maronites, who have become the nationals of many countries and cultures where they immigrated long ago, and not even like Arabs and Muslims from existing sovereign countries and nations who either maintain a double citizenship or have relinquished their old identity and substituted for it a new one, as many immigrants into the West, for example, do. Even the Diaspora Irish, who are spread all over the world at the same time that they have their independent Irish state, do not resemble to Jews inasmuch as their exile is not of as long a duration as the Jews (two centuries compared to two millennia) and as much as the Irish people worldwide sense affinity to their brethren, even they do not entertain the close sense of Jewish solidarity where American Jews financed the universal struggle for the freedom of Soviet Jewry ("let my People go"), the removal of Ethiopian Jewry to Israel and the aid to Israel since its inception. Neither do the large Chinese minorities in the West and in Southeast Asia ("China Towns" in practically all large cities) practice anything close to Jewish solidarity in their relations to their motherland. May be it is the size that accounts for the difference. China is so large and its population so numerous that the large distribution of its people worldwide cannot preserve the tightly intimate relationship of a small people. Similarly, Indian minorities, which are themselves divided into sub-ethnic groups (Sikhs, Tamils, Bengali, Parsi etc.), and are found in Africa, Southeast Asia, the UK, the Americas and the Arab Gulf States, are far from exhibiting anything close to the worldwide close relationship between Jewish groups.

Unlike all those minorities, the Jews constantly prove, once and again their worldwide commitment to each other, and to Israel as their unifying theme, for even when they criticize the Jewish state, out of their genuine disagreement with its policies, or for fear of dissenting from the official attitude of their hosting state towards Israel, or in extreme cases of proving their independent judgment from other Jews, there is usually an element of concern on their part towards the image of the Jewish state for its affects them as Jews. If they did not really care, they could have slipped into the total abandonment of Judaism and assimilation into their respective host cultures, as many have indeed done over the centuries, either willingly or forcibly. But the extraordinary resilience of Jews, compared to others, in holding on tenaciously to their faith, ethnicity and culture over two millennia, remains incomparable. There may be nonetheless a partly comparable situation when Islam is concerned: there too there is a worldwide myth of solidarity, for the existence of the Islamic *umma* which represents the universal community of all Muslims has symbolized since its inception the totality of its members as if they were limbs of the same organic body, much like the Christian *ecclesia* which was presented in medieval art as a human organ with multiple arms. That means that the *umma* was and still is thought of as an organic body, and any pain or harm done to any limb of it is felt in a Pavlovian fashion throughout all the rest and necessitates a response. That is the reason Islam does not permit the entire Muslim community to remain silent when any part of the Muslim world is under attack, much less does it permit to collaborate with Infidels when they battle against Believers. When American troopers of the Muslim creed either refused to serve in Afghanistan or in Iraq, or went into an orgy of shooting and killing of their fellow-soldiers in America or in the various front lines, it was not just an outburst of irrational rage, but a religion-bound imperative that they could not contravene.

Conversely, Jewish soldiers on both sides of the divide in World War I, and hundreds of thousands of them during the Second World War, fought on the side of the Allies, including the British, and many perished, despite the fact that the British openly sided with the Arabs against them, while many Arabs and Muslims were allied to the Nazis. Again, maybe for the Muslims the prohibition to fight other Muslims stemmed out of a religious tenet which was reinforced by the existence of so many Muslim entities (57 since the 20th Century) the fact that there were many Muslim nations and countries, while Jews emphasized their nationality and political loyalty, since they had none of their own, which allowed them to be pitted against each other across the lines of rivaling nations and countries. But once Israel was founded in 1948, the extraordinary new phenomenon of a Jewish state immediately posed the issue of double-loyalty, a question never posed for the Irish, the Muslims, the Chinese and the Indians in the service of other nations. The only exception was perhaps the Japanese in America in W W II, who were suspected of double loyalty, maybe due to the impregnable nature of Japanese nationality in Japan itself, where it is almost impossible for foreigners to be naturalized and where the Korean minority who had lived there for generations has been deprived of local citizenship and have to satisfy themselves with the lower status of a non-national minority.

More recently, a differentiation has been developed between loyalty and allegiance, the latter meant in the political sense, namely when a national of any country, regardless of his or her faith, ethnic affiliation, language one speaks, who feels and behaves as belonging and embracing the same national group defined by his country, language and culture, and obeying the same social pact that ties all other nationals together. At the same time, however, a person can adhere to his or her civil loyalty, that we also dub as fealty, to one's tradition, customs, religion, ethnic group without compromising one's allegiance to one's state. Jews, since they consider themselves both a people (Jewry, the Jewish people, the Hebrews, the Israelites) and a faith (Judaism), all encompassed in one, their state also combines both aspects (Israel, the Jewish State, or as the French dub- it the Hebrew State), Israelis sense both allegiance to it and loyalty to their Jewish culture. The Arab-Muslim minority in Israel, while it could be expected to feel allegiance to it in its political sense, while adhering to their loyalty to their faith, culture and tradition, do not in fact, as when they constitute minorities in other parts of the world, stand up to these reasonable expectations. And this unusual characteristic of Islam, which cannot distinguish between allegiance and loyalty is what makes it problematic as a minority almost anywhere around the world. The traditional way to express allegiance to a Caliph or national authority in Islam is the *bay'a,* which is actually a pact, a religious oath of fealty and political allegiance at the same time. It is religiously recognized because it is made either directly by the subjects to their ruler or on their behalf by a body of religious scholars, the '*ulama*'. A religious act cannot be replaced by another formality, even when the *bay'a* is skipped in the modern world, because the ceremony of installing a President or a Prime Minister, or the process of "elections", when and where they exist, are seen as a substitute for the original act of fealty. It is interpreted as meaning that allegiance is given to the new Chief not because he was elected among several competitors but because it is to him personally that the people feel committed.

Thus, a difference has developed between Jewish and Islamic minorities in the Western world. While Jews jealously keep to their allegiance to their country of dwelling as long as they reside there, and when they sense that they can no longer adhere to it they immigrate elsewhere (usually to Israel or other Western liberal societies), they in most cases maintain a "moral loyalty" to Israel which in no instance displaces their allegiance, and pious Muslims cannot usually tell one from the other. Religion being part of the culture, and the social and political order part of religion, any pious Muslim would face a harsh contradiction if he were to commit himself to a political system which does not agree with his faith. For example, Islam determines that sovereignty does not belong to any individual but to Allah, and therefore allegiance to Him, to His Prophet and to His Holy Word, precedes commitment to any man-made rule, constitution, law or court ruling. Islam proclaims the Lord as the Supreme Sovereign, causing any claim to crown man and people as the ultimate source of power, as in liberal democratic systems, would be held as a profanation of the Divine Will and punished accordingly. Zealots among ultra-Orthodox Jews may also advocate similar tenets, but the rigidity of their doctrine is mitigated by the concept of "submission to the rule of the Gentiles". It is paradoxically in Israel that some ultra- Orthodox Jews challenge the validity of the legal and political systems of the country, but there they are overwhelmingly outnumbered by those who made peace with the idea that "for now" they accept the secular system. Among the Muslim communities in the West, which are many-fold larger than their Jewish counterparts, they are so numerous and growing in self-confidence, that they have begun demanding in several places that their *shari'a* be applied to the general public.

For that same reason, Muslims have been few in the Western armed forces and in the political systems of their countries of habitation, while Jews, especially in politics, are present way out of proportion to their numbers. When Jews become senior members of important committees in Congress, they can act wholeheartedly for America's interest, but when pious Muslim members of Congress enter the fray, they bring with them Islamic residues of biases and prejudices like the built-in anti-Semitism that they cannot waive as non existent, as has been revealed recently in the conduct of Congresswomen T'laib and Omar who were elected for the Democratic Party to represent their Muslim constituencies. For example, when the Holy Qur'an proclaims the Jews as "descendants of pigs and apes", and that they are doomed to eternal misery, and when Muslims state daily in their prayers that Jews have drawn upon themselves the wrath of Allah, no Muslim is expected to respect them or treat them as human beings. For, while human attitudes can evolve and change, the Word of Allah is immutable and eternal. Similarly, when Muslims are repeatedly enjoined to kill Unbelievers wherever they find them and to refrain from befriending them, how in the world can they survive as a minority in an environing society on which they depend totally?

The Jews draw particular attention in the world about their extraordinary solidarity, much more than the religiously binding commonality of sentiment that is shared by all members of the universal *umma*, not only due to their small numbers, which compel them, like within small surviving minority groups which must close ranks to survive (Druze, Kurds, Alawites, Assyrians, Copts and others) but also, like some of those minority groups, they combine ethnicity with religion. In fact, it is the religious prohibition to intermarry outside the faith which dictates inbreeding, ending up in the creation of separate ethnic groups. In some of those groupings where no conversion is possible (like the Druze and Copts) the lack of outside occasional injection of alien genes, renders the co-habitation of religion and ethnicity even stricter and close to total purity, unlike Judaism, for example, where conversion though infrequent is possible. Jews remain unique nonetheless in the sense that their identity contains a strong element of nationality. For even though the three millennia of the Jewish story contain much history and little geography, namely the tale of the people and their wandering and suffering around the globe, but rarely the story of a territory, there was always in their imagery and prayer a nostalgic look upon the Holy Land as a place to yearn to return to. Not that other minorities did not equally aspire for territorial sovereignty, like the Kurds who were often close to realizing their dream but ended up as minorities in Turkey, Iran, Iraq and Syria, or dispersed in other Diasporas, but the Jews are part of the few who succeeded to realize that dream, in spite of their exile from their turf, and to accompany it with the revival of their own language, on the same old territory, while maintaining their ancient faith and rituals.

This is where Zionism came in, which invoked the name of Zion, the alternate name of Jerusalem, which often refers to the entire Land of Israel. As a movement of national liberation, intending to gather in Zion the dispersed Jewish people in order to afford it to regain its sovereignty as a free and independent nation on its ancient turf, by means of its revived language and culture, it became since the end of the 19th Century (1897 when the first Zionist Congress was convened in Basel by Theodor Herzl its founder) the launching pad of a plan of reconstruction, which within 50 years, as predicted by its founder, grow into a first independent Jewish entity in 2,000 years. It took another half century for it to grow into a modern and advanced country in its regime, technology, medicine, agriculture and science, much beyond what its founders had imagined, and prominent amidst the failing states of the Middle East which surround it. It now accommodates some 7 million ingathered Jews (half their total number in the world), affording them protection and the opportunity to live free from oppression and humiliation, proud of their land and culture and a guarantor of Jewish safety everywhere. Indeed, as reflected in the proclamation of Israeli independence in 1948, which stated its centrality in and preoccupation with the entire Jewish people around the world, Israel has stood in the forefront of the struggle against anti-Semitism and kept vigilant in the defense of any Jewish minority anywhere suffering from any mistreatment, deprivation or persecution. Domestically, this positively patronizing attitude towards Jews worldwide, which stems out of the innate sense of solidarity, has been translated in Israel's life into an extraordinary care for its citizens, especially when they are abroad. For example, anyone who gets into trouble while on a journey or falls victim to a natural calamity, there is a rescue campaign organized by the authorities, closely watched by the media and the public in Israel, to which donors' funds flow, often beyond the need. So it goes for any manifest case of poverty, malady, imprisonment or other *malaises* striking individuals or groups, which are monitored and watched by the public, who is always ready to shoulder responsibility for its solution. During the Indian Ocean *tsunami* of 2004, for example, many thousands of people, mostly locals, but also many tourists, perished or were reported missing. There were many aliens among them, including several hundred Swedes and a couple dozen Israelis who were on vacation in Thailand. While for others it took weeks to account for them, and some were never found, the immediate Israeli rescue team was there on the ground in no time and did not leave until all Israelis were accounted for, and the story reported hour after hour to the entire concerned Israeli public.

The Jewish state has become such an accepted feature of the world scene, that it has also adopted the "normalcy" of itself incorporating a large Arab minority of over 20% (almost 2 million inhabitants out of over 8), since Jews have turned from a dispersed and persecuted minority around the globe, deprived of national sovereignty, into a full-fledged self-confident and proud independent state, that is now itself accused by its large Arab minority, of having turned it from the majority of Palestinians prior to 1948 into a minority under Israeli rule thereafter. This reversal in the fortunes of the two populations (the majority and minority) has had to tackle several unprecedented and unique problems:

1. Jews had been subjected to Islamic rule in the entire Islamic space, for over a millennium, under the appellation of *dhimmis*, ("protected people", a well-defined subaltern status on the religious, economic, social, political and judicial levels) in the Islamic *shari'a* which governed all Islamic countries and was symbolized by the humiliating payment of the *jizyah* (a poll tax) that the Believers were exempt from. For the Arabs/Muslims to see the status of the inferior Jews elevated to become the rulers and their own to be diminished to a minority, is unacceptable. Of course, there are also Muslim Minorities in Europe and elsewhere, but that is by choice for the most part, while in Palestine their demise was visited on them against their will.

2. The Arab population which lived in Palestine until the foundation of Israel in 1948, constituted two thirds of the local population (one million people out of a total of 1 and half million, with the remaining third encompassing the minority Jewish population). Therefore, the 1948 war, which reversed that situation, is considered by Israeli Arabs, who prefer to be dubbed "Palestinians" like their brethren across the border, as their disas-

ter (*nakbah*), much to the chagrin of the Jewish majority which joyfully celebrates their freedom and independence.

3. Due to the continued conflict situation between Israel and the Palestinians (and much of the rest of the Arabs), the Arab minority in Israel finds itself emotionally and politically divided between their country (Israel) and their people (the Palestinians), a classic situation of irredentism, friction and violence. More often than not, due to the continually escalating conflict between Israel and some of its Arab/Muslim neighbors, the Arabs of Israel usually display their open support to other Arabs rather than to their country and find themselves in a permanent state of conflict with it.

4. The Israeli Arabs lay claim, like the rest of the Palestinians, to their "right of return", to their original locations from which they had fled or were forcibly removed in the 1948 War. Granted that most of them have become refugees in the adjoining Arab countries, many thousands of them qualify themselves as "internally displaced", namely that they were uprooted from their villages in 1948, although they remained as refugees within the boundaries of Israel. As long as they are not allowed to return to their destroyed locations, on which other settlements have grown in the meantime, they cannot feel at peace with their country- Israel.

5. Israel has passed its own "Law of Return", allowing any and all Jews of the world to immigrate to Israel and resettle there, signifying that the demographic balance in favor of the Jews has been constantly improving, despite the much faster natural growth of the Arabs, who have grown more than ten fold (150,000 in 1948 to close to two million in 2019), similar to the growth rate of the Jewish population (600,000 in 1948 to about 7 million in 2019), mainly by Jewish immigration from the outside. Arabs claim, and not without justification, that as natives they are morally and legally more entitled to return to

the land than "foreign Jews", flocking in from the outside. If their plea were to be satisfied, the large numbers of refugees and their successors over four generations (5 million) would together with the existing Arab population of Israel outnumber the Jews and take over the country, putting an end to the Zionist dream.

The accusation of "double loyalty" has been usually lodged in situations of this sort, but particularly against Jews who have been spread all over the world and have been sensitive to this claim since the birth of Israel in 1948, although with less justification than many others. Arabs of Israel, for example, have constantly demonstrated their loyalty to their people rather than to their country as in the existing dire state of conflict this manifestation of loyalty to the enemy side has become a daily matter. And yet, they regard this conduct as "natural" and matter of course, and any criticism of it as an uncalled for "attack against Arabs", although usually their rights are respected and they enjoy a degree of freedom that few Arabs have in their own Arab countries. Conversely, consistent with the permanent state of humiliation, and persecution the Jews had been subjected to in their millennium of subsistence in the Muslim world, immediately upon the birth of Israel in 1948, practically all the million Jews who had lived in Islamdom for centuries, were constrained to leave under the accusation of their loyalty to Israel, although they were no more culprits that the Japanese in California during W W II, who were interned by the American authorities. In both cases, the accusation was false. Similarly, Koreans in Japan are permanently held in contempt and suspicion, and usually refused Japanese citizenship, despite their many centuries of existence there and the fact that it was Japan who had occupied Korea for half a century, not the other way round.

For Jews universally, nonetheless, the accusation of double loyalty pops up constantly, as one facet of anti-Semitic sentiment, the moment Zionist and Israeli sovereignty were re-launched in the 20th Century. For, while Arab and Muslim terrorist attacks by European and American nationals of the Arab/Muslim creed never raised the issue of "double loyalty" to the Arab/Muslim country of origin, the Jewish minorities everywhere are watched under the microscope and constantly scrutinized for their loyalty, sympathy or support for Israel. And if they are "caught" expressing any positive sentiment toward the Jewish state, the accusation putting in doubt their allegiance is hurled in their faces as "evidence" of their treachery. They forget that during W W II, while Arabs and many Muslims collaborated with the Nazis, half a million Jews in America fought in the ranks of the American armed forces on both the European and the Pacific fronts, much more than any troops that Israel has ever fielded in its wars combined. But when the French or British Muslims from Algeria or Pakistan commited horrendous acts of terrorism agaisnt their host countries, no one has heard such a suspicion rise either in the media or in popular belief. Indeed, in the case of the Islamic minorities, and this is unique to them, the question of double allegiance does not apply to country, nation, ethnicity or clan, but to religion, and there it is absolute, on-sided and indivisible. While Jews can only be positively loyal to their Jewish nation, which they maintain concurrently with their existing nationality wherever they live, Muslim minorities are negatively predisposed to any faith that is not their own and are duty-bound to operate against it "in the Path of Allah", and that is precisely what they do when they can. Hence stem all the differences between Jewish and Muslim minorities worldwide, the fact that there is Islamic terrorism and not a Jewish one outside the Middle East, and the phenomenon that Jewish minorities participate in their countries' life and welfare and contribute to their arts, science and creativity, while Muslims are for the most part active in gnawing at their hosts' welfare and wellbeing and bent on their destruction in order to replace them with Islamic hegemony.

Chapter One

The Waning Separation of Many Disparate Civilizations

The delightful and diversified world where we live actually has been the fruit of its tremendous cultural, racial, ethnic, religious and linguistic making, and of its accessibility through mass tourism in modern times to most common people. The many tens or hundreds of millions of tourists who tread the transatlantic air routes and the continental highways of the world bring multitudes of Chinese and Nigerians to Israel and Thailand, Americans to Nepal and Argentina, and Israelis to every corner of the globe. Israel, as one example, has been since its inception surrounded by only hostile neighbors. Thus, her people were unable until recently to simply cross the border to the environing Arab countries, and explore next door's cultures and ways of life; most young Israelis, upon completing the two or three year mandatory military service during which neighboring cultures were viewed through the barrels of their guns, fly to the farthest flung destinations (the Amazone in South America, or India and the far East) to experience other cultures that they had been deprived from encountering before or to acquaint themselves freely via direct contact with new landscapes and cultures. This means that the curiosity to know others, contact them and share their experiences is innate in human beings and in need to be put constantly to the test.

Of old, people went to visit or study at places of their choice, having been enchanted with Italian art and food, the Greek landscapes and classic culture, the British Museums, the Chinese Forbidden City or the Scandinavian Lappish civilization. In old days, it was fascinating to go, visit specific destinations for a well defined purpose and to satisfy precise needs. So one traveled, smelt the odors, savored the tastes, heard the sounds and saw the sights, thus sensing the entire cultural experience, reading the materials to enrich oneself and taking the pictures, and then trekking back home, full of impressions and fairy tales, to tell friends and relatives, and show them the visual evidence, so as to embolden them to go and see for themselves. But now, never in human history has there been such a massive movement of people from one place to another, as there is now, with the tourists normally yearning to see and experience instantly new places and people and then return to their routine lives in their home countries, as if travel had become a must in every modern person's curriculum, as if rendering visits to other cultures and places no longer required any predisposition or keen interest in a location or a topic, and as if the impact the trip left on the traveler failed to matter any longer. At any rate, that quick and superficial impression would be shortly supplanted by another, to the next destination, which will be also added to the list of "*déjà vu*".

Europe of the 21st Century, the main destination of tourism worldwide, has been facing its worst refugee crisis since the Second World War, with more than 1 million people applying for asylum in 2015 and again in 2016. As the systems that were designed to manage these flows have been under intense pressure—not least than the Common European Asylum System (CEAS) the international community has been tackling new ideas to manage mixed flows and create sustainable long-term solutions for refugees. This major movement of populations into Europe at the same time that massive popular tourism is reaching new peaks, lends an unprecedented visibility to foreign presence in all European touristic sites, and dilutes more than even before, the native cultures where the old-fashioned tourist has been investing his emotions, expectations and funds so as to spend a period of time in his or her favorite cultural site. And he wonders whether this is what he came all the way to visit. And when such scenes are met by unpleasant sights of loud speech, improper conduct, disturbance of public order by some unruly or uncivilized visitor, or a totally unacceptable and unexpected outburst of public anger or violent demonstration, then the entire experience of cultural intake that the visitor had come for is frustrated. Of course, when similar outbursts are joined by local equally violent or unpleasant occurences, these scenes are not made more easily digestible.

To diminish the potentially negative impact of unruly migrant-refugees the host countries try to distribute them evenly between various parts of the country, but, being free and democraric countries, on the one hand, and sensitive to human rights of the incoming migrants on the other, they cannot constrain the innate desire of the refugees to drift towards regions where their co-religionists or compatriots had settled before, and so you have enclaves of new immigrants, likc thc citcs around Paris, or ccrtain ncighborhoods of Malmo, Amsterdam, or Cologne, where entire quarters become Muslim, or otherwise alien, and in the long run so much teeming with crime that they no longer are accessible to the general public, and sometimes even grow out-of bounds for police and emergengy services, and in any case become a land of strangers for some fellow citizens in their own country. EU policy debates about moving asylum seekers from overburdened frontline countries, such as Greece and Italy, to other member states rarely consider how migrants form and act on preferences for certain destinations—and how difficult it may be to change these views. As maritime arrivals climbed in 2015, EU policymakers struggled to mount a coordinated response. A range of *ad hoc* crisis-response tools emerged, but many officials worried that if another migration emergency were to hit Europe, the European Union may still be unprepared. But due to the dismay and confusion in Europe, versus the determination of the Muslim influx in Europe that is motivated not only by need and an outburst of humanitarian compassion which facilitates its absorption, but also by a doctrinaire ideological zeal to increase Muslim presence in Europe, the efforts of many Western countries to maintain their singular cultural uniqueness seems to have grown into a losing rear-guard battle.

Europe's reaction to this massive flow, being disorganized, in the vein of "too little too late", came mainly by popular pressure of the populace who could not tolerate watching helplessly while their culture and national ambience they had grown under have been eroded and "polluted" by outside accretions that were not always pleasant to watch or to experience. And since they felt they were powerless to arrest this process of deterioration, they reacted either physically by mounting counter-demonstrations, or launching acts of counter-terrorism, or else organized politically in nationalist parties which gave rise to nationalist governments. Sometimes, governments followed suit by legislation, putting lids on Muslim immigration (like in Sarkozy's France), making tough statements against Muslim immigrants (like President Macron in France), or reversing their open immigration and consequent multi-cultural policy(like the British and the Dutch)[2], or else imposing such restrictions on candidates for naturalization, such as a proven knowledge of the host countries' languages and history (like Holland, Spain, Austria) so as to limit dramatically the numbers of incomers and to limit the damage done to the local culture when so many ignorant aliens are injected into it. Nonetheless, the pace of metamorphosis of European cities under the impact of Muslim immigrants and tourists, has not remarkably slowed down due to their high visibility with their foreign dress, loud speech and growing arrogance, as their self-confidence as the future masters of the

____

[2] R. Israeli, *Retreating from the Mirage of Muti-Culturalism? The cases of Holland, Britain and Israel;* Strategic Books TX. 2016.

land keeps sky-rocketing.

So, Europe's struggle to preserve its particular national cultures in the face of the immigants' onslaught against them, can be traced especially in everyday events and even anecdotes which can be illustrated in infinitely minor incidents, maybe insignificant in themselves, but in their aggregate they not only amount to a critical mass which impacts the existing cultural infrastructure of each country, but also reflects the often subliminal struggle between the host culture to survive in its beauty, attractiveness and richness, and the guest intruders to affect its course to their tune. Before we provide concrete examples of this continual competition, we may generalize by reminding the Europeans of the "oriental open markets" in their cities, which add color and diversity for some, but noise, disorder and stench for others; the minarets that Muslims apply to construct for their mosques, which are proof of the renowned Western tolerance for other faiths, but a constant noisy irritant to neighboring dwellers who are awakened in odd early hours by the calls to prayer of the *Mu'azzin*; Muslims squatting in streets, plazas and other public places for public prayer, which are a sign for some that the host state does not afford them enough prayer houses to accommodate their worshippers, while for others these are open challenges by a tolerated faith to the generosity of the hosts who are aghast with the penetration of a competing religion into their public square, especially when a reverse Christian trend of that sort is not allowed into Muslim countries; Muslim women veiled in European streets, as their free expression of their style of dress, while many, like France, do not allow the total masking of human bodies beyond recognition in the public square and in public institutions; rising crime in Muslim neighborhoods and by Muslim individuals, which ends up spreading Islamic radicalism in the European jails where the culprits are incarcerated; and the daily reports in the European media about Muslim terrorism, joint anti-semitic demonstrations, often accompanied by violence, of Muslims and their extreme right and radical left partners in the streets of Europan cities; often, reports also emerge of forced marriages, poligamy, "honor killings" in families and other odd customs and traditions imported by immigrants but are looked upon in disdain and disgust by native Europeans.

These challenges to European values prove every day anew what the Europeans and the world stand to lose if they are unable to control the current process of erosion of their life style. In 2015, for example, when the massive attacks against civilians in France took place, it was the onslaught on freedom of the press that was assassinated with the murder of the *Charlie Hebdo* magazine, and the liberty to perform art that was massacred with the killing of hundreds of free viewers in the *Bataclan* theater. It was also visitors of open *cafe* houses on the sidewalks of the splendid avenues of Paris, a pleasure that tourists from around the world travel to the French capital in order to experience, who were hurt. To Jewish residents of the museum-like city of Paris, who were murdered in their Kosher supermarket, it was demonstrated that the illusory peace and liberty that they used to enjoy under the legendary symbols of the French Revolution, have gone with the wind, and no amount of policemen in the streets of that glamorous city can erase the new depressing atmosphere of emergency and vigilance that has been imposed by the new social make-up of France. Not any more, any way, than when the massive over-running of dozens of celebrating civilians by a maddened Arab truck driver who sought to destroy the end of the year public festivities of the lively *corniche* of Nice, which had become a glittering symbol with its luxurious hotels and seashore of the French *Riviera*. Who would wish to effect his annual pilgrimage to enjoy the delights of France in a France whose foci of attraction had grown into localities of death?

And those were not the first and only manifestations of violence that have altered Europe for ever, both in the eyes of its citizens and newly nationalized immigrants and for the tens of millions of visitors who stream there continuously. They were preceded by the

Rushdie Affair in 1989 and the Cartoon crisis in 2005-6, which implanted in the hearts of Europeans a reign of terror, that was accepted by some European leaders as a fact of life when they chose to "apologize" to Muslim countries for the wrong they did not do. Before that, the Twin Tower and the Pentagon disasters in New York and Washington, which demonstrated how serious and adamant were Muslim radicals to condemn the West to resign to the new supremacy of Islam and submit to it, and then the train station in Madrid and the London underground, followed by Brussels, Manchester, Cologne and all the rest, as the bastions of freedom of the world crumbled helplessly before the new barbarians and the erstwhile great powers of yesteryear were caught powerless to control the new situation, much less to remedy it. The citizenry of European previously self-confident states and cities grew scared, unable to put its trust any longer in wavering and untrustworthy weak leaders, who instead of providing solutions were themselves paralyzed by their own impotence and capitulated one after the other, yielding to demands of the terrorists and of the increasing Muslim population, acting like fire fighters whose only desire was to extinguish the flames around them, hoping to be reelected in a few years, rather than seize the bull by its horns and bring it down. Women of Europe, not to speak of Jews, became terrified by the increasing rate of rapes, beatings and murder, while security forces were increasingly unable/unwilling to deal with the crisis and the politically correct decision makers reluctant to direct them to do so.

Apart from these major axial events which dotted contemporary European history, an infinite series of small events unfolded every day, everywhere thoughout the continent (much less in America due to the lower rate of Muslim population- 2% compared to 5-7% in Europe), which passed almost unnoticed, but their cumulative effect is what has been transforming the West in the long haul. The West, unwilling to face the grim future awaiting it in the process of this matamorphosis has usually elected to ignore those bits and pieces which indicated this general trend, which were all clearly announced in advance by their perpetrators. In a *Letter to America*, published in the organ of the Hamas in Gaza, *Al-Risala* (the Message), but indeed directed to the entire Western civilization, Atallah abu al-Sabah, who boasted a PhD degree, indicating that he was a well educated man, supposedly versed in higher education and probably trained in the West, wrote in the immediate aftermath of the September 11 horror, while the world was stupefied and hurting:

I am confident that you will be facing for a long time to come, the mirror of your history. Thus, you will be able to realize how oppressive, corrupt and sinful you have been, how many entities you have wiped out and how many states you have destroyed. Do you remember what you did in Korea and Vietnam? Do you recall how you turned Hiroshima and Nagasaki into piles of radioactive rubble, which contain death for the two ruined cities, now and in the future? Not one single human being was left in those two cities that the fire has not deformed, not a baby who was not torn to pieces, nor a bird which was not drowned in a sea of flames!!!

Oh America, the sword of oppression, arrogance and crime!!! Do you remember how you smashed man's humanity? Do you remember how you mistreated the Blacks under your aegis? Can you describe for us the humiliation, disgust and contempt you meted out to those unfortunate people, whose only sin was that they were born to black parents? It was your white son who chained their necksin slavery,after he had hunted them down in African forests and along its coasts. They were born free but they were enslaved in your virgin land...

Did you ever ask yourself about what you did to the original inhabitants of your land, the Apache Indians?

You trampled them down under your white feet, and then used their name, the Apache, for the helicopters that carry death, destruction and annihilation to owners of rights [the Palestinians] who dared to clamor for the rights. This is a heinous and destructive conduct, which made us hate the Apache, before we could realize that they had been themselves victims, just like us...

Did you ever ask yourself what was the sin of the children of al-'Amariya and Kana [locations on the Lebanese-Israeli border, hit during border clashes initiated by Palestinian troops], or the reason for the continuous injustice you have been bringing down to Baghdad, Jerusalem and Jenin [all loci of conflict] and on all those who do not see eye to eye with you, or refuse to walk the road of those sycophant and emasculated [Arab rulers] that you address as "excellencies" and "majesties"? America, did you ever ask yourself why do you produce cluster bombs, nuclear and hydrogenc bombs, biological weapons for mass killings, and F-16 planes? Even should we accept the contention that you do it for your own war preparedness, why do you put these weapons in the hands of every murderer, war criminal and enemy of humanity, such as [Serbian War Commander]Karadzic, [Israeli Prime Minister] Shamir and [his successor] Sharon?

America, have you ever tasted horror, pain and affliction? These have been our lot for a long time, and they have filled our hearts, torn our guts and burned our skin. This has become daily routine for us, and carried out by your favorite [proxies] with high proficiency. They indeed destroy our shacks in Jenin, and what has happened tonight there, is no different from what has happened to you. Every so often [Vice President] Dick Cheney and his girlfriend, Condolezza Rice, set out to calumniate us, to castigate us, to incite against us. And we lined up and asked Allah to make you sip from the cup of humiliation, until Heaven responded. Now, America, consider whether you are able to forgo your fanaticism, your arrogance and your vanity... While we have accepted your mediation for the sake of peace... you have opened the gates of the Pentagon for every Jew to acquire a knife in order to slaughter us. You have thus planted the seeds of hatred against yourself... You did not think that the roots of those plants would grow to poke your eyes, even as they were placed on top of the World Trade Center. Those plants have also grown to hit at the heart of the Pentagon, the most heavily guarded facility on earth. Can you not see that the outgrown roots have reached the very eyes of your strong Secretary of Defence, Donald Rumsfeld, who thought he was immune to revenge for what he did?

America, why did you evacuate the Sears Building, the way we do every night in order to flee from your laser-guided missiles? Are you scared, just like us? Do the giants also experience fear and run for their lives just as the oppressed do?... It turns out that you are weaker than the weak and miserable like all the refugees whom you forced out of their villages on the Palestinian seashore, together with their wives, children and torn clothes... America, where is your famous CIA, which can detect even ants on a rock? You did not see the grievances of those who have struck you... for your blindness could only see through the eyes of traitors and spies... America, where is your second eye, the *Mossad*, which you always made us believe could detect anything?

Can we expect that this time you will reconsider and avoid attacking a drug factory in Khartoum, or in Libya?

Or will the appetite for revenge again blind your sight and lead you to discharge your wrath on Al-Amariya or Beit Hanun? What good did your Navy or ballistic missiles and nuclear reactors do to you? How have your satellites or AWACS, NATO and world leadership come to your help? All those were paralyzed when the sword of vengeance got to your neck, in this unprecedented feat in world annals... You surely understand that unless you repent from your corruption, you are bound to be hit once and again by the same perpetrators...

America, reexamine your decisions to cast hundreds of veto votes [at the UN] with a view of denying humanity its rights. Look at your humiliated face, and check whether it is not due to those votes. This will teach you to stand by justice and the righteous, even if they are weak, and then perhaps the dust of humiliation will be removed from your face[3].

Much along the same lines, the editorial of the same journal, also written by an educated and supposely "enlightened" Dr Ghazi Hamad, called the US to task, stressing the rule that "punishment fits the crime", and wondering why th US has not learned any lessons from the killing of her marines in Lebanon, th destruction of her HQ in Khobar (Saudi Arabia), the bombing of her two embassies in Africa, the incapacitation of USS Cole in the Yemen, and the attacks against her forces in Japan and the Gulf. These two blatant examples of projecting the blame on the victim of the September 11 horrors, which showed no sympathy for the families of the dead, and were probably boosted by the atmosphere of jubilation in the Palestinian street on the morrow of those attacks, would soon give

---

[3] Atallah abu al-sabahSabah, 'Atallah abu al- "A Letter to America", *al Risala,* 13 September, 2001, cited in *MEMRI,* "Terror in America", No 1.

way to the denials that Arabs and Muslims could have had anything
to do with that horrendous act of murder and destruction. So, on
the one hand, Arabs and Muslims in general were not displeased by
the disaster that befell America, as the symbol of the West, but on
the other hand, when they began to recoil before the gravity of the
horror and to fear the wrath of the US response, they ran for cover:
they had neither seen or heard; it was all the fault of others; it was
the US, the West and Israel to blame. They attributed no crime to
Japan before Hiroshima, no Arabs and Muslims were mentioned as
major traders who hunted down Black Africans and ferryied them
to the Americas, or as the conquerors of vast territories and peoples
whom they subjected to Islam and erased their civilizations. Their
vast acts of terror, which peaked in September 11 were ignored as
the reason for Apache helicopters reacting against them, nor were
the waves of terror visited on Israel which murdered entire families
in buses, restaurants and the streets of its cities. All that was meted
out on the West not as a punishment, to their mind, as crime and
chastisement are conceived as stemming out from each other in
their worldview, but as a revenge, to see the West humiliated, diminished, threatened, at the mercy of the upcoming Islamic world.

In those and another multitude of write-ups which followed Sep
11, America as the representative of the West in general is depicted
diminished and weak, in fact a paper tiger, ripe for reprisal and
vengeance until mercilessly tottered. Its CIA, and allied Israeli
Mossad are mocked as weak and blind, and certinly ineffective in the
face of the rising power of Islam and its capacities, which are merely
defensive against an arrogant and aggressive Western civilization.
They first denied they had a hand in September 11, at the same
time that Bin laden was boasting of his feat, and the streets of Cairo,
Casablanca, Gaza and Quetta were teeming with jubilant crowds
who were celebrating the humiliation and downing of Western and
Jewish "arrogance". Muslims around the world, often contrary to

the apologetic attitudes of their governments which felt embarrassed to share in the orgy of popular joy in their streets and were scared of US reactions, wiewed their sense of retaliation as a sign of the upcoming switch in world hegemony to their side and sensed able and proud both to summon President Bush to convert to Islam, and to threaten American decision makers to change their policy of support to Israel, or else... America and the West, to their mind, had to draw lessons from the strikes against them, to accept and resign to them, instead of retaliating against them. To step up pressure against them, since they were close to capitulate, more terrorist attacks were launched against them on their territories, both in Europe and the Americas, and even in far away Australia, boosted and supported by the intensifying influx of Muslims to those continents, legally if possible, illegally if necessary, since the holy goal of Islamizing the world justified this means of "peaceful Jihad" when feasible, and the violent one when there was no other way.

A columnist in the London-based Arabic *al-Sharq al-Awsat* put the blame on President Bush, who was "hardly elected" to his post and needed the drama to draw behind himself the bi-partisan support of the US, and on Secretary Powell, due to his military background which conditioned him to conduct war, not diplomacy[4]. Another alternative scenario was the Jewish-Zionist plot, because the Jews "controlled the world media, economy and politics" and "wished to press America and NATO even more thoroughly to submit to Zionist ideology" and "further promote the Zionist slogan of Islamic terrorism"[5]. Another columnist urged the Arabs to take a firm stand so as to wash their hands clean of any accusation and to transcend their defensive and apologetic stand and move to the offensive[6]. Another Jordanian writer was "personally certain that

---

[4] *Al Sharq al-Awsat*, London, 14 September, 2001, *Memri*, "Terror in America", No 4.
[5] *Al Dustour*, Jordan, 13 September, 2001, Ibid.
[6] Ibid.

no Arab or Muslim stood behind this act, because it was Zionist organizations which were interested in perpetrating this crime in order to draw the attention of the world while they were destroying the Aqsa Mosque".[7] While an Egyptian journalist claimed the "right to be happy and joyful for the American losses, because they have finally tasted the flavor of death"[8] his editor defended his right to celebrate "because that was the first step in the 1,000 mile journey toward the rout of America by knock-out"[9]. Other columnists called upon the US to choose between "respecting other nations or dying"[10], with the organ of the "Liberal Party" of Egypt, rejoicing that America proved a "paper tiger", and they rejected the pressures on its readers to contain their joy at the sight of "America crumbling instantly under the attack"[11]. A viewer of that horror, described shamelessly and cruelly those events as:

> Moments of a beautiful and glamorous hell, the best and dearest of my life. I saw the towers, the walls, those symbols of power which constituted a modern and scary monster, penetrated by a courageous hornet… The hornet stung that mythological monster, who looked horrific as it cried, shouted and collapsed like a hell. All the media which ply to America, broadcast those pictures that all the past and future generations will envy us for having been privileged to witness[12].

All this amounted to Arabs and Muslims not only rejoicing at America's plight but also perceiving it as frightened, helpless and

---

[7] Ibid.

[8] *Al-Arabi*, Egypt 16 September 16, 2001

[9] Ibid.

[10] Ibid.

[11] *Al-Ahrar*, Egypt,, 14 and 17 September, 2001.

[12] *Al-Usbu'*, Egypt, 17 September, 2001.

teetering towards its demise, hence the need to keep harassing it to bring her to her end. This prevailing feeling in the Islamic world has been backed by the authoritative voice of Sheikh Qaradawi the most prominent Islamic jurist in the Sunnite world, who had in the past sanctioned acts of *Islamikaze* (erroneously called "suicide bombings"), arguing that the martyrs who performed these acts, as in the case of September 11, actually wage an active Jihad seeking the extermination of the enemies of Islam, and thereby killing themselves, although he was against indiscriminate killings, save in case these acts were perpetrtated against Israel. Nonetheless, he qualified his ruling with so many caveats as to make it ineffective, or at least questionable, thus lending legitimacy to similar acts in Europe in order to speed up its demise:

1. It was the West which has turned Islam into its enemy since the Crusades, by coveting Muslim lands and resources, while Islam, in his words, did nothing to justify its enemy status. He just forgot to mention the Muslim conquest of vast lands in the Middle Ages which threatened Europe at the time, and the present-day Islamic onslaught on Christian minorities within its borders or other nations outside of them. It was Qaradawi who justified the continued, indeed encouraged, the influx of Muslims into Europe, as a sort of peaceable Jihad to Islamize that continent;

2. If the West attacks Muslim countries (such as Iraq and Afghanistan or Libya) Muslims cannot ally with it, unless it is proven that they authored an act of terrorism; just to harbor terrorists (as Afghanistan did) does not mean that the harboring country can be accused of participating in the murder;

3. The September 11 attacks against the US are the fruit of hatred, whose roots must be investigated, for if Bin Laden were to be killed (as he was indeed to be many years later), another 1,000 like him would emerge, especially that neither

Bin Laden nor the Taliban could have had any involvement in this.

4. The Shari'a forbids Muslim collaboration against other Muslims. This would be a sin and an act of aggression. Moreover, every Muslim country is obliged to rush to the help of any other Muslim land under attack, with both fighters and funds.

5. It is also prohibited to surrender a Muslim to non-Muslims; this would otherwise oppose common sense since Islam does not recognize any geographic borders, race, color or language differences between Muslims. They are all one *umma,* united under Islam and in Islamic fraternity;

6. It makes no sense that Pakistan should assist foreigners to invade its Muslim neighbors; no Mulims scholar would countenance such a prospect, and I do not understand why Pakistani *ulama* can allow this to pass;

7. If Bin Laden should prove guilty, I have no objection to having him handed over to Muslim justice in Egypt or Saudi arabia.But wo can prove that he recruited, trained, financed and disptched the perpetrators? This would be very difficult, for terrorists exist all over the world and it is not inevitable that Bin Laden or al-Qa'ida should be involved.

8. There is no doubt that the Zionist entity is the one who stood to gain from this crime; the US supports Israel, and Israel is the greatest terrorist in the world.

9. There are two lines of terrorism: the one pursued by people who defend their rights and homeland, which is sanctioned by the Qur'an, as the Believers are enjoined to "cast fear"[13] in the heart of the enemy. This is the kind of terrorism practiced by the Hamas against Israel as well as other organizations like al-Qa'ida and ISIS against the West. If this is terrorism, then this is the best kind of terrorism, because it is a Jihad for the sake of

---

[13] The Arabic term is *irhab*, which translates into the modern word of terrorism.

Allah. The other kind of terrorism, which is practiced by Israelis is illegitimate, bcause it kills and desecrates Muslim holy sites. But even though the US supports this Israeli terrorism, we should not attack civilians in the US. We could instead boycott the US and compel it to retreat as we did in Durban in 2001.[14]

What is appalling is that these points of view of Qaradawi are shared by vast strata of Islamic societies as had been previously shown elsewhere[15]. Some leaders, political, intellectual, cleric or artistic, who either openly loathe the US or see no prospects of joining it, do not mince their words when they analyze their perceptions of the September 11 events. So much so that one of them, an Egyptian movie critic, Samir Farid, wrote that he was ashamed of the commentaries he read in the Egyptian press which reported about popular processions in towns and villages which exclaimed the abominable slogan:"We shall redeem you with our soul and blood, O Bin Laden!! "[16]. But he was the one civilized exception, for even the Chair of the Arab Writers Association found no other place than the *Literary Weekly* in Damascus to vent his disturbing though widespread trend of thought which was found to merit depiction in that supposedly humanistic and artistic journal, in harrowing detail:

> I usually ache for the death of innocent people,but the day the power symbols of America collapsed on September 11, reminded me of the daily funerals of so many innocent people in occupied Palestine... of the day of the Americano-British aggression against Libya, when they tried to destroy the house of its leader while he was

---

[14] *Al-Hayat*, London, 3 October, 2001.

[15] Raphael Israeli, *Islamikaze: Manifestations of Islamic Martyrology*, Frank Cass, London, 2003, the Introduction.

[16] *Al Hayat*, London, 3 October, 2011.

asleep, but they only succeeded in burying his daughter under the ruins. So my soul was full of disgust and bitterness towards a country whose history of oppression and support for the racism of Nazi Zionism and the apartheid in South Africa... The American Administration which is ruled by Zionist decisions and supports the occupation and the racist deeds of the "Israelis" has numbed my feelings. It has contaminated my soul, and when I saw the multitudes running away in terror in the streets of New York and Washington, I was telling myself: "Let them taste from the cup they have forced upon all nations and upon us in particular..."

When the Twin Towers collapsed, I felt as if I were extricated from the bottom of a tomb, as if I were hovering over the arrogant mythological symbol of American imperialism, whih has covered up the crimes it had committed... My lungs filled with pure air and I breathed deeper than ever before... Even when I thought about the innocent who were buried under the rubble... I was sorry that my humanity had been soiled by Zionist America and world Zionism... But minutes later I learned new facts from the media: that Arabs and Muslims are accused as the culprits, and threats were voiced calling for revenge against them... This has returned me to the spiritual tomb where I had been submerged by the aggression., arrogance and distortion of facts. But my stamina which saved me from drowning enabled me to breath again over the surface: we shall live, be victorious and bring justice to the world, because we are ready to sacrifice ourselves for our existence, our rights, justice and the world's humanity... The American people has to wake up to the image that its policy has created of it, namely the dirty policy that does not bring respect to its initiator...Maybe even the American brain will understand that military and economic power deprives it of true humanity...

Americans have to understand that their support for Zionist racism and its Nazi deeds, causes the entire Arab nation to rejoice when America suffers death and destruction... The symbolism of destroying one of the five wings of the Pentagon and of killing one thousand people there is far more important than the fact that it continues to exist and to threaten other nations, especially Afghanistan and Bin Laden. This means that it is enough that one person has decided to die for his honor, rights, nation, faith and civilization, in order to attain his goal against a superpower in the heart of its territory, for nations to wake up and evince this kind of willpower, and set out to resist tyranny, dictators, racists and imperialists who drink their blood... It is easy to imagine what happens next...

Something has collapsed in America and this is the beginning of America's collapse as the sole superpower... The collapse will be followed by the building of a new base for the victory of the oppressed and miserable people. For all tyranny will come to an end, force will be routed by force, and there will be no limit to human will when it determines to confront the arrogance of power... Just as I am certian that many of the victims do not deserve compassion due to their belonging to the blood suckers of other people, one should not rejoice at the loss of human life. My humanity that American and Zionist policy has attempted to numb, gains the upper hand in the final analysis over hatred and hostility[17].

---

[17] *Al Usbu' al-Arabi, The Literary Weekly,* Damascus, 15 September, 2001. Cited by MEMRI, "Terror in America", No 10.

The sense of universal confrontation between Islam and the West, which precisely strengthens the Muslim determination to transport their growing self-confidence in their ultimate victory to their countries of asylum in the West, and even more so in places where geopolitics has turned them into minorities on their native turf, like Kashmir and Palestine/Israel, on the one hand; and the suicidal permissiveness in the liberal democratic host countries which let these developments unfold, is what permits the Muslim challenge to Western countries grow more hostile and threatening to their core values, while the host countries seem to grow numb and incapacitated to respond in self-defence while their respective cultures are being diluted, sidetracked and actively combated. Muslims coming to the West, either as tourists or more so as immigrants, arrive with their Muslim luggage endorsed by the highest authorities in the faith. We have seen above what Sheikh Qaradawi professes openly in terms of the final victory of Europe by Islam, but he is not a lonely voice. Al-Azhar University in Cairo and its dons, who represent the "moderate"Islam of the Sunnite establishment, and are in hemselves threatened by Muslim radicals, proclaim in no uncertain terms:

> We are in the midst of a fateful confrontation[between Islam and the West], whether we like it or not. This confrontation was declared by our rivals, and we are all its target. Muslims will be attacked everywhere in the world, bcause the target of American attacks is our faith. They are fighting our faith under all kinds of headings such as terrorism, cultural hostility and [Muslim] uprising [against the West]. The bottom line is that Islam is the target... The West also senses that it is threatened by Islam, therefore they formed a coalition against it... Why don't we unite too around the saying:" There is no God but Allah, and Muhammad is the messenger of Allah?". Allying with America is an act of apostasy, therefore the

Afghan opposition ought not to collaborate with America, but go hand in hand with their compatriots and co-religionists, lest they be cursed by Allah and His angels[18].

Another religious scholar, Dr Shahin,said that based on the Qur'an, the term *irhab* (terror) carried a positive connotation inasmuch as it urges the Believers to sow terror in the hearts of the enemies of Allah, to dintinguish from the modern day terror which maybe a sort of madness carried out by individuals but has nothing to do with states. Therefore accusing Islam of terrorism is a mistake, the Muslims being the "symbols of peace in the world, and the Muslim *umma* having never attacked a neighboring nation"[19]. Dr Shahin, would have a hard time showing why and how Islam had expanded since its inception through conquest, unless we accept the Muslims' classic argument that those occupied peoples and territories had refused to surrender "peacefully" to the rule of Islam under the prevalent war cry *Aslim - Taslim*(become Muslim amd you will be safe), therefore Islam had to subjugate them by conquest in "self-defense". Moreover, it would be impossible for him to explain why, when Islam is accused of terrorism, he advances the claim that terrorism is individual and therefore cannot be imputed to states; but at the same time any nation fighting that terrorism is itself accused of "state terrorism against the weak"[20]. In other words state terrorism in Muslim eyes is the one waged by those who resist Islamic terror, like the Americans, the Indians, the Chinese and the Israelis. The notion that terrorism is defined according to the means of combat and its targeted victims, not by who wages it and against whom, simply escapes the Muslims minds, except when themselves become its targets. For example, Bin Laden became a terrorist when he

---

[18] Sheikh Abu al-Hassan, the Head of the fatwa Council, 11 October, 2001. Cited by *MEMRI*, "Terror in America", No 28.
[19] Dr Shahin, 16 October,2001, Ibid.
[20] Dr Mat'ani, 22 October, 2001, Ibid.

turned against his country (Saudi Arabia), while previously, as long as he as his likes acted against Israelis, Jews and other non-Muslims, he was a "*halal*" jihad fighter. For Dr Farmawi and others, for instance, Bin Laden was never seen as a terrorist while the American war against him in Afghanistan was an act of "oppression, barbarism, travesty of justice and hooliganism", and he urged his coreligionists to "wake up before the American Crusaders reach us"[21].

What boosts ever more significantly the Muslim attitude of arrogance and defying self-confidence in the streets of Europe and America is the capitulating spirit adopted by Western societies, which pretend not to hear or comprehend Muslim warnings, threats and physical intrusion, and evince tolerance and "understanding" towards this spitting at their face as if it were providential rain on arid land. Take for example, the regime of intrusion into the privacy of air passengers worldwide, which was inaugurated in recent decades due to the hijacking of airplanes introduced by Arab and Muslim terrorists. Instead of fighting it aggressively, by excluding from international air traffic all the nationals of countries whic gave shelter to those terrorists and so eliminate the scourge at its roots, the West surrendered to it and instituted the rule of intrusive inspection of all travelers' lugage, thus sumitting to this mode of collective punishment of the entire Western population for a crime that Muslims committed, while whining continuously against the "collective punishment" to which they were submitted by Western and Israeli counter attacks when they bombed the lair of those criminals. From the Muslim viewpoint Jihad is calculated to bring "justice" and "peace" to the world, naturally Muslim justice and peace that can only be dispensed by the Muslim legal system within the *Pax Islamica*. Hence the current clamor of Muslims for justice, or peace with justice. However, while the Western moral and legal tradition has developed a certain vision of these concepts, partly

---

[21] Dr. Farmawi, 11 October, 2001, Ibid.

based on the biblical prophecies of "beating swords into plough-shares", so that nations shall wage war no longer, and partly on the Roman concepts of *justicia* and *pax,* in Islam there is no theoretical equality between all nations, for the only prevailing one is the *umma* of Islam, "the elected nation of Allah", whose divine mission is to propagate the Word of Allah among nations, peacefully is possible, forcibly if necessary until they "see the light" and submit to Islam. Only then can peace and justice be served.

The belief in Islamic superiority goes hand in hand with the abysmal contempt many Muslims feel towards Infidels, especially Christians and Jews whom they perceieve as the direct challengers to Islamic hegemony. This contempt has been fed by the inexplicable gap between their innate inferiority which has been cast upon them by Allah Himself and the injunction to fight them [22], on the one hand, and their rather stunning success as advanced, rich and powerful nations in the modern world, on the other. Particularly unacceptable and incomprehensible to Muslims is the status of the Jewish communities in the West, especially in the US where they enjoy a far greater influence in the economic, scientific and artistic spheres than their small numbers would warrant. Especially humiliating to them is the fact that the Muslim communities in the West,

---

[22] See e.g. the Qur'anic

1. Sura 9:29: "Fight against those to whom the Scriptures were given. Who believe not in Allah nor in the Last Day, who forbid not what Allah and His Messenger have forbidden and follow not the True Faith, until they pay the tribute *(jizyah)*out of hand and are humbled".

2. Sura 5:51: "Oh, you who believe! Take not the Jews and Christians as friends. They are friends to one another. Whoever of you befriends them is one of them. Allah does not guide the people who do evil".

3. Sura 9:30-31: "The Jews say that Ezra is the son of Allah, and the Christians say that the Messiah is the son of Allah. Those are the words of their mouth, con forming to the words of the Unbelievers before them Allah, attack them!!! How pervert they are!!! They have taken their rabbis and their monks as lords besides Allah, and so too the Messiah son on of Mary though they were commanded to serve but one God. There is no God but He. Allah is exalted above that which they deify beside Him".

with their large Arab component, are nowhere near them in terms of impact. Therefore, when they confront Westerm and Israeli troops in various fronts, or when they penetrate into their territory by immigration, they act on the principle that if they cannot rise to their rivals' level, their only remaining option is to bring them down to their own level by terrorizing them and undermining and destroying them from within, as the only way to erase their own humiliation.

Consider what a Palestinian textbook for children, unwittingly financed by donations from the EU, puts forward as regards the prospects that await their benefactors who are busy giving shelter to the multitude of refugees from the Muslim world:

> In the present period... of unprecedented material and scientific advances... scientists in the West are perplexed by the increase in the number of people suffering from nervous disorders... and the statistics from America in this matter are a clear indication of this... Western civilization flourished, as is well-known, as a consequnce of the links of the West to Islamic culture, through Arab institutions in Spain and in other Islamic countries where Muslim thinkers and philosophers took an interest in Greek philosophy... Western civilization, in both its branches- the Capitalist and the Communist- has deprived man of his peace of mind and stability when it turned material well-being into the supreme achievement...., his money leading him nowhere execept to suicide...
>
> There is no escape from a new civilization which will rise in the wake of this material progress and which will continue it and raise the man to the highest spiritual life along material advance. Is there a nation capable of fulfilling such a role? The Western world is incapable of fulfilling it... There is onlly one nation capable of discharging

this task and that is our nation... No one but we can carry aloft the flag of tomorrow's civilization... We do not claim that the collapse of the Western civilization and the transfer of the center of civilization to us will happen in the next decade or two, or even 50 years, for the rise and fall of civilizations follow processes, and even when the foundations of a fortress become cracked it still appears for a long time to be at the peak of its strength. Nevertheless [Western civilization] has begun to collapse and to become a pile of debris... We have awakened to a painful reality and to oppressive imperialism, we drove it out of some of our lands and we are about to drive it from the rest...[23].

Anyone raised in this ambience and educated in this system would expectedly conclude that in view of the coming Western apocalypse, it is worthwhile to help undo Western civilization in order to speed up the process, and that since Islam is designed by Allah as the successor, it becomes a sort of a religious duty, a cultural Jihad, to undermine the West from within. Many Muslims have indeed smiled under their mustache at the sight of the ruins of September 11, as the first debris of the collapsing Western civilization. The rest can be helped or forced. Some Western-educated Muslims who dwell in the West, have begun detecting the unravelling of the West and their own sudden re-awakening after September 11. They naturally found solace and encouragement in the "words of support" as they interpreted them from within Western society itself, and also viewed them as "proof that their missionary Islamic messages were being absorbed by their traditional rivals

---

[23] *Outstanding Examples of Our Civilization for 11th Grade*, pp. 3-16. See R. Israeli, "Education, Identity State Building and the Peace Process: Educating Palestinian Children in the Post-Oslo Era", in *Terrorism and Political Violence*, VOl12, No 1, spring 2000, p. 87.

within the Western-Christian world. They were confident that time will come when when their host society will see the light and convert to Islam. Instructive in the regard are the words of Dr Fathi of the Harvard Medical School who reported to the Arabic press after the September 11 drama his first hand impressions which augured the end of Western culture and the advent of the Islamic era:

> … From Day one the media began hinting that Muslim and Arab hands were behind this event… We convened an emergency meeting of the Islamic Center in Boston and decided to organize blood donations, to be covered by the media… We all tried to hang on to any bit of information that would distance this criminal act from Islamic and Arab hands…, for we wanted to prove our humanity as we were attacked on all sides, and we were afraid that our preaching for Allah was set back 50 years in the US and the entire world… On Saturday, 15 of September, I took my wife and children to the largest church in Boston… to represent Islam there, at the invitation of Boston senators… We were welcomed as if we were foreign ambassadors… The senior priest defended Islam in his sermon and introduced me to the audience as the respresentative of the Muslim Association of Boston. Following his sermon, I read a statement of the Heads of the Muslim religion which condemned the events… and explained the principles of Islam and its sublime teachings…
>
> After that, I read translations into English of verses from the Qur'an… Those were moments I shall never forget, because the entire audience broke in tears when they heard the Words of Allah… One of them told me: "I do not understand Arabic, but what you said certainly sounded like the words of Allh". Another woman left a

note in my hand upon leaving the church in tears. It said: "Forgive us for our past and present. Please continue to sermonize to us." Another person, also in tears, stood at the gate of the church and said: "You are just like us, nay, better!"

On Sunday, September 16, we issued an invitation to the public to visit the Islamic Center that lay between Harvard and MIT. We expected 100 visitors, but we got 1000…, including university professors, priests… who were invited to speak, and all of them expressed solidarity with Muslims… There were many questions from the public who wanted to understand the teachings of Islam, not one of them was hostile. Quite the contrary, they were in tears when they heard about the lofty principles of Islam… Many of them had only heard of Islam through the incitement of the media… I was invited to repeat the same at another gathering in the church the same day, and the sights were the same…

On Thursday, a delegation of 300 professors and students from Harvard, accompanied by the American Ambassador to Vienna, undertook a visit to the Islamic Center. They sat on the floor of the mosque… We talked to them, explained Islam and cleared it from the suspicions that had been attached to it. I once again read from the Qur'an and their eyes filled with tears. Many of them were so excited that they asked to participate in the weekly classes that the Center holds for non-Muslims…. On Friday a Muslim delegation convened with the Governor of the state, where the introduction of Islam into the school curricula was discussed so as to avert racism against Islam which originatesd from American ignorance of the Islamic faith…

This is an example of what is happening today in

Boston and other American cities. Our proselytizing not only was not set back 50 years as we have feared… quite the contrary, those 11 day days that elapsed since 11 September were the equivalent of 11 years of proselytizing…. I am writing to you today with full confidence that Islam will expand all over America and the entire world, by the will of Allah, much faster than at any time in the past, because the world is all too eager to know Islam[24].

---

[24] Article by Dr Fatihi, in *AL-Ahram al-Arabi* of 20 October, 2001. It is noteworthy that the motif of tears "when one hears the sublime verses of the Qur'an" goes back to early Islamic history which relates that the Chritians of Najran in southern Arabia burst into tears when they heard the Prophet reciting to them the Words of Allah, and they converted on the spot. See MEMRI Report 36.

CHAPTER TWO
The Chaos of Multi-Culturalism

What caused Europeans to finally opt for the maintenance of their separate national identities and cultures, and the Muslim immigrants to be encouraged in their bid to erase Western culture so as to remold their host societies to their taste, was no doubt the cultural chaos that the policy of multi-culturalism has provoked throughout the continent, when the newcomers pretended to teach the original Europeans what Western values, like democracy, freedom, human rights and tolerance were. September 11 was the occasion for Islam to come out of its hidden apologetics and instead of providing excuses for that horror committed by Muslims, it presented its faith as the coveted creed of the world, whose glamor not only was not tarnished by the cataclysm, but on the contrary provided the opportunity to Muslims worldwide to show the lofty quality of their faith and to convince anyone who cared to listen that such a religion could not possibly have prompted its believer to perpetrate the horror. Many Muslims expected that once they showed Islam's mettle, the entire world would go their way docilely and embrace the principles of Islam which were the golden rules of tomorrow. If so, it became a tenet of Islamic activistm to Islamize human civilization by immigration and *da'wa* (missionary work) so as to dilute the leftovers of Infidel cultures and incorporate them all into Islam- the faith of the future.

Therefore, while prior to the momentous events of World War Two, which tore countries apart, caused untold death and destruction worldwide, and turned accepted norms and conventional wisdom upside down, the world's cultures, religions, ethnic and linguistic groups were centered on the local, national or regional turf, within clear boundaries, except when war or forced colonization brought a culture to encroach upon another's territory; after that momentous war, new patterns of population movements were conceived, by force or under agreement, by design or plying to evolving humanitarian conditions, under one pretext or another, which generated admixtures of populations, religions, customs and languages, thereby creating new frictions, instability, suspicions, fears and clashes between civilizations, climaxing in acts of terrorism that the world has failed to devise ways to fight.

One has to take cognizance, however, of the fact that some of the colonized nations before the war, had had their part in promoting their own self-confidence and sense of superiority over others, attitudes that had caused them to mistreat different cultures and minority groups within their borders, or to evince their hostility toward them by invading and subjugating them to their rule beyond their borders. That was in fact the nature of all major empires, where the ruler, be it Mongol, Abbasid, Ottoman, British or French, imposed his own rules over the subjected populations. The result in all cases was the imposition of the hegemonic power's culture, language, often religion and mores over the occupied populations. Very often, the subject peoples chose to adopt the ways of the rulers and learned how to assimilate themselves into their culture (in the Western colonies that was called "westernization", "modernization", and in Islamdom "Islamization"). Christian missionaries who came on the footsteps of their colonizing authorities usually elected to characterize their mission as "salvation", the "Gospel of Christ" and the like, and their task a *mission civilisatrice*.

What happened after World War II, and the turmoil it caused in the world, was not only the massive movements of independence in the colonized world, but also a reverse tendency of the colonized nations to migrate *en masse* to the lands of their previous occupiers. The reasons, or pretexts were not missing: the Western manpower having been depleted during the War on the one hand, and the immense needs of rehabilitation and reconstruction having never been so pressing and acute, on the other, the easy answer being to import a "provisional workforce" (in German they called it the *gastarbeiter*, the term "guest workers" pointing to their temporary status). On the importers' end, it was convenient and fast to rely on their previous colonies to recruit the requisite foreign man power, due to the supposedly linguistic and cultural heritage that the colonizers had left behind: the British in India and Pakistan and the Middle East, the Dutch in Indonesia, the French in North Africa; the Germans elected the Turks, their allies from World War One, who though ignorant of German culture and language, were the most emotionally approachable for temporary work; all were sure to be repatriated to their countries of origin at the end of their working abroad episode.

At first, in the 1950s and 1960s, most workers arrived on their own, conscious of their provisional status, and they were well content to dispatch home the proceedings of their labor and to visit occasionally their families back home during work vacations. But life necessities proved stronger than the intentions of the host nations and the rhetoric of the politicians. Soon, people began to either bring in their families or to intermarry with local women and start their own families, and many of them produced a second and third generation, which was now fluent in the languages of the adoptive countries, and whose expectations and demands kept growing: education for their children, family reunions with their relatives left behind, local citizenship in order to obtain also civil rights, and social and religious services to fit their needs. The individuals who had migrated to the West to find work and improve their standard of living, and were Muslim for the most part, were by the 1980s and 1990s solidly organized according to countries of origin, linguistic or ethnic groups, or religious congregations of various denominations, although mostly hailing from Islam.

Not only did most of the immigrants, who had by now attained a critical mass (over 10% of the total population in France, maybe 7% in Germany and an average of 5-6% in most of the rest of Europe, and much less than that in southern Europe (3% in Spain and Italy), and even less in the Balkans and Eastern Europe, which perceived the Islamic "menace" earlier than the others, and have taken energetic measures, much to the chagrin of their partners in the EU, to bloc Muslim immigration almost totally. The promoted fear from that "menace" emanated from the history of the Islamic invasions in Europe: in the 8th Century Islam had invaded Europe from the southwest, occupied the Iberian Peninsula and advanced into southern France, until arrested by Charles Martel in Poitier in 732; as they were finally expelled from there in the 15th Century, the second attempt was launched by the Ottoman Empire from the the direction of the southeast, when they occupied the Balkans and ultimately advanced to the gates of Vienna. The new contemporary "invasion" it has been claimed, was made by "peaceful" means, through mass migration, to which the West must ply due to its standards of civil rights and commitment to absorb "political refugees" running away from cruel and undemocratic regimes, which also happen to be located in Islamic countries in Africa, Asia and the Middle East. The greatest practitioners of this policy in the West naively sang the praise of what they dubbed "multi-culturalism", being unaware of its subversive effects or simply choosing to ignore them.

The end result has been that no Western country has kept its character, demographic homogeneity, religion or even its predominating language. When one strolls in the streets of Stockholm, Hamburg, Geneva or Rome, Paris or Nice, London or Birmingham, one observes a landscape never seen before: a confusing mixture of peoples, looks, languages and modes of behavior, which necessarily dilute the local culture to the point of becoming unrecognizable. In other words, one can no longer go to Sweden, Britain or Switzerland to delight in their environment, ambience and culture, for that culture exists no more in its original form. This admixture has been blessed by UN idealists, and some naïve Western leaders, before they woke up to its dangers, as "serving the cause of peace and understanding between nations", and by the migrating nations of the Third World who lust for an unlimited open door in the more advanced, prosperous and free West. But its greatest drawback has been its unilateralism: it is only the Islamic world which falls upon the West and alters it to its tune, while the reverse simply does not happen, for the Islamic world remains in its purity without outside interference, as though colonization had reversed course, and it was now the turn of Islam to impose a temporary multi-culturalism on Western lands in preparation for taking them over as a first step towards ruling the world.

In countries of immigration, like the US, Canada and Australia, the situation is not much better. There was a predominant Waspish element at the outset, but then the various waves of immigrants have been changing the character of those countries to the point that talking about an American culture, or a Canadian culture or an Australian culture has become laughable, for such things do not exist anymore. In the US, one century and a half after the bloody civil war which was waged on the noble question of repealing slavery, which tore the country apart and caused hundreds of thousands of dead and wounded, clashes between white and black have become a daily affair, with tensions mounting, bitterness and resentment increasing, and no prospective solution in sight. To a great extent, the Islamic element in this multi-cultural situation has become identical with the Black issue in exacerbating the moods and proving the unfeasibility of multi-culturalism in the long run. In Canada, the French separatist movement for a "free Quebec" persists, and the continued influx of immigrants, inter alia from Muslim countries continues to build up a Muslim community which has already been colored with extremism and some attempted acts of violence. In Australia, the mixture of races and cultures, which has gone so far peacefully, has united most Aussies against the manifestations of occasional terrorism on the part of Muslim immigrants who have embraced Islamic values more than the dominant Anglo-Saxon culture which has been joined by growing portions of peaceful Asian input.

To illustrate the destructive effects of this blind "multi-cultural-ism", which culminated in dotting the map of Europe with growing caches of weapons, terrorist gangs and committed ideologues, we can cite the cases of some countries, like Britain and the Netherlands[25] that have mostly suffered from its consequences. But all of them, backed by others, like Germany and the EU institutions, have elected to dub the scattered acts of terrorism by the Muslim immigrants as "criminal" in order to differentiate them, as it were, from the vast masses of "peaceful Muslims" who were moving to the European continent, ignoring the fact that wherever a Muslim community grew, it was bound to fall, sooner or later, under the spell of militant preachers who would incite violence and terrorism. In fact, however, those who engaged in terror were not criminals in the traditional Western sense. For criminals usually break the law for material gain: money or other assets, while Muslim terrorists did not aspire for any material benefit, and are on the contrary putting their lives on the line, for ideological/religious purposes. Thus, as long as European and American leaders and scholars were reluctant to call a spade a spade, and refrained from dubbing them what they were-- Muslim terrorists- multi-culturalism continued to entrench itself on the continent and terrorism went on unchecked. And

---

[25] See R. Israeli, *Retreating from he Mirage of Multi-CUlturalism?: The Cases of Holland, Britain and Israel,* Strategic Books, TX, 2018.

when they woke up, it was too late to turn back the clock. It was only in Summer 2019 that President Macron of France had the courage to avow publicly that Muslim radical elements in France sought to alter French political culture their way, and that the Republic was determined to resist that endeavor. He reiterated that pledge in October, 2019, when a Muslim convert employed at the Police HQ in Paris assasinated four of his colleagues at work, much in the fashion of the American-Muslim military psychologist who had gunned down his peers in Texas a decade earlier.

The first observation anyone makes who happens to render a sporadic visit to any country where multi-culturalism is experienced, is the salient differentiation between the various populations one runs across in the streets of cities: light complexions and dark ones, civil clothing of the current fashions, for men and women, along with traditional dress, with robes for men and veils for women, stands for fast food emitting familiar and luring tastes and fragrances, along with foreign odors and repulsive tastes, something so distasteful as sometimes turning to nauseating, though not due to their intrinsic disgusting nature but to their unfamiliarity with the place where they are emitted. In short, when things seem to be out of place, people get disoriented; local residents accustomed to certain landscapes, faces, colors, tastes and smells, sounds and languages, are no longer sure where they have landed or where they have ventured. Exception is made, of course, in countries like Brazil, where material and temporal multi culturalism had been at the foundation of the country from its inception. At the same time, in other parts of South America, the descendants of the Inca, Maya, Aztec, and other local civilizations are still marked by their physical traits and cultural and economic marginalization, namely ontinued socio-cultural frictions, but usually short of violence. But wherever Muslim minorities are added to the mix, exhibited religious components are bound to emerge and to cause disruptions which often may escalate into open violence due to their uncompromising nature.

One is tempted by the appearance of the popular resistance to world globalization, during the recent E-7 and E20 conferences, where the violent demonstrations tended to encompass parts of the immigrants into the Western countries, to conclude that multi-culturalism is only one manifestation of the conspiracy of world globalization, which as it endeavors to mix economies into one system that is remote- controlled by the big corporations, it also strives to control the peoples of the world by mixing them together into one spineless mass of nation-less people who are not bound by patriotism, ideology, culture or language, but are only committed to a single world economic system. This is precisely the crack where Muslim minorities penetrate Western democracies, taking advantage of their liberties and civil rights to undermine them from within, for while they ostensibly support a world government, and in the process disrupt the system in the host countries of multi-culturalism, they are determined and persuaded that the future belongs to Islam and that the waning of Christian Europe and the West in general, augurs the emergence of the Muslim world and its taking control of world dominion.

Certainly, many practitioners and promoters of multi culturalism use that terminology, not due to its philosophical or moral or humanitarian implications, like the presumption of a universal world where the human individual is more important than nations and states, and that all human creatures are equal and deserving of the same right to happiness and access to the goodies of life, but to serve what they consider as their long term interests. For example, many politicians who watch with an open eye the constantly decreasing reproduction rate in the West, which is due mainly to the pessimism with which prospective parents view the future and are therefore reluctant to marry, much less to engender children, realize that unless they import human reinforcement from the outside, they would face in one generation an acute shortage in manpower to replace workers in the factories, take care of the aging populations, and strengthen the productive part of society which alone can produce enough wealth to sustain the rest. This might be viewed as a very positive mode of thinking, not very characteristic of governments in Western liberal democracies, which usually sacrifice the long haul for the immediate interest of winning the next elections. But the chosen solutions do not have to be so precipitous, and could be much more cautious, gradual and digestible than the massive import of destitute Muslim refugees who are by definition potentially inimical to the Western nature of the country and its people.

By multiculturalism one usually means a social pluralism in which one ethnic, religious or linguistic group does not predominate over the others, no group is required to waive its character in order to accommodate the others, and no dominant ethos- historical, cultural or otherwise is permitted to marginalize the others. This is perhaps possible in immigrant societies, like the US, Canada and Australia, where national character has been in a state of flux since the inception of those countries, as the nature of the land, its regime, societal structure and culture are constantly changing to the tune of the incoming immigrants. But even then, those countries had chosen their basic foundational character as Waspish, Western, democratic, Christian and overwhelmingly Anglophonic, and all newcomers knew that they had to abide by those rules and adapt to them if they wanted to become part of their host societies. So did Latinos, Europeans, Arabs and Jews who immigrated to those countries, and to a great extent also the Asian immigrants of Indian, Japanese, Korean, Vietnamese or Chinese origin. The only problematic element which has wrecked that peaceful evolutionary pattern, by which immigrant societies have been absorbing their newcomers without any need for multi culturalism, has been the Islamic one. Due to its refusal to melt into this sort of society where its distinctive character would be diluted and then lost, and to its readiness to use force and violence to enforce its distinctiveness, it has differentiated itself from all other minorities, who may also have refused to melt and disappear but at the same time reconciled to the idea that assimilation was unstoppable in the long run and that they had no other recourse than accept it, which they had done implicitly the day they had relocated to their new land.

Multiculturalism as a political philosophy involves ideologies and policies which vary widely, ranging from the advocacy of equal respect to the various cultures in a society, to policies of promoting the maintenance of cultural diversity, to policies in which people of various ethnic and religious groups are addressed by the authorities as defined by the group to which they belong. Multiculturalism that promotes maintaining the distinctiveness of multiple cultures is often contrasted to other settlement policies such as social integration, cultural assimilation and racial segregation. Multiculturalism has been described as a "salad bowl" and "cultural mosaic". Two different and seemingly inconsistent strategies have developed through different government policies and strategies. The first focuses on interaction and communication between different cultures; this approach is also often known as interculturalism. The second centers on diversity and cultural uniqueness which can sometimes result in intercultural competition over jobs among other things, and may lead to ethnic conflict. Controversy surrounding the issue of cultural isolation includes the ghettoization of a culture within a nation and the protection of the cultural attributes of an area or nation. Proponents of government policies often claim that artificial government- guided protections also contribute to global cultural diversity. The second approach to multiculturalist policy making maintains that they avoid presenting any specific ethnic, religious, or cultural community values as central. It has been referred to as "a kind of Esperantic Disney World," a *tutti frutti* cocktail of cultures, languages and art forms in which 'everything becomes everything else'.

Thus, the pro-multi-culturalist movement in the West (and Japan for that matter) finds its rationalizations in the pressing needs to fill in its depleting demographic reserves, due to the negative procreation that generates a negative population growth; in the future needs for labor manpower; in the influx of young people to replace the constantly aging local populations; and in maintaining an amiable relationship with the Muslim world where those migrants might originate from. Governments in place also vouch for increased influx of immigrants into their territory, not only to prove that their policies have worked, but to expand their political base by incorporating the supposedly grateful immigrants into their political parties and ensure their continued hold on power. Governments in liberal democracies must act like fire brigades which have to extinguish fires at every turn to keep their populace satisfied and be voted in in the next elections, and could not care less about the grim future that awaits their countries two or three decades hence, when they are no longer in power. Only totalitarian regimes which are assured of the longevity of their regimes can plan for the long haul, and they devise their five-year plans in consequence. It is a fact that the more undemocratic regimes in Europe, as one travels eastward, where until recently doctrinaire Communist regimes predominated, the more restrictions on Muslim immigration into their borders.

But the Muslim immigrants, who are allowed into the West under the liberal-democratic governments who promote multiculturalism, wiew things slightly differently: they endeavor, first and foremost to increase their numbers by encouraging more immigration in order to reach the critical mass, and more conversion to Islam of the Westerners who are lured and fascinated by the successes of Islam in Europe, or think that they read into the future more intelligently that their compatriots. Secondly, they demand, in the name of the civil rights they acquire that *Shari'a* laws and Muslim customs (like wearing the veil, erecting minarets, forcing marriages, and imposing honor killings) be made to apply in their host countries. The incompatibility between the two systems is illustrated by the fact that the numbers of Muslims in jails in the West by far surpass their rate in the population. Thirdly, they prevail upon their adoptive countries to direct their foreign policies to their tune, for example with regard to a negative attitude towards the US and its policy in the Middle East and in favor of the Palestinians, and to shackling the West in any future conflict with or inside any Muslim country. They attain that goal by congregating in certain voting constituencies and making sure that no member of Parliament in their voting zone could be elected unless he or she supported more Muslim immigration, and favored their political and international agenda even against the government's stated policy.

Reinforcing communal cohesion so as to become a political force to be reckoned with, these immigrant communities self-impose isolation in their own neighborhoods and begin developing dissenting groups which may evolve into hostile anti-societies in the long haul. This process has been identified with Muslims in China since the 8th Century, and is enduring in Muslim villages and townships in Israel, and in the Muslim quarters in Detroit and London. Secondly, an independent Islamic educational system is installed worldwide through the lavish establishment of mosques, schools and Islamic centers throughout the world, especially taking advantage of their liberty to do so under the liberal regimes of the West, despite the continued persecution of Christian minorities in Islamdom and the banning of the Christian Mission in many Muslim countries, most of all Saudi Arabia, which does not even permit non-Muslims into its borders. The famous educational system that Fethullah Gulen built in the US is only one spectacular example of this quiet and subtle, but steady, subversive and effective penetration into Western society in order to transform it.

In multiculturalism as a term, there is much ambiguity since it can serve many social and political causes, and it is not merely used to promote cultural pluralism in countries which, due to political and historical circumstances, find themselves grappling with a plurality of ethnic or cultural groups. Multi culturalism is not a choice made voluntarily by countries and people, who usually elect uniformity, homogeneity and familiarity of their citizenry, which can more easily draw a social contract and avoid social and political frictions between various parts of the population and especially when they are alien to the naticve culture. However, rare are the countries where there are no minorities, and where their presence is not spread everywhere; so, when aggrandized by their numbers, and they are unwilling to yield to the predominant culture, or are enhanced by a religion like Islam that rejects any form of government that is not their own, brings us to the collision course. Watch the case of Yugoslavia which after Tito' s death broke up into its components. But in that case, the ethno- religious groups were also territorial and facilitated their secession into Orthodox Serbia, Catholic Croatia and the Muslim majority Bosnia, and enabled Muslim Kosovo to break up from Serbia,though large minorities of every other ethnicity remained in each of them, which posed unresolved ethno-religious problems thereafter. Other authoritarian countries, like Syria, Iraq, Libya, also broke up into their ethnic, tribal and religious components when the leaders who held them together passed away or weakened.

That was the situation when domestic historical conditions had shaped the regimes of multicultural countries. But the problem of multi culturalism is more often visible when applied to aboriginal ethnic groups, like the Indians of the Americas, the aborigines of Australia and New Zealand, or to foreign groups who immigrated to the countries in question and maintained their distinctiveness. The Palestinians, including Israeli Arabs, for example, regard themselves as natives of their land and they rebel against the imposed Jewish government upon them. But they should perhaps refrain from embracing those precedents, which have kept the native aborigine population marginalized and impoverished. Besides, while the other natives in other countries were *in toto* taken over by those who colonized them, Israeli Arabs are only a small part of the Palestinian people which dwells elsewhere and strives for its own sovereignty. Foreign immigrants have usually done well when they accepted the dominant cultures they knew when they immigrated, save for Muslims who, due to their identification with the universal Muslim community, the *Umma,* have had more difficulties than other minority groups to adapt to the new cultural background and acculturate into it. Different is the situation when a culturally different territory is amalgamated with another country or culture, like Hungarian Transylvania and Voivodina which were integrated into Romania and Serbia, respectively, or the Arab areas of the Galilee and the Negev which became part of Israel. There, multi culturalism always runs the risk of escalating into *irridenta* and endless political clashes like those occasioned by the German Danzig Corridor in Poland and the Sudeten in Czechoslovakia on the eve of W W II, or the Russian minorities in the Ukraine and the Baltics today.

Academics and armchair political strategists can theorize at ease about the morality, fairness and desirability of multiculturalism, or its interculturalist version, but only people who have experienced its related misfortunes, either from the minority aspects which abound in bitterness, sense of discrimination and wish to disengage, or from the majority angle which is replete with suspicions, fear, terror and estrangement in its own land, can deliver a worthy judgment of their defects and the possibilities of remedying them. Therefore, there is no much use to the various anthropological and sociological theories to this effect, nor is there any point to rely on this or that political philosophy to unravel the complications caused by these unfortunate situations, especially when they are intertwined with economic interests and political power. The gamut of definitions and interpretations voiced in this regard has so widened as to encompass ethnic, religious and linguistic minorities, but also minority nations, indigenous peoples and even the disabled as a minority group. Most of all, these academic debates have been focusing on whether multiculturalism is the best way to deal with immigrants and refugees, be they gradually and legally invited in, sorted out and absorbed according to state organized blueprints, or fleeing zones of combat and flocking across borders uninvited, capitalizing on Western democratic societies' customs and moralities which compel them to absorb refugees, rescue people in danger and extend immediate humanitarian aid to them. But these humanitarian measures, which are unique to the West, do not specify what happens next. Are they unlimited in time, space and volume, or limit the numbers of absorbed incomers, and the length of time of their accommodation in the host countries to accord with the economic capacity of the host country, the size of its population and the ethnic and religious feasibility to receive and absorb the newcomers without causing disruptions to the fiber of the existing societies?. For example, populations running away into enemy countries, or from hostile cultures and religions, are the shelter countries expected to take them in, and obliged to absorb them and for how long?. These are some of the dilemmas many Western countries have been tackling these days once the idea of multiculturalism has proved inadequate to resolve them.

When it comes to Muslim refugees, especially when radical Islamic groups and individuals seek asylum in countries they plan to undermine from within, the situation becomes even more complicated, because Muslims do not accept any rule which is not theirs. This state of affairs is exacerbated by the fact that Jihadi movements like ISIS, al Qa'ida, Hamas, Hizbullah, and Islamic Jihad are waiting in the aisles for the opportunity to penetrate target countries for their work of *da'wa* or subvesrsion, constantly reinforced by Muslim youth volunteers who reside in the same Western countries they plan to penetrate. These Muslim radicals are also aided by the erstwhile moderate Islamic countries, like pre-Erdogan

Turkey, and pre-Khomeini Iran, which have shifted towards radicalism and turned their old alliances with the West and Israel into a virulent anti Western stance. Thus, Western countries must become more vigilant when they are sought for shelter to Muslim regugees. Worse, as the numbers of anti-Western Muslim countries and movements keep increasing, their worldwide presence in all parts of the globe causes the state of siege around the West (and Israel) to feel tighter and the chances of accommodation between these clashing civilizations ever slimmer. While great powers and advanced countries can wield enough wherewithal and weave appropriate alliances to defend themselves and overcome the threats, small and vulnerable countries like Holland and Israel, whose populations are limited and the fear of being inundated by Muslim populations is great, feel and behave differently. Their means are also limited, and their very existence hangs on a patron state or an organization like the US, NATO and the EU. So, they perceive the emergence of radical Islam and the menace it poses to their existence as very concrete, immediate and overwhelming. In this state of affairs, movements of Muslim terrorists who have shown in the past their mettle in destruction and death, in hatred and cruelty, loom larger than life while their threat to Western lives too has grown very real and imminent.

The modern Western world has become accustomed to discuss openly and debate publicly the rationality and justification of policies, domestic and international. But Muslims, while using the same vocabularies in order to make themselves understood to the West, keep using misnomers[26], and are followed by docile Western politicians and scholars, to an extent that old notions have been confused with new ones, words lose their significance and expressions of political correctness have handily replaced linguistic accu-

---

[26] R. Israeli, *Misnomers and Cultural Choices: How Islam Tries to Impose its Norms on non-Muslims,* Strategic Books, TX, 2019.

racy. Words are used to mean different things to the point that we find it increasingly awkward to transmit certain messages, and have to create new phrases and coin alternative words in order to avoid misunderstandings. Cases in point have been the widespread usage of "Islamist" (to distinguish from Muslim) as if there were two separate doctrines of Islam, one to serve the moderate "peaceful" Muslims, and the other to express the Jihadi tendencies of the radicals, and "suicide bomber" where there is no suicide, not even the semblance of a suicide in the thinking of those terrorist killers. For Muslims, there is one Islam, for Jihad is not only the domain of the radicals, and the "suicide bombers" (elsewhere dubbed *Islamikaze* by this author)[27] are martyr fighters for the cause if Islam in general.

If, as some claim, there were a certain percentage of Muslims who are "radical", "fundamentalist" or simply "Islamists", while the majority is Muslim of the good brand, which politicians like Bush and Blair wrongly called "peace-loving", then how come that we see vast crowds, which seem to represent the local majorities, in every place where Muslims burst out in violence, be it in Cairo, Gaza, Quetta, Teheran, Kabul as during the Cartoon Affair in Europe in 2006, or when the Muslim populace jubilates when a disaster hit the West or Israel? What happens to those supposedly peace-loving majorities who are not supposedly represented by the violent crowds? And when Muslim columnists, including Western-educated and degree-holders, write in the mainstream journals of the Muslim world, including in "moderate" and "pro-Western" countries, like Egypt, Saudi Arabia or Jordan, genocidal wishes and virulent recriminations against the West and Israel, and expressions of joy after September 11 or every time a bus or a restaurant blow up in the West or in Israel, with dozens of victims, are those celebrating frenzied crowds representative of "radicals" or of "Islamist"

---

[27] R. Israeli, *Islamikaze: Manifestations of Islamic Martyrology*, Frank Cas, London, 2003.

individuals?[28] Then, where is the difference between "peace-loving" Muslims and so-called "Islamists"? While there are theological differences of nuance between Sunnites and Shi'ites, and within the Sunnites between the four Schools of law (*madhahib*), for instance between the puritanical Wahhabis of the Hanbali cult and the more lenient Hanafites on matters of *Shari'a* law, there appears to be unanimity among them with regard to Jihad wars and the contempt and hostility towards the West, because they all draw from the same medieval Abu Yussuf and Ibn Taymiyya and the more modern Hassan al-Banna, Sayyid Qut'b or abu al-'ala' al-Mawdudi. Understandably, not every Muslim would observe to the letter the strictest prescriptions of those scholars, but at the same time no sweeping and authoritative alternative doctrine to those great luminaries has emerged to challenge them, let alone replace them.

Those referred to by Westerners as "Islamists" call and regard themselves simply as plain Muslims, who are perhaps more zealous than others and wish to fulfill Muslim goals here and now, but essentially hailing from the same Islamic doctrine. But are they so distinguishable from other Muslims that they deserve to be treated as if they were different Muslims or as if they had invented a different Islam? All religious Muslims venerate the great masters of radical Islam like Hasan al-Banna, Sayyid Qut'b, Mawdudi and Qaradawi, even if they are not categorized as "radicals". The latter relate to the masses of common Muslims the way activists or militants in a political party refer to the rank and file of sympathizers who only vote when the day comes, but are not involved in any day to day politics. But we do not distinguish between "radical" and "common" party members. Yes, they differ, in both cases, as far as the degree of commitment, activity and observation of details are concerned, but we cannot set them apart ideologically, and they

---

[28] See R. Israeli, *Islamikaze:Manifestations of Islamic Martyrology,* Frank Cass, London, 2003, Chapter 1, pp. 11-32.

continue to belong to the same core of belief and conviction. For if there were a "liberal" or "moderate" tendency in Islam, it would be evinced, first of all, by theologians of Islam who would stand up courageously and battle against the ideas and theses of the "Islamists". However, while truly moderate and daring individuals of Muslim descent (and sometimes conviction) do exist, principally in the safety of the West, we cannot discern any significant trend of moderation and "peace-loving" inclination which rallies behind it masses of Muslims. So, what is erroneously dubbed "moderate" or "non-Islamist" Islam, is actually the silent majority who is, unfortunately, more likely than not to follow the outbursts of jubilation when the West and Israel are harmed, to watch bluntly anti Western and anti-Semitic series on television which depict American or Israelis as blood-drinkers, world -conspirers and children-killers, and to avidly absorb genocidal statements by their leaders and clerics and reiterate their belief in the same non-sensical slogans and conspiracy theories that are circulated in their media. One year after September 11, Dan Rather of CBS News undertook a worldwide survey of Muslim (not Islamist) reactions to those horrific events. From a sample of 8 Muslim countries, between Morocco and Pakistan, where he polled the literate population in remote villages in each one of those countries, the overwhelming majority of the populace, which was not "radical", spelled out their conviction that the horror was "of course" perpetrated by the Jews, the *Mossad*, the CIA, or in collaboration of the two, and such delusive fairy-tales.

Did the Palestinians suddenly become "Islamists" when the radical Hamas won elections among them in 2005? No, they remained as Muslim as they were before the elections. They burst into unabashed joy when September 11 happened, much to Arafat's embarrassment who sent his security forces to disband those "radical" children to avoid further disgrace. Why did they do that? Because they were indoctrinated by their school textbooks, which assured them of the imminent victory of Islam against the "corrupt and tyrannical" West. They burst forth in jubilation when Israeli and Western families were shown torn into pieces, and they re-enacted harrowing scenes of explosions against Israel, showing cardboard buses or restaurants burning and limbs of children flying around, with huge crowds of children, passers-by, shop-keepers, students and policemen clapping hands and rejoicing. Even their universities and school plays staged such re-enactments. Could all those be "Islamist"? No, in their eyes, Israelis and the West are perceived as the enemies of Islam (not of "Islamists"), therefore one should rejoice at their defeat, and because they are not defeated often enough for the Muslims' taste, no Muslim can skip the delight of re-playing that defeat and savoring it in slow motion. Another question is why America and Israel are particularly targeted and their national flags usually accompany each other, when a Muslim frenzy of burning and destroying burst forth in any part of the globe. The answer is two-fold: first both of those countries stand out as the consummate representatives of strength, modernity, prosperity and success, something which only brings out the impotence and backwardness of the Islamic world. That is the source of "humiliation" that Muslims reiterate so often and so intensely, for only the existence of that successful world permits Muslims to grasp what they missed, and they get truly humiliated by the hopelessness of their lagging behind. Secondly, their dream to remedy the situation by creating a *Pax Islamica* to encompass the entire universe, has been scuttled principally by Israel in its immediate vicinity and by America worldwide, for the US is the only power able and willing to stand up to them and obstruct their goal of establishing a world caliphate. That double frustration has been shared by Muslims in general, regardless of whether one categorizes them as "Islamists" or otherwise.

After September 11 a talk show was held by *al-Jazeerah* network (representing what is known as "moderate" and "peace-loving" Islam) where the question was posed to the panelists and the viewers about whether Bin Laden was a terrorist or a hero. The only truly moderate panelist, a Tunisian, was mocked and humiliated by his co-panelists and by the moderator of the show for daring to dissent from the otherwise unanimous opinion which crowned Bin Laden as a national hero. Viewers who called or emailed from the entire Islamic world, were almost unanimous in the same consensus. That was not a poll among "Islamists", but among the rank and file of Muslims, most of whom were supposedly the educated owners of PC computers. Yet, their reaction was "Islamist" in substance. So, where is the distinction? Yes, there are *Islamikaze* activists who are ready to blow themselves up for the cause of Islam, in the process killing Westerners and Jews. But they are only a handful, who are recruited, trained, financed, indoctrinated and dispatched by a vast infra-structure of Muslim states, organizations and individuals, and surrounded by the sympathy and admiration, often adulation, of the vast masses of the Muslim public and the mainstream press in countries that are clients of the US or signed peace with Israel. Who is then an "Islamist" among all those layers of activists and supporters, and who is the "moderate" and "peace-loving?". In the US and Europe, it was found that several Muslim intellectuals, leaders and clerics, who gained favor with the authorities and access to the highest echelons of power, for their supposed "moderation", and their openness to "dialogue", were later arrested for their illicit fund-raising for Muslim terrorist organizations, for incitement to terrorism or for suppressing women's rights; did they suddenly turn from "moderate" to "radical"? No, they were the same Muslims who were perceived previously as moderate when they acted or refrained from acting in a certain way, but became "Islamists" when they were caught red-handed when engaging in subversive acts against their host countries. In both instances they acted as Muslims in the name of Islam; it is Western and Westernized Muslim scholars who attached to them those epithets which they themselves never recognized. Most Muslims who cite the relevant passages from their sources to justify their deeds, and they do so regularly and perenni-ally, are also used to make blunt anti American and anti-Semitic and genocidal statements, and no amount of rhetorical maneuvering can mitigate that fact.

It seems that the fictional distinction that is drawn in the West between Islam and "Islamists", which is usually made either by Western scholars and politicians or by Muslim moderates who live in the West, emanates more from an instinct of self-defense and survival than from a sober observation of reality. In Muslim coun-tries themselves it is often hard to tell who is who, inasmuch as Palestinian, Saudi, Egyptian and Pakistani clerics who belong to the "moderate" establishment, often issue *fatwas* and deliver sermons that are every bit as "extremist" as the "radical" ones, and even imported or home grown Muslim clerics in the West do not make any effort to distinguish or to distance themselves from "Islamists", because they themselves cannot tell the difference. Western scholars and politicians, who want to cater to Islam, for electoral or other worldly perks, on the one hand, but cannot ignore the rage of their own people against violent Islam, on the other hand, find shelter in that distinction which allows them to claim that the Islam they support or defend is "moderate", while the violence that their peo-ple condemn emanates solely from the "extremist Islamists". At the same time politicians and scholars critical of Islam need that dis-tinction to shelter themselves from accusations of "racism", as if multi-ethnic and multi-racial Islam were a "race", or of anti-Muslim bias and hatred. Muslim scholars and public figures who live in the West resort to that distinction in order to avoid a blanket condem-nation of Islam of which they are part, and to escape suspicions by their coreligionists that they "sold-out" to the West or that they committed an act of "treason" against their culture and religion. Many of them find it more expedient to claim that they are "secular Muslims", a notion that is unacceptable to Islam in all its nuances, and some of them convert to Christianity in order to feel free to lash out at their previous religion, though they know that they are handily offset by the much larger numbers of Westerners who convert to Islam.

Matters are further complicated and made less comprehensible to Western minds by the paranoia and conspiracy theories that are very widespread in the Muslim world, among "Islamists" and others alike, whether Muslims are modern and Western-educated or traditionalist and obscurantist. Those theories that are rampant even among Muslims living in the West, would insist that world leaders who support Israel are Jewish (like Presidents Reagan and Bush), that the UN of all places, is the mastermind of the Jews who utilize it as the tool for their world dominion, and that the major violent acts that shook the world, like the world wars, the world revolutions and September 11, are all the fruit of Jewish creation and execution, with or without Western connivance and collaboration. Their minds are so permeated with these non-sensical theories that they become impervious to logical, rational debate that is open to argument, discussion and to persuasion. Therefore, the difficulty of dealing with Muslim minds consists not only of removing the mountains of pure delusion that choke their free thinking, but also of persuading them that the very attempt to counter-argue those futilities is not necessarily part of the world conspiracy that is being woven against them. It is possible to explain their imaginary picture of the world by their need to project on their enemies the conceptual and analytical shortcomings that bewitch them, but it is impossible to move them out of the illusory scenarios that they have constructed around themselves and then they cling to them with a tenacity that defies and contradicts Western standards of conduct. The result is that even when Muslims initiate and launch an act of violence, they accuse the West of it and dub it, or what led to it, as an act of "aggression" of which they are the victims and which calls for their retaliation.

As long as the Muslim anti-Western and anti-Semitic discourse was internal, little attention was paid to it in the outside world. But since the end of the Afghanistan War (1979-89) which also signaled the end of the Cold War and the return of the *Mujahideen* to their Muslim home countries, tremendous energies were released by the *Afghanis* (i.e, the foreign Arab battle-hardened graduates of the war in Afghanistan) which were channeled both domestically (Islamist activity in Algeria, Saudi Arabia, Sudan, Lebanon, Egypt, Jordan, Pakistan and Taliban Afghanistan), and internationally to wage a worldwide Jihad, led by Bin Laden's al-Qa'ida, and ISIS, but carried out simultaneously on Arab, American, African, Asian and European soil. The rising prices of oil afforded some oil-producing Muslim countries and their rulers the possibility to finance the spread of Islam of the puritanical and violent brand in the West and to absorb some of the unemployed *Afghani Mujahideen,* while the others were turned loose and ended up in the battle fields of Iraq, Lebanon, Bosnia, Chechnya and Palestine, and then Syria, or became mercenaries of violence in America and Europe. The Danish Cartoon Affair of 2006 proved a golden opportunity for Muslim regimes who began to feel the heat of terrorism breathing down their necks, to re-direct the rage and fury of their masses outwardly against the West and Israel, regardless of whether we define them as radicals or moderates, for Western institutions were attacked in Libya, Egypt, Palestine, Syria and Lebanon, and the boycott of Danish products was launched by Saudi Arabia and other Gulf states which are usually considered "moderate" and "pro-Western".

When one examines the spread of Islam into Europe one must take stock of all those considerations, and come to the conclusion that it is not enough to account for Muslims' immigration into the Old Continent and its transformation at their hands, but also go into the dialectic between European counter-measures after the major acts of terror that occurred there and the Muslim worldview which regards those defensive measures as aggression, persecution, racism, discrimination against the ever-docile and always "poor", underdog and helpless, innocent and "victimized" Muslims who had just come to seek work. When Britain or Germany idolized multi-culturalism as a way to "enrich" European culture, and celebrated the fake "difference" between moderate Islam of the mainstream and the violent few troublemakers, the Muslims regarded that goodwill gesture by and large, as an attempt to dilute Islam and split it apart in order to dominate and eliminate it. Only their unrestricted and violent activity in Europe, they thought, and favorable recognition of their own mores and norms, such as wearing the veil, forcing marriage on their women or pursuing "honor killings", or showing leniency towards group rape by Muslims of European women, would be acceptable as a fair behavior of the host countries towards them. In other words, not satisfied with full equality of opportunity, freedom of speech and of religious cult, Muslims demand special privileges for themselves, like the prerogative to train terrorists or incite violence against other fellow-citizens, because in their skewed view of democratic society, only too much freedom and *laissez-faire*, even at the detriment of the host state and society, is enough freedom for them. When they burn down a Jewish synagogue or beat a Jew in Berlin or Paris or Melbourne, they expect their adopted countries to accept that as a matter of course, and they are often aided in that belief by the local extreme-left or extreme-right, or church organizations that boost Muslim demands due to their common anti-Semitism or in order to appear as "progressive" multi-culturalists.

Reverting to the right terminology, calling a spade a spade, is not only our duty to scholarship, which recognizes no biases, no self-serving ideologies and no catering to political correctness, also re-establishes straight lines of communication between authors and readers and between scholars and their peers, and forces upon everyone in the field to play by the same rules. It is unthinkable, for example, that ideology-driven volunteers, who are ready to make the ultimate sacrifice for their convictions, should be denigrated as "suicide-bombers", however they may deserve denigration, or that anyone who lacks in courage to criticize any aspect of Islam should hide behind the spurious excuse of refraining from bashing "Islamism", while Islam pure and simple remains untouchable and beyond reproach. One should also recognize that injecting massive doses of Islam into an already difficult dispute, has turned the Muslim- Western confrontation into a bloody and *Intractable Dispute*[29] (listen to Bin Laden's and to Iran's and other Muslim radical threats toward the West and take them seriously, and do not dismiss them as pure rhetoric and boasting. Watch the senseless and cruel execution of Daniel Pearl in Karachi and others in the killing fields of ISIS, or the terrorist acts done by al Qa'ida and others of their likes, and listen to the threats and attacks against Jews in Europe and on Israel's borders by Hamas and Hizbullah), and you will get a sense of this asymmerical and uncompromising battle. Acting so, the dispute was pushed one notch up, because from the quantitative issue it used to be, involving territories, compensations and other measurable and negotiable assets, it grew into a qualitative problem dealt with in absolutes, in Allah-given terms, which are not subject to negotiation, let alone compromise and settlement. Anyone reading the Hamas Charter[30] or viewing the Hamas conduct on Israel's borders with Gaza, cannot have missed this trend since it was elected by Palestinians to guide their destiny. In short, Westerners should realize that it is Islam, not Islamists are their ideological rivals and potential enemies, and terrorist movements like the al Qa'ida and Taliban, the Hamas and Hizbullah are the long arms which resort to *Islamikaze* to sow terror in the West and discourage it from resisting this onslaught. Diluting the Islamic rivals by sin-

---

[29] See a book of this title by this author: *The Intractable Dispute: Why Are Muslims and Arabs at Loggerheads with Jews and Israel.* Strategic Books, TX, 2019
[30] See R.Israeli, "The Charter of Allah: The Platform of the Islamic Resistence Movement", in *Fundamentalist Islam and Israel:Essays in Interpretation,* University Press of America, Lanham, 1993, pp.123-170.

gling out Islamists among them, diminishing their death and terrorist contractors by calling them "suicide bombers" and denigrating their home grown idealist followers by dubbing them criminals, not only does not address the problem of Islam in general, but lends to it legitimacy.

CHAPTER THREE

The Pitfalls Impeding One Integrated Culture

Many countries in the world were born under the constraint of an organic diversity of populations, and they have tackled the issue for better or for worse, as a given that they did not either control or could alter. But Western democratic countries, which had been until W W II used to the familiarity and pride in homegrown national ethos, culture, language and ethnicity, and to the unchallenged homogeneity of the country to which very few minorities or alien individuals were quick to adopt and melt into the lot, were faced after the war with the influx of foreigners, mainly from their former colonies, and their seemingly best way to absorb and integrate those newcomers were various attempts at some form of multi culturalism, although this term was not used then. At first, the straightforward thought suggested that any immigrant should integrate into the existing culture and become part of it, although in some cases the stigma of color made some of the immigrants more salient and distinguishable from others, and made the process of integration slower and more difficult. But in time, with the growing numbers of migrants, whom Europe felt the obligation to welcome from its previous colonies, questions were raised about their mode of integration, for various alternative ways loomed in the horizon which called for trial, and rapid assimilation of the masses of newcomers was no longer viewed as the exclusive way of their absorption, as many of

them, especially among the homegrown second and third generation, adhered to movements to revive their original languages, cultures and mores which started emerging.

As the international community became more and more aware
of human rights and dignity, and of the rights of individuals to their
own cultures, the host states of these diverging migrants had to
constantly install new ways and test new methods of dealing with
the issue with a view of acculturating the immigrants, because this
was essential for their integration, which they themselves had been
desirous to achieve, but also wished to respect the the tendency of
the younger generation, which was integrating in their newly
acquired language and political and social system, but they also
wanted to preserve their original heritage that their parents had
imported with them but were gradually abandoning. The problem
of the absorbing countries was whether to subordinate the revived
heritage of the new comers to the national civil curriculum which
was common to all citizenry, or the other way round. Those who
supported a *laissez faire* policy of non interference with the immigrants' choices, found themselves at some point encouraging dissent
and rebellion against the countries that have given asylum to the
migrants and generously allowed them to make their choices, which
had put on a par the imported cultures with the national educational systems. That contradiction was bound to undermine integration and hamper the acculturation process of the new comers, the
result of which we see today in the growing ghettoization of the
immigrants and in their alienation, and sometimes open hostility,
toward the predominant culture of the countries of asylum. A case
in point was played out in a national stadium in France, which
hosted an international soccer game between a local team and an
Algerian visiting team. The national anthems of both countries were
played, as of custom, and when the Algerian national hymn was
sounded, the audience duly stood to attention. But when the turn
of the *Marseillaise* came, the Arab part of the audience began booing

vociferously, to the stunned reaction of the French notables present and the French audience at large, which could not comprehend this purposeful show of hostility and disrespect, which did not spell out acculturation, and certainly not civility.

One basic aspect of a multicultural or pluralistic society, at least in Western democratic societies, is the expectation that every cultural group culture is recognized and respected equally. This has been the stated policy of those countries where the presence of a diversity of cultures within the common national identity requires such a recognition and respect. But here is the first difficulty. In the US, Canada and Australia, for example, there is already an established recognition of the primacy of the English language as the *lingua franca* of the country, and except for the special case of French in Quebec, there is no chance that any other language, for example Chinese or Hindi, could be adopted as another official tongue, even if the numbers of immigrants from one of those countries should attain a critical mass of claiming parity with the established linguistic patterns of the land. Thus, to speak about equality between all cultural groups is a fiction. These three Anglophonic countries, which are founded on a policy on a selective immigration quotas so as to leave intact the Waspish nature of the land, have naturally become since the 1970 the early precursors of multiculturalism and the models thereof. So much so that the Canadian Royal Commission on Bilingualism and Biculturalism is often referred to as the origin of modern political awareness of multiculturalism. Only following those countries, European members of the EU adopted that policy, unaware or ignoring the differences that made that course possible and feasible in the former due to their being countries of immigration whose national culture and ethos were being gradually shaped as they went along, while the European states, with the exception of binational and bi ethnic Belgium, and Switzerland that is divided between three ethno-linguistic groups (German, French and Italian) had been cultivating their homogeneity and cultural distinctiveness for centuries, and therefore their multi culturalism was necessarily harder to pursue. However, some left leaning ideology- driven Western governments, chief of which was Tony Blair' s Labor cabinet in Great Britain, adamantly pursued this course, while some right wing governments which followed them, but understood the pitfalls of this policy, started to retreat from it as soon as they could, for example David Cameron's government in Britain and his counterparts in the Netherlands and Denmark. In his last speech in Parliament before his retirements from politics, Blair confirmed that immigrants ought to be integrated into the existing national and cultural system, not encouraged to cultivate their own separate one, which gave rise to the homegrown acts of terrorism in London in the summer of 2005. That was a retreat to monoculturalism, which was soon echoed, though not in so many words, by Chancellor Merkel of Germany. Nonetheless, she reversed course again in 2015 when she agreed to absorb any number of Muslim refugees from the Middle East, but under harsh criticism at home she withdrew again from that position and qualified and limited it once again. Other Europeans who experienced multi culturalism but were smitten by its consequences, like Sarkozy of France and Aznar of Spain, were honest and courageous enough to admit their mistake and became staunch supporters of monoculturalism, which could tolerate only a limited and digestible number of minorities.

Maybe the most vocal politician advocating the retreat from multi culturalism has been the Dutch head of the Freedom Party, Geert Wilders, the country which had been the most advanced in implementing that ill- advised course and in obvious reaction to it. He was the one who understood that the problem was not extremist or radical Islam but Islam in general, and therefore he launched severe broadsides against that faith, which cost him indictments and court trials, together with scorn on the part of his fellow politicians and their left wing colleagues throughout Europe who refused to recognize the danger. But his radical speeches and public denounce-ments of Islam also won him a considerable support on the part of Dutch people who also awoke to the menace, thus magnifying his political support at home and inspiring a similar rise of right wing parties in Belgium, Germany and elsewhere. The only grave error those politicians made, which mobilized popular support against them was the apparent "Islamophobia" that transpired from their political messages, as they condemned Islam and its beliefs in extreme and derogatory fashion, and thus mobilized a wide liberal public in Europe against what appeared as intolerable "racist" and xenophobic utterances hurting Europe' s image as the land of toler-ance and human rights. Had Wilders and his counterparts in Europe focused on the damages Islam has been causing to the national ethos and culture in various European countries instead of condemning it wholesale, and had they stressed that they had noth-ing against Islam when it stayed in its own turf and did not try to invade Europe and attempt to impose on it its deficient standards and subversive mores, they would have had no quarrel with it, and they would have probably increased their political base instead of watching it barred from actual power. So, in spite of the abuses by Muslim immigrants in Hamburg, Malmo, Manchester and Sidney, where women were attacked and terrorist activities committed, part of which are not reported in the media in order not to inflame the moods, the inflammatory rhetoric of the right wing politicians like Wilders has often backfired against him and his likes.

So, when Geert Wilders of the Freedom Party left a courtroom in Amsterdam on June 23, 2011 where he was acquitted of all charges of discrimination and inciting hatred against Muslims, it seemed to him as a great leap forward in a week that saw the end of the decade-long Dutch experiment with integration via multi cul-turalism, the very concept he was fighting tooth and nail. Judges ruled that although the comments the politician made in the Dutch press and on the internet between October 2006 and March 2008 comparing Islam to Nazism may have been offensive, they were nonetheless legal and part of a legitimate government debate only a few years ago. He himself retorted that "The good news is that it's legal to be critical about Islam, and this is something that we need because the Islamization of our societies is a major problem and a threat to our freedom. And I'm allowed to say so." But a directly concerned Dutch Muslim was soon on record claiming that Wilders was creating hate against Islam, and his young daughter stated that when she watched him on TV he scared her. But none of them mentioned in the least what their Moroccan compatriot had done when he murdered the much controversial Dutch cinema producer and artist Theo van Gogh in an Amsterdam street and left him bleeding with a dagger and a note of warning stuck in his chest. Wilders, like other prominent critics of Islam in Europe, and his compatriot member of Parliament from a Muslim Somali background, Aayan Hirshi Ali, had to pay also a personal price, in addition to their shaming in public for their views against Islam, and for calling to ban the Qur'an and discontinue Muslim immigration to the country. For they needed to maintain personal body guards wherever they went, due to the threats they constantly received from their enemies. Ali, had ultimately to abandon her shelter country and immigrate to the safety and the anonymity of living in New York.

Europeans and other Westerners began to awake, in the wake of the disastrous terrorist acts against their citizenry by Muslim terrorists, to the necessity that time to fight back had dawned, and retreat to the old 19th century notions of nationalism and statism that had become imperative, if the West was to defend itself against the new onslaught of Muslims on it. The nation states had been founded on the principle that each nation was entitled to its own sovereignty and to engender, protect, and preserve its own unique culture and history. Therefore unity, uniformity and homogeneity were seen as an essential feature of the nation and the nation-state –, namely unity of descent, unity of culture, unity of language, and unity of religion, for the common citizens to feel part of the nation and comfortable living in it. And those were precisely the components of nationalism that the Muslim influx was violating, making many commoners to feel alienated strangers in their own country. Some countries, like Nazi Germany, had even taken the extreme measure of ethnic cleansing, like expelling or physically eliminating Jews, Gypsies and other racial entities that were not defined by Aryan traits. Now, all that the reacting Europeans to their overwhelming predicament was to ask to be left alone and be allowed to restore the lost national familiar characteristics that were endangered by the pressure to accommodate the new waves of encroaching Muslims. They meant no ill towards anyone, they just wanted to preserve their national turf and find themselves, once again, bathing undisturbed in their own culture that they loved and were now terrified to see dissipating before their eyes. They had joined the European Union in order to strengthen their defenses against the powers that be, not in order to find themselves invaded defenseless and left to the mercy of political correctness, soothing sermons by politicians and clergymen, and reassuring pledges by the invaders that they meant well and no danger was posed by their influx.

As part of the retreat from the disappointing multiculturalism that failed them, Europeans and other Westerners instituted new rules in order to cut the influx of Muslims into their countries, and to compel those who did get in to guarantee their quick integration into the existing culture before they could be naturalized, by learning the national culture, history and language, by studying and internalizing the local system of law and the judiciary which enforced it, and by understanding that the local laws in which they integrate will always be superior and override any other rules or mores they would have imported with them. Even Angela Merkel, the champion of multiculturalism in Europe, had admitted in October 2010 to a group of her CDU youth in Potsdam, that her attempts to build a multi cultural society had totally failed[31]. Germany's special endeavor in that regard certainly emanated not only from the need to toe the line with the rest of Europe, but to erase the stains of the Nazi past where racial profiling and relentless persecution of non Aryan minority groups had brought disgrace and rage against her throughout the world. Curiously enough, Sweden, which was the first country in Europe to adopt officially multiculturalism when it tabled in Parliament a resolution in 1975, under a social democratic government, has remained the most liberal country of asylum to incoming Muslims, as it permits more of them in, despite the terrorist attacks and the abuses her citizens have been subjected to in the Muslims ghettoes to which police and other social services do not dare enter. For some historical or psychological reason, it is hard for Sweden to admit an error and to reverse its policy, but this seems far more understandable than Angela Merkel's stance when she admitted the error but pursued with vengeance, at a stepped up pace, the policies she had dismissed. At any rate, Sweden's rationale was that in view of the equality of opportunity that she accorded to the new immigrants, mostly Muslims, she allowed them to retain their own languages and cultures, and from the mid-1970s, the goal of enabling the preservation of minorities, and creating a positive attitude towards the new officially endorsed multicultural society among the majority population, became incorporated into the Swedish constitution as well as cultural, educational and media policies. But the obstruction of the Muslim integration into society by the adopted measures of distinctiveness that had been adopted by the government despite the anti-multiculturalist protestations of the Sweden Democrats, survived side by side with multiculturalism which remains official policy in Sweden, and the acculturation of Muslims into Swedish culture remains as remote as ever.

---

[31] *BBC News.* 2010-10-17.

Interestingly enough, two Asian countries, South Korea and China, provide the best arguments with regard to a policy of multiculturalism. South Korea has, due to the hard work of Christian missionaries become, after the Philippines, their greatest success in Asia, with a third of the population converted into Christianity. In the years 2009 and 2010 there was widespread discussion in its media whether it was becoming officially a multicultural country, after it had been in fact for years. But the media did not have in mind the Western faith that distinguished a large portion of the population from the rest, because for them Christian Koreans were still culturally Korean, and what they meant was the one million strong foreigners which constituted a foreign culture. This unusual approach, which did not view religion as a cultural divider is unique to East Asian religion which always lived side by side wih others and considered each other as different ways to the Truth. The number of foreign residents in South Korea has grown to such an extent, and mixed marriages between foreigners and locals have become so widespread that the Korean government has been earmarking some of its social welfare programs as multi cultutalist. That sounds progressive and modern in bustling and prosperous Korean society. *Joong Ang Daily* wrote

> If you stay too long, Koreans become uncomfortable with you. [...] Having a 2 percent foreign population unquestionably causes ripples, but having one million temporary foreign residents does not make Korea a multicultural society. [...] In many ways, this homogeneity is one of Korea's greatest strengths. Shared values create harmony. Sacrifice for the nation is a given. Difficult and painful political and economic initiatives are endured without discussion or debate. It is easy to anticipate the needs and behavior of others. It is the cornerstone that has helped Korea survive adversity. But there is a down-

side, too. [...] Koreans are immersed in their culture and are thus blind to its characteristics and quirks. Examples of group think are everywhere. Because Koreans share values and views, they support decisions even when they are obviously bad. Multiculturalism will introduce contrasting views and challenge existing assumptions. While it will undermine the homogeneity, it will enrich Koreans with a better understanding of themselves."[32]

The problem of Chinese Muslims[33] is much more serious and pregnant with real dangers, because it is similar in some aspects to that of Muslims in the West, with the big difference that in China they are considered a native religion, not an immigrant one. Nonetheless the small Muslim minority of a couple of tens of millions in the billion and half nation, has always been considered outsiders if not foreigners, due to the separate way of life that differentiated them from the rest of the population in history, and especially due to their repeated rebellions against the authorities in the 19th and 20th Centuries which had threatened China with secession. The Muslims in China, who are spread all over the place, and thus differ from other national minorities, like Mongols and Tibetans, who are attached to a specific territory that they can claim, are nonetheless divided ethnically into the Hui in China Proper and the Turkic Uighurs in the northwest. Especially the latter, who are watching their cultural turf colonized and taken over by the Chinese Han, have mounted unrest since the 1980s, to conform with the mounting wave of Muslim fundamentalism elsewhere, and following the example of their nearby

---

[32] *Underwood, Peter. "Multiculturalism in Korea".* JoongAng Ilbo. South Korea 26 August 2010.

[33] See the two main works of this author: 1. *Muslims in China: a Study of Cultural Confrontation*, Curzon and Humanities Press, London and Atlantic Heights, 1980; and 2. *Islam in China:Religion, Ethnicity, Culture and Politics*, Lexington Books, 2002.

Kazakh, Kirghiz, Uzbek and others who have attained independence from the disintegrating Soviet Union. Since they dwell in the security and strategically sensitive Xinjiang, they are also viewed as a security risk and many restrictions have been put on them. Thus, unlike the Koreans who consider the presence of foreigners in their midst a multi cultural issue that needs to be addressed and resolved in those terms, the Chinese do not regard it that way since they view it as a security issue which can potentially give rise to terrorism. In other words, the Westerners who used for years to look at the few Muslim immigrants the Korean way, as a multi cultural issue, have shifted to the Chinese way when terrorism has transformed its native Muslims into a security hazard.

There have been various responses of the European countries to their encounter with their Muslim immigrants, from the soft, accommodating and welcoming approach of Sweden and Germany, even when multi- culturalism was avowed as a total failure, through the resignation of France and Belgium to living with this reality, lest they be accused of "racism" and "Islamophobia", and to the negative approaches of Central European and East European newcomers into the EU, like Hungary and Poland, which elected to preserve their predominant national character over the fashionable lure of multi-culturalism. Others, like Britain, Denmark, Spain and Austria, who began smilingly and approvingly, but turned around and adopted tougher positions towards immigrants and multi-culturalism when Islamic terrorism began to change the moods in those host-countries. Europe, like the rest of the world, had been stunned by the horrors of September 11 (2001), and they sent delegations to Washington to present their condolences and sympathies to the US, convinced that they were immune to such events and refusing to believe that such horrors could ever affect them. But paradoxically, as soon as the US began to react to terrorism by fighting it actively on its own turf, and in Afghanistan, Somalia and Iraq, it found itself almost alone but for the loyalty of Tony Blair of England and John

Howard of Australia, who harnessed the public opinion and resources of their countries to that battle.

With hindsight, one can assume today that the European reluctance to get "stained" by active battle against Islam had emanated precisely from its fear that it might have to toe the same line if, incredibly as it sounded at the time, Europe might also be exposed to the same terrorist threat. And again paradoxically, it was Britain's Tony Blair, who supported President Bush wholeheartedly in Iraq, who became also the champion of multi culturalism in Europe, maybe to atone for the damage caused to his image in the EU. The mirror image of Britain in those years, was the Spaniards' decision to heed the Muslim threats against aligning with America, and to remove from power their Aznar government, who was totally in favor of Bush and Blair's policies against terrorism, and elected instead a labor government which immediately abandoned their American alliance and repatriated their symbolic contingent from the war arena. That was an example of both determination in standing up against terrorism on the one hand, and capitulation to it on the other. In either case, Islamic terrorism did not spare anyone of those countries and caused them to a great extent either to retreat from multi-culturalism or at least to remain skeptical about it. Those countries behaved like soft states that had lost the will to stand up to terrorism of the new barbarians, and to profess the old values that had been the backbone of their traditional ethos. It is worthwhile recalling that in past millennia the rich, powerful, self-assured empires of Rome, Persia, Byzantium and China had also much to lose, yet they were unwilling to fight anymore. These empires subsequently lost their battles to Vandals, Arabs, Turks and Mongols, respectively, because the latter had nothing to lose, looked with contempt upon life, but coveted the wealth of their neighbors and concluded that it behooved them to seize it rather than let it languish in the hands of those declining empires which they ultimately attacked and destroyed.

Of course the parallels do not indicate a perfect similarity between the two parts of the equation, except that in both cases the target countries had become weak enough in the eyes of their predators, and paralyzed by their wealth and soft lifestyle, to make them easy prey for attack and conquest. European multi-culturalism, i.e. the European will to dilute itself and let its culture be swallowed up by Muslim newcomers, who are determined to alter it and change it to their tune, has colored Muslim conviction that they are on the way to victory, by increasing their demographic, political and cultural pressure correspondingly with the weakening of their host countries to resist, since the latter have systematically elected human rights over law enforcement, and achieving apparent safety by appeasement over active defensive measures to protect their citizens and way of life. And even when clear threats of Jihad were heard in London, Paris and Berlin, these warning signs were ignored by European governments. For example, then British Home Secretary, Jack Straw's liberal policy, for which he was to repent only too late, found it more convenient to embrace incoming Muslims, for the sake of multi culturalism, rather than to heed the menace of terror. In so doing, he acted irresponsibly. For governments are not judged by their liberal intentions or the good-heartedness of their policies or idealistic values, but by their success or failure to defend their citizens, when they allow terrorists to wreak havoc on their country and expose their myopic leadership's misunderstanding of the growing Muslim threat when they permitted their ideological blinders to guide their way. The fact that only after the large terrorist acts in Britain in 2005 have the British government awakened to act too little and too late, and to reverse its policies and take even harsher measures than public opinion or Parliament would allow, was in itself an indication of its inability to foresee what was coming and to prepare its citizenry before terror struck.

The US was no different, for in spite of the documentary evidence gathered on film by Steven Emerson in the early 1990s under the threatening heading of *Jihad in America,* the US approach to potential terrorists was very human and liberal, in line with the huge multiculturalist melting pot that prevailed in America since its inception. Indeed, Muslim associations were permitted to collect money under the cover of "charitable" institutions, and even to conduct military training with live ammunition, which Emerson documented in New Jersey, partly under the doctrinal supervision of the blind Sheikh Abdul Rahman, a fugitive from Egyptian law, who was later involved in the first explosion of the Twin Towers in 1993. While these threats were developing, they did not seem sufficiently alarming for the FBI to awaken to its responsibilities in internal security. It was the first attempted sabotage of 1993 which brought about the arrest of the Sheikh who had masterminded it. Both models of Western democracy, the US and Britain, needed a traumatic jolt before they moved to act in earnest. In the US it was the watershed event of September 11, 2001; in London, the July 7, 2005 bombings. And in other countries: the March 2004 train bombings in Madrid; in France the 2005 violent riots; in Amsterdam the Van Gogh murder; in Asia, the Bali horror; and finally in Scandinavia, the Cartoon Affair. In all instances the jolt was brutal for it shattered the naivete of European populations who had believed in the multiculturalist coexistence with their Muslim immigrant populations and in the feasibility of their integration into the European cultural and societal tissue.

Take for example, once again from Britain, the case of Abu Hamza al-Masri, who took refuge in the country in 1994. He never hid his destructive intentions and his subversive plans, but was not heeded until convicted in 2006 for the crimes that he had committed in the previous decade. That means that what has changed is not the man or his deeds, but the permissive and nonchalant attitude of the British leadership that was nurtured by multiculturalism, which was reversed by the London terror of 2005. Abu Hamza, of Egyptian origin, had arrived in London and became the Imam of the Finsbury Park Mosque. He headed the *Ansar al-Shari'a* (Supporters of the Shari'a), a movement that would have surely been outlawed in Cairo, wherein he promulgated the cause of the violent Algerian Armed Islamic Groups (GIA). Both his native Egypt and Yemen demanded his extradition. He emerged from a background of moral corruption, something that was sure to make him more radical than others, as if he wished to catch up on his "lost" years[34]. Thereafter he moved to Afghanistan with his family prior to the Taliban regime, at a time when the *Islamikaze* camps[35] were disseminated throughout the various domains of the regional warlords[36]. He fought then against the withdrawing Soviet troops and was severely wounded by a landmine which removed both his hands and destroyed one of his eyes. That was to augment his aura as a tested Jihad fighter and what is called his "charisma of infirmity".[37]

In 1994 Abu Hamza, a civil engineer by training, found refuge in liberal and refugee-welcoming liberal Britain at a time when the entire West was off guard with respect to the international Islamic terrorist networks that were being erected around it and in its midst, like al-Qa'ida and *Ansar al-Shari'a*. Reminiscing about that period of easy going Britain, he complained that while he had never lived on his hosts' money, those British "Infidels" levied taxes on him when he worked for them as an engineer, and therefore that justified in his eyes his latter broadsides against the West which "had plundered the lands of Islam". He never explained why he

---

[34] For Abu Hamza's background, see *al-Ayyam* (Yemen), August 8, 1999; *the Christian Science Monitor*, September 27, 2001. Both cited by MEMRI No 72, October 16, 2001.

[35] For this term, the combination of Islam and Kamikaze, see R. Israeli, Islamikaze: Manifestations of Islamic Martyrology,, Frank Cass, London, 2003.

[36] For trhe description of those camps, see R. Israeli, "Islamikaze and their Significance", in *Terrorism and Political Violence*, 9:3, 1997, pp. 96-121.

[37] Other famously handicapped charismatic leaders were Delano Roosevelt (Paralysis), Moshe Dayan (lost one eye) and Ahmed Yassin, the founder of Hamas (wheel-chair bound).

chose to live in the land of those alleged "robbers", unless we take his words at face value: "I am a cripple and I use their country to spread good, to counter the British authorities who use it to spread corruption". These are not thoughts or statements made by people intent to merge and integrate into their country of shelter, nor were the British multiculturalists who ignored them making great proof of responsibility towards their countrymen. In spite of his continuous complaints that he was persecuted by the authorities, to cover up for his obviously subversive deeds, his activities went on unhindered until he was briefly arrested in 1999 and then released, and finally arrested again in 2004 and then indicted and convicted in 2005-6 in the aftermath of the London bombings. On his convictions he told his many interviewers that within a decade or two the Islamic flag would flutter over Downing St 10 and the Elysee in Paris and clearly and seriously stated that Islam did not come to England to integrate into it but to change it. On his Internet site he claimed that Yemen was the best launching pad for the worldwide Islamic Revolution after Afghanistan had been taken over by the US[38]. And it was from Yemen that he directed his attention in 1998, after having left his London mosque to take care of his " Aden Abyan Muslim Army". He apparently masternminded an abortive attempt against the life of the Yemeni President and the kidnapping of foreign tourists. In a press conference which he conducted in London in 2000, he called for the overthrow of the Yemeni regime and urged foreign visitors to leave Yemeni soil. In a letter to the London-based Arabic daily *al-Hayat*, he warned the ambassadors of Britain and the US that they should leave Yemen, lest a "painful strike against the enemies of Islam" might be carried out against them. He also attacked the Arab monarchs and depicted the deceased King Hussein of Jordan as "roasting in Hell" for his

---

[38] www.al-bab.com/yemen/hamza/hamza.htm

pro-western conduct.[39].

Al-Masri, like many of his coreligionists throughout Europe, whose writing on the wall was not heeded by the local governments, who preferred to evince their humanitarian concerns for the immigrants rather than to investigate the dangers they posed to the host countries, has also aggressively shown more concern for Muslim communities elsewhere than for the welfare of the states where they sought asylum under the multicultural promise. In 1999 he convened a conference on Chechnyan Muslims and incited his audience against a group of Russian reporters who were on hand to cover the debates. On the same occasion, he voiced support for the Chechnyan attacks in Moscow in the summer of that year[40], cruelly anticipating what would his position be when such acts of terrorism would occur in the country he chose as his refuge. All this took place under the open eyes of the British authorities, with many similar acts in other parts of Europe, which seemed not to see or care, foolishly believing that that words did not hurt and deeds would not follow that systematic incitement, because the multicultural blinders had caused them such a thorough blackout that they could no longer perceive the reality of the terrorist infrastructure that they allowed to be erected as they were watching. Tony Blair, Jack Straw and their likes should have known that in the well known hate literature, defining and dehumanizing the enemy were the precursor of delegitimizing and ultimately using violence against him, unless they thought that Britain was immune to that rule, or that the incoming Muslim immigrants were friends of Britain and of Western culture that they sought to displace and replace, as the latter terrorist attackers have indicated. Abu Hamza's choice of Yemen as the ideal launching pad for the Islamic revolution emanated from his and others' belief that it remained the only country

---

[39] Ibid.
[40] *Online Journalism Review*, November 15, 1999.

in the Arabian Peninsula that "had not yet surrendered to the United Snakes [sic] of America", and he was certain that after the takeover of that country by Muslim radicals, other Muslim countries would also fall as the domino effect unfolded. He denied in one of his interviews that he had called upon his followers to kill foreigners in Yemen, specifying that he meant Infidels (*kuffar*), unless they converted to Islam, or paid the poll tax (*jizya*h) that *dhimmis* ("protected" infidels) were obliged to do under Islam. Otherwise, he asserted, "their blood and wealth are not protected". He also admitted that he had operated in Algeria and Egypt, but only because reform from within was impossible there, due to the corrupt regimes in place, and he came to the conclusion that only a Muslim invasion from the outside would trigger the Islamic Revolution and the warranted change. And that invasion he envisaged as stemming from Yemen and then fanning out worldwide[41].

Could anyone who followed this line of incitement and action cast any doubt about Abu Hamza's intentions for Britain and the rest of Europe, and for the role of the Infidels in that scheme? What were the British authorities waiting for, before they nipped in the bud those intentions? No, multiculturalism obliged them to hope for the best and to put their trust in the best intentions and instincts of the Muslim immigrants, which may have been peceful at their base, but suffice for a small element of Muslim radicals to act as the leaven in their community and to trigger acts of violence among a basically indifferent crowd, to cause turbulence and raise havoc in the entire populace, as the homegrown terrorists of 2005 were to prove. Abu Hamza indeed acted along those lines: he not only promoted Muslim terrorism, but also recruited young British volunteers for indoctrination in Afghanistan and Pakistan, collected funds for Muslim organizations to finance those activities, knowing that British suicidal liberalism would swallow and ignore all that.

---

[41] *Al- Ayyam* (Yemen), 11 August, 1999.

He held "Islamic Camps", usually in the grounds of unsuspected mosques, offering "military training for Brothers, self-development skills, martial arts, map reading etc., all intended to distract the young 30 men in attendance from television, and the obscenity of Christmas"[42]. Incidentally, the website that carried this public announcement was decorated with a picture of a hand grenade. Some of those trainees who found their way to Afghanistan were killed there, but this did not come to the attention of the media until the horrors of September 11[43], though they probably served as an inspiration for the Muslim terrorists of July 2005 in London, and certainly for the young Muslim Britons and the thousands of other European Muslims, who flocked to the killing fields of ISIS in Syria and Iraq in 2013-6.

During the Second Conference of the Islamic Movement held in London in February, 1999, Abu Hamza told the gathering of 500 Muslims of a plan to "blow up civil and military aircraft, so as to challenge Western monopoly of the skies". He even gave details of "new flying mines connected to balloons, currently being experimented in Afghanistan", and hinted that sometime in the future such an operation would be carried out against Britain or the US[44]. But the famous British Intelligence and authorities probably thought he was hallucinating and elected to look the other way, so persuaded were they of the worth of the detrimental multicultural approach. There are indications that Abu Hamza was one of the very few who knew about the coming September 11 plan; that he was busy with masterminding a plan to kill President Bush during the G-8 meeting in Genoa two days before the New York and Washington attack, so that an America in disarray over the death of its president would be less able to respond effectively to September 11; and that he held a meeting in his mosque in London on June

---

[42] *Christian Science Monitor* January 13, 1999.
[43] *Daily Telegraph*, October 5, 2001.
[44] *French News Agency (AFP),* February 28, 1999.

29th, 2001, where the idea of attack using aircraft was raised[45].

The most relevant aspect of Abu Hamza from the western point of view was his encouragement of violence[46], which he cultivated and elevated into an ideology in its own right. He advocated the use of violence for the double purpose of toppling the existing regimes in the Arab and Muslim world and replace them with Islamic governments of his own kind, as well as boosting the diffusion of Islam worldwide. But even his statements to that effect, backed by deeds which reflected that intention, did not seem ominous enough for European multi-culturalists to shake off the inertia of their slumber and self- assurance that all was well. At a gathering in early 1999 commemorating the removal of the last Ottoman Caliph by Kemal Attaturk, the father of modern Turkey, he openly asked Muslims to resort to the sword to implement the blueprint for domestic and international upheaval. One of his supporters, Muhammad Yussuf, seconded his mentor's appeal by urging his followers not only to fight back against the West in the Balkans and the Middle East, but also to establish a "strong fifth column" within the Western world[47], something that could explain his own self-imposed exile in London and his cultivation of violence in the name of Islam there and elsewhere. All that was said and done repeatedly 6 years prior to the London underground explosions but Jack Straw (and Tony Blair for that matter) neither saw nor heard any of that, despite the early warnings of some reporters and academics[48], where accurate details were given of his incitement among young Britons, his recruiting them to train in Afghanistan and his vocal support for Islamic violence. In 2001 Abu Hamza got involved in a press conference

---

[45] http://dsc.discovery.com/news/briefs/20010910/abroad.html.

[46] See R. Israeli, *Muslim Minorities in Modern States: the Challenge of Assimilation,* Transaction, NJ, 2009, pp. 5-12.

[47] *Middle East Times,* Issue 13, 1999. Cited by MEMRI 72, October 16, 2001.

[48] See R. Israeli, ISlamikaze: Manifestations of Islamic Martyrology, Frank Cass, 2003, London.

geared to "clear" his name from the "abominable accusation" that he had relinquished the use of violence, something that would have been antithetical to the nature of his ideology and actual struggle. Indeed, according to the London-based *Al-Quds al –Arabi*, Abu Hamza had been "accused' by Abdul Hakim Dyab, another Egyptian radical expatriot who also found refuge in London, of having dismissed a *fatwa* of the Palestinian radical cleric, Abu Qatada, that Muslims should kill the wives and children of Egyptian police and army officers as part of the struggle against the existing Arab regimes[49]. Naturally, Abu Hamza denied the allegation and defied his accuser.

That accusation was too much of an affront for Abu Hamza. In his rebuttal in the same paper, he claimed that he did not recognize the term "violence" in his vocabulary, because it had become a weapon used by the world media to designate anyone who defended his faith and honor against existing Arab regimes which rule through "legislative and oppressive measures". Therefore, the very term "violence" seemed deceptive in his eyes and incompatible with religious Islamic law and the struggle for the survival of Islam. He asserted that *mujahideen* had never recognized that term because the ruling regimes have utilized it to sustain their own monopoly in their own use of terrorism, while conversely resorting to it to eliminate the Muslim religious concept of "doing good and avoiding evil". Needless to say that for Muslim radicals like Abu Hamza, their own terrorist behavior is "good" while any attempt to resist it is inherently "evil". This kind of thinking also helps explain why for Muslim radicals the Western definition of terrorism is inacceptable inasmuch as it addresses itself to a means of combat to attain a political goal, even if that involves acting against innocent people, while the West addresses itself to the core issue of the struggle and does not justify all means to attain it, for terrorism is terrorism. His

---

[49] *Al Quds al-Arabi*, (London), July 21, 2001

own words are instructive in this regard:

> As a rule, Islam teaches that holding opinions different
> from one's own should be treated gently and with flexi-
> bility, provided they are willing to listen and comply, and
> provided that one's tolerant efforts do not lead to the
> blurring of rights and boundaries... Treating gently any-
> one who blocks one's ears and imposes perversion,, her-
> esy, abomination and humiliation upon Muslims in their
> own countries by the use of force is a kind of idiocy and
> loss of rights and of religious precepts... What can be said
> of Arab regimes which have enacted abominable laws,
> have implemented them and usesd tax money to finance
> military personnel for the protection of suich abomina-
> tions, instead of protecting Jerusalem and its people?...
> This is the mark of Cain, which is unprecedented in the
> history of Egypt[50].

The pro-multi-culturalist movement in the West (and Japan for that matter) finds its rationalizations in the pressing needs to fill in its depleting demographic reserves, due to the negative procreation that generates a negative population growth; in the future needs for labor manpower; in the influx of young people to replace the constantly aging local populations; and in maintaining an amiable relationship with the Muslim world where those migrants might originate from. Governments in place also vouch for increased influx of immigrants into their territory, not only to prove that their policies have worked, but to expand their political base by incorporating the supposedly grateful immigrants into their political parties and ensure their continued hold on power. Governments in liberal democracies must act like fire brigades which have to extinguish

---

[50] Ibid.

fires at every turn to keep their populace satisfied and be voted in in the next elections, and could not care less about the grim future that awaits their countries two or three decades hence, when they are no longer in power but the consequences of their destructive policies will become evident. Only totalitarian rulers who are assured of the longevity of their regimes can plan for the long haul, and they devise their five-year plans in consequence. It is a fact that the more undemocratic regimes in Europe, as one travels eastward, where until recently doctrinaire socialist regimes predominated, the more restrictions on Muslim immigration into their borders.

But the Muslim immigrants, who are allowed into the West under the liberal-democratic governments who promote multi-culturalism, wiew things slightly differently: they endeavor, first and foremost to increase their numbers by encouraging more immigra-tion in order to reach the critical mass, and more conversion to Islam of the westerners who are lured and fascinated by the suc-cesses of Islam in Europe, or read into the future more intelligently that their compatriots. Secondly, they demand, in the name of the civil rights they acquire that *Shari'a* laws and Muslim customs (like forced marriages, honor killings) be made to apply in their host countries, the fact that their numbers in jails in the West by far surpass their rate in the population notwithstanding. Thirdly, they prevail upon their adoptive countries to direct their foreign policies to their tune, for example, on the negative attitude towards the US, their policy in the Middle East and in favor of the Palestinians, and in shackling the West in any future conflict with or inside any Mus-lim country. They attain that goal by congregating in certain voting constituencies and making sure that no member of Parliament in their voting zone could be elected unless he or she supported more Muslim immigration, and favored their political and international agenda even against the stated government policy.

Reinforcing communal cohesion so as to become a political force to be reckoned with, they self-impose isolation of Muslims in their own neighborhoods wherever they finds themselves as a migrating minority, beginning with Muslims in China since the 8th Century, to the Muslim villages and townships in Israel and the Muslim quarters in Detroit and London. Secondly, an independent Islamic educational system is devised around the globe, through the lavish establishment of mosques, schools and Islamic centers throughout the western world, taking advantage of their liberty to do so under the liberal regimes of the West, despite the continued persecution of Christian minorities in Islamdom and the banning of the Christian Mission in many Muslim countries, most of all Saudi Arabia, which does not even permit non-Muslims into its borders. The famous educational system that Fethullah Gulen built in the US is only one spectacular example of this quiet and subtle, but steady, subversive and effective penetration into western society in order to transform it.

****

The question of inadaptability and incompatibility of Islam with other cultures, which does not allow it to submit to any other but Islamic rule, stands as the main reason for the friction and unrest it occasions under any "Infidel" rule. Usually, the problem is ascribed to the wide, amorphous and unpredictable coalition of radical Islamic movements and countries, which can strike anywhere directly, via their ISIS, al Qa'ida, Hamas, Hizbullah, and Islamic Jihad branches on Israel's borders, or anywhere else around the globe. Worse, as the numbers of anti-Western Muslim countries and movements keep increasing, their worldwide presence in all parts of the globe causes the state of siege around the West (and Israel) to feel tighter, and the chances of accommodation between these clashing civilizations ever slimmer.

Above all, the doctrine of *Islamikaze,* erroneously called in the West "suicide bombing" and by other Muslims *istishhad* (martyrdom), which means active death in martyrdom, that had been sanctified by the Muslim Brothers in the 1930's and 1940s, against the British in Egypt and Palestine, and against the Jews in Palestine and Israel. It was taken up by the Hizbullah in Lebanon, against US and Israeli presence there in the 1980s, and has become of universal usage by all Muslim terrorist movements, who had repeatedly warned the West of their contempt to life, because as martyrs their real eternal life is assured in Paradise, in contrast with the Western approach which sanctified life. As the Israeli presence in southern Lebanon wore on, those operations were intensified until they became the routine trademark of the violent encounters between the Hizbullah and Israel, and between Islamic radicals and the West. Unlike the Shi'ite martyrs who emulated the martyrdom of Hussein in Karbala, who have acted with the goal of self-inflicting pain and suffering, the modern *Islamikaze* have in mind inflicting death and destruction on the enemy, even at the cost of their own lives. The long succession of *fatwas* delivered to justify these acts, has indeed provided the rationalization for the mostly Sunnite *Islamikaze* groups to launch their deadly and massive attacks on Israel and the West. It is quite amazing indeed to watch the Sunnite radical groups adopt the Shi'ite ways, not only by embracing the Iranian and Hizbullah *modus operandi*, something that has been evinced in the collaboration of Iran and Hizbullah with the Hamas and Islamic Jihad, but also by creating their own version of the supreme sacrifice and suffering. In the battlefield of terrorism in the Path of Allah, we have seen 19 adepts of al-Qa'ida committing collective acts of *Islamikaze* within one hour of each other on American soil on September 11. Al-Qa'ida fighters in Afghanistan, Iraq and now Syria, have defied death in the face of American and Syrian air power, as do Hamas and Islamic Jihad operatives in Gaza, or the Muslim terrorists of *Lashkar-e -Tayiba* in Kashmir or in India proper, or the *Boko Haram* in Nigeria as do their fellow radical Muslims in Syria and Iraq, who slay their own compatriots with the same senseless and blind zeal as they do when they attack foreigners. This universalization of Sunni Muslim terrorism also carries with it a growing daring in the operations, to the extent of its banalization in view of its frequency, diffusion and beastly cruelty. Not only the massive attack of September 11, but especially the almost daily attacks on Israel and its civilians during the 1990s and 2000s by the Hamas, the Islamic Jihad and even PLO-related Palestinians, and the recurrent acts of terror throughout the Western world, from the US to Australia, have rendered these harrowing acts routine to the point that they became "part of life", as if they were God-ordained and impervious to human preventive initiative.

Even though Israel has become "accustomed" to the horrendous sights of Arabs and other Muslims celebrating over the spilled blood of their victims, when delirious and ecstatic Muslim crowds evince outlandish eruptions of jubilation when news break regarding "successful" attacks against Israel or the West, with no one in sight to rein them in, what followed in those orgies in the cities of the Muslim world, while Israel and the West were mourning their dead in a somber dignity and internalized pain, their Muslim supporters were distributing sweets, dancing in the streets amidst cries of "Allah Akbar!", as if to attribute to Allah their great feats of murder against their sworn enemies. They then go again into the repetitive ritual of burning the flags of their enemies, or trampling them under their feet as if possessed by frenzy. Since the demonstrators are not for the most part the participants in the real events themselves, who often those perish as *shahids*, they sometimes reenact the horror symbolically to share it with the public, praising Allah for His intercession on their behalf. In Nablus, during the Palestinian *Intifadah* that broke out in October 2000, a most disturbing exhibition was presented to the general Palestinian public in the city public square, which showed in inhuman detail the replicas of detached limbs and body pieces of Israelis who had perished in a blown-up restaurant by a Hamas terrorist. It was only the reports by deeply disgusted foreign correspondents, and the protest of Israelis who did not want to relive that horror by seeing it replicated on the screens, which convinced the Palestinian Authority to move the exhibition indoors, not to close it down and arrest its promoters.. It is understood that by widening the scope of the viewers of those scenes among the public, to the point of rendering them a sort of street theatre, even if most viewers were not part of the radical Islamic movements, the organizers expected to elicit respect and esteem for the self-immolating heroes, and to encourage the new recruits of tomorrow who are bound to emulate them. In other words, unlike the inward-turning stories of their suffering enacted by the Shi'ites for the sake of commemoration, identification with the martyrs and self-hardening in order to stand the excruciating trials to come, radical Muslims today elect to harden their crowds and cultivate their audiences by boasting about the gruesome suffering they inflicted upon the enemies of Allah.

Having learned to take seriously the stated intentions of annihilation against westerners and Israelis, because they are aware, and many of them had experienced themselves living as *dhimmis* in the Islamic world, just like many Christians had done in the past in occupied Christian territories by Muslims, and as many Eastern Christians continue to do today. Because many Arabs and Muslims are under a pressing psychological need to erase the humiliating anomaly which permitted Christians and Jews, the submitted *dhimmis* of yesteryear, who had lived for centuries at the mercy of Muslims, to emerge as sovereign nations which today predominate in the world, and stand up against them after they had even colonized them. The mistreatment of Christians and Jews under Islam, in the Middle East, North Africa and the Iberian Peninsula, has been a matter of some controversy. Scholars like Bernard Lewis, Marc Cohen, and Moshe Maoz, have taken the more lenient attitude towards the various Muslim regimes, pleading for understanding of the context of that era. Others, like Michael Curtis, Bat Ye'or and

Andrew Bostom, and lately Dario Fernandez, have demonstrated and solidly documented the sorry story of the extermination of entire Christian and Jewish communities, or their forced conversion to Islam in the domains of Islamdom. Be it as it may, the humiliating effect of the *dhimmi* status of the Christians and Jews under Islam has been universally recognized as having generated such a deep hatred and hostility towards Christianity as a universal rival and towards the Jewish minorities throughout Islamdom, until the latter was converted to anti Zionism when Israel was born in 1948. During the years of Islamic conquest, expansion, annihilation of some existing Christian and Jewish communities, occupation, forced conversion, and cruel subjugation of the non-Muslim communities which survived were practiced on a large scale. The general picture, however, was even much bigger and much more painful than the persecuted Christians and Jews themselves suspected in their particular locations, for Islam went on a triumphalist journey to rule the world, as a divine vocation, and convert its population to Islam, except for the followers of the monotheistic creeds, who were offered the generous choice between converting and being integrated into the dominant Muslim society, or keeping their faith under the *dhimmi* status and paying in return for their protection the poll tax, the *jizyah,* which was levied in a humiliating manner, to exhibit in public the inferior status of the non Muslims and encourage them to convert.

The Muslim-occupied territories where those people lived were dubbed *Dar al Islam,* the Abode of Islam, or *Pax Islamica,* while the rest of the world, was termed *Dar al Harb,* or the country of war, meaning that war was to be in a perpetual tool in the hands of the Islamic rulers until and unless was they submitted to Islamic rule. For Muslims then, taking over others territory was Allah sanctioned, by means of a holy war, that is *Jihad,* and anyone who did not submit to that divine edict was the enemy of Allah. Thus, unless Christians and Jews remained as *dhimmis* under the boot of Islam, their arrogant assumption of building their own independent states, and beating Islam in almost all confrontations with it since the beginning of modern times, is an aberration of history and of the Path that Allah had prescribed for the world. Since the Crusades, which were in fact an attempt to recover the territories thy had lost to Islamic conquest and expansion, and up until shortly prior to the end of the last Muslim Caliphate, namely the Ottoman sultanate in the WW I, the West was often on the defensive from Islam, although already in the 18th Century it started to conquer and colonize the Muslim world and bend it to its will, and even imposed the Capitulations regime on the weakening Caliphate. But the mounting power of the western democracies has since reversed the situation and put the West on top of the world, an affront that Muslims cannot forgive of forget. But, while most of the Islamic world has been aware of its weaknesses and backwardness, and realizes how much it depends on western powers, the radical Muslim movements among it, led by charismatic people like Osama Bin Laden and his followers, have taken the requisite initiative and mobilized all the temerity and religious zeal worldwide required to revive the spirit of Jihad, defy the hegemony of the West and launch an all out unconventional war against it to bet it into submission. If they cannot raise their own level to be like the West, they must defeat it in order to erase the humiliation that afflicts their present state.

The modern Western world has become accustomed to discuss openly and debate publicly the rationality and justification for policies, domestic and international. But Muslims, while using the same vocabularies in order to make themselves understood to the West, remains replete with misnomers to an extent that old notions have been confused with new ones, words lose their significance and expressions of political correctness have handily replaced accuracy. Words are used to mean different things to the point that we find it increasingly awkward to transmit certain messages, and find that we have to create new phrases and coin alternative words in order to avoid misunderstandings. Cases in point have been the widespread usage of "Islamist" (to distinguish from Muslim) as if there were two separate doctrines of Islam, one to serve the moderate peaceful Muslims, and the other to express the Jihadi tendencies of the radicals, and "suicide bomber" where there is no suicide, not even the semblance of a suicide in the thinking of those terrorist killers. For Muslims, there is one Islam, for Jihad is not only the domain of the radicals, and the "suicide bombers" are martyr fighters for the cause of Islam.

Chapter Four
Separation and Wealth of Cultures

Multi-culturalism was devised under the false assumption that the admixture of the incoming outsiders with the local tradition and culture would create a homogeneous and harmonius new culture where all would feel comfortable and welcome. The fallacy lied in the fact that while liberal Europeans were prepared for such a mix and became the champions of a world culture that denigrated their own local religion, the incoming Muslims were content to see their norms, ideas and notions being recognized and legitimized in their host countries, but were firm in their resistence to give in on their imported Muslim tradition and mores. The reason was clear: while for Europeans it was a matter of liberal incorporation of foreigners into the local fibre, on which they could make far-reaching concessions, for the Muslims it was a matter of religious commitment on which there could be no compromise. This fact was best illustrated by the stunning phenomenon that many more immigrants who are members of the Muslim minority in Amsterdam, Paris and London visit mosques on Fridays than local Christians who were members of the Christian majority visited churches on Sundays for worship.

The best gauge of the failing European attempts to create one new integrated culture, are the trials pursued to transform accepted norms that were abandoned in practice, and the flowery ideological rationalizations which had to be reversed. England, Germany and Holland, for example had indeed genuinely attempted to digest the Muslim demands for their dress, public worship and behavioral norms to be universally accepted, unlike France, Switzerland and Central European countries which forbade them, but when they realized that the Muslim immigrants took those accommodations as signs of capitulation of the host societies, they tried to back track. Those mostly accommodating countries also emitted ideological justifications for their concessions, such as liberalism, tolerance, multi-culturalism, diversity and enrichment of the local culture, not to speak of the reinvigorating demographic growth and the labor market, or repenting for past guilt, but ultimately they had to review their naïve policy of openness and reverse it, *inter alia* under the pressure of the populace which was shifting toward the populism of the right-wing parties which promised a return to nationalism, traditional values and checks on more immigration.

There have been various responses of the European countries to their encounter with their Muslim immigrants, from the soft, accommodating and welcoming approach of Sweden and Germany, even when multi- culturalism was avowed as a total failure, through the resignation of France and Belgium to living with this reality, less they be accused of "racism" and "Islamophobia", and to the negative approaches of Central European and East European newcomers into the EU, like Hungary and Poland, which elected to preserve their predominant national character over the fashionable lure of multi-culturalism. Others, like Britain, Denmark, Spain and Austria, who began smilingly and approvingly, but turned around when and adopted tougher positions towards immigrants and multi-culturalism when Islamic terrorism began to change the moods in those host-countries. Europe, like the rest of the world, had been stunned by the horrors of September 11 (2001), and they sent delegations to Washington to present their condolences and sympathies to the US, convinced that they were immune to such events and refusing to believe that such horrors could ever affect them. But paradoxically, as soon as the US began to react to terrorism by fighting it actively on its own turf, in Afghanistan, Somalia and Iraq, it found itself almost alone but for the loyalty of Tony Blair of England and John Howard of Australia, who harnessed the public opinion and resources of their countries to that battle.

The evolution of European policies went step by step along with the daily frictions and clashes that emerged within the host societies which often tried to be tolerant, flexible and generous toward the newcomers, and the immigrants who soon gained self-confidence, accumulated political power, and boosted by outside radical clerics, started to advance claims and demands that made their absorption a mounting challenge to the countries of asylum. For following the days of euphoria, generosity, sharing and charity, sympathy and goodwill towards the "poor and destitute" refugees, came outbursts of rage, demonstrations (by both hosts and guests), terrorist attacks, gang rapes of local women and a mounting suspicion replaced the initial fascination and curioristy with the sights, sounds, tastes and smells that the newcomers started spreading around. Events that are reported daily on European and world media, often under the alarming headline of "breaking news", inevitably drive to the head of Westerners' agenda the preoccupation with Muslims' intrusive conduct into their erstwhile tranquil living, and many of them to question the wisdom of having brought upon themselves that trouble that has come to disturb their existence.

Examples are many and they abound correspondingly with the influx or more and more Muslim immigrants. There were some landmarks which horrified vast Western crowds, like the September 11 murders in New York and Washington in 2001, the Van Gogh assassination in the heart of Amsterdam in 2004, the Madrid and London train explosions in 2004-6 and the Danish Cartoon Affair of 2006, and then the dramatic terrorist acts in Paris, Brussels, Nice, Manchester, London and Berlin in Europe, matched by similar horrors in Florida and California in the US which shocked the word, but their effect soon declined to reemerge soon after in the next outrageous explosion or mass shooting. But most of the long-term, enduring and subversive impact on Western civilization, which has been changing it by gnawing at it continuously, has been the result of a slow build-up, almost imperceptible of small, usually routine acts and intitiatives which get the European eye accustomed to them as trivial and unimportant, but their aggregate impact turns out at the end to be game-changing.

A case in point unfolded in Britain, when a Dudley City Councillor called for plans to create a "Muslim village" in the town center after it was revaled that the contoversial project would receive 150,000 pounds funding from taxpayers. Liberal Democrat leader, Dave Tyler, said he wanted to see everything about the "Pride of Dudley" project out in the open, emphasizing that "poeple are very agitated at the prospect of having a large mosque on their doorsteps. The problem we have got is that we do not know enough about this- it was sprung on us as a community and the public are wary". Dudley Council confirmed the project, to include a large mosque, sports hall, fitness room, healtrh clinic, etc. It would receive the funding over a two year period from the government's Neighborhood Renewal Fund[51]. In February, 2007, the local Planning Committee refused permission for the mosque, but the bid to build it was expected to continue. Local Christians were concerned about security issues, community cohesion and the Islamization of the town. Stephen Green, the National Director of *Christian Voice*, said:

> I am delighted that this mosque application has fallen
> at its first hurdle. It had started off claiming to be the
> "Pride of Dudley". It had a minaret that would have

---

[51] "Full Facts: Plea on Muslim Village", *ExpressandStar*, April, 2007.

made it the tallest building in Dudley, an important spiritua;l statement for Muslims with strong political overtones. Even the latest project had a minaret of some 65 feet[52].

The plans sparked a protest campaign described as "the biggest in living memory" after more than 22,000 people signed petitions and and wrote 944 letters of objection. The Development Control Committee rejected the 18 million pound plans. Muslim leader, Khurshid Ahmed condemned the decision as the "death of democracy". In 2005, the original 15 million pound proposal, fearuring a 110 foot minaret had generated 2000 objections after protesters claimed the tower would dwarf other landmarks like the castle. With the issue becoming increasingly political, Ahmed followed Council advice and modified the plans, cutting the minaret to 65 feet, dropping the "Pride of Dudley" title, and completely separating the community center from the mosque. Mulim leaders insisted no public money would be spent on the mosque and no council money would be needed for the project as a whole.. Funding, it was claimed, would come from Europe, centrl government grants and money from community organizatuions and sporting bodies[53].

Similarly, a study published in the US at about the same time revealed that Mulim groups had been striving to establish enclaves in which they could uphold nd enfore a greater compliance to Islamic law, and that what had been happening in Europe with regard to Muslim rising profile was being transplanted to the US too.[54] Europe was not the first precedent, however, since more than a decade earlier, the same phenomenon was reported among the

---

[52] "Dudley Mosque Refused Planning Permission", *Christian Voice*, 27 February, 2007.

[53] "Land Plan Becomes Raging Issue", ExpressandStar, 24 April, 2007.

[54] David Kennedy Houck, "The Islamist Challenge to the US Constitution", Middle East Quarterly, Spring, 2006.

Muslim community in Israel[55] and among other Muslim minorities under non-Islamic rule in Asia[56]. According to David Kennedy, while the US Constitution enshrined the right to religious freedom and the prohibition against a state religion, when it came to the right of religious emclaves to impose communal rules, the dividing line was more nebulous. For example, could US enclave home-owner associations and other groups enforce Islamic law? But those questions were no longer academic theory and had become a very pressing practical issue. Muslim organizations established enclaves at first in Israel and some Asian countries as we have seen, and then transplanted that model to Bosnia and Kosovo, and later crossed the Atlantic, prompting some Islamic community ledaers in the US to challenge the principles of assimilation and equality once central to the civil rights movement, seeking instead to live according to a separate but equal philosophy. The Gwynnoaks Muslim Residential Development Group, for example, has established an informal emclave in Baltimore because, according to John Yahya Cason, Director of the Islamic Education and Community Development Initiative, "there was no community in the US that showed the totality of the essential components of Muslim social, economic and political structure". Kennedy asserts that Baltimore was not alone, for in 2004 a local planning commission in Little Rock, Arkansas, granted the Islamic Center for Human Excellence autho-rization to build an internal Islamic enclave to include a mosque, a scholl and twenty two homes. While Imam Csaon says his goal was to create a "clean community, free of alcohol, drugs and free of gangs", a positive endeavor in itself, the implication for US juris-prudence of such enclaves are much greater. For example, while the Little Rock enclave might prevent the sale of alcohol,can it punish possession, and in what manner? Can it force all women, be they

---

[55] R. Israeli, *Muslim Fundamentalism in Israel,*, Brassey's, London 1993.

[56] M. Yegar, *Between Integration and Secession:the |Muslim Communities of South-east Asia*, Lexington Books, Lanham, 2002.

residents or viitors to don the hijab? The group had foreign financial support, presumably by groups envisaging the Islamization of the US, which are much larger umbrella organizations, like *Islam 4 the World,* an organization supported by Sharjah, one of the constituent emirates of the UAE in the Gulf. It may be assumed that like other its neighbor Qatar which supports the Muslim Brotherhood, Sharjah too wishes to secure itself from radical Islamic threats by supporting one of its branches.

Kennedy admits that the parameters of Muslim enclaves are ill-defined as yet, but the tendency to construct more and more of them does not augur well in terms of the "separate but equal" ideology they espouse. In September, 2004 the New Jersey branch of the Islamic circle of North America rented a park in New Jersey for the "Great Muslim Adventure Day", the advertisement announcing that "the entire park for Muslims only". He also cited the example of a similar event in close-by Canada, where radical Muslims took advantage of its liberal flexibility to their benefit. In fact, in October 2003, while Canada legislators assumed that the Muslims would still hold national law to be paramount, the Islamic Institute of Civil Justice (IICJ), created Muslim arbitration boards and stated its intent to arbitrate on the basis of Islamic law in Ontario. Canadian Muslim women groups opposed the application of the *shari'a* that would supersede their far more liberal and egalitarian rights. Only in November 2005, was the Arbitration Act amended to abrogate all existing religious arbitration. Kennedy, who studied the issue, warned that larger such enclaves within the US may signal that US jurisprudence will soon face a similar developments. For diehard Muslims can abuse the tolerance offered by the liberal policies of the Western judicial environment.

What happens in the US, Canada, Israel and other liberal democracies, who for fear of being dubbed "racist", "islamophobe", "discriminatory" or "oppressive" tend to neglect their own future and to ignore their national security, by placating their intrinsically hostile Muslim minorities which disdain local laws and regard *Shari'a* as superior to them, also happens in Europe more and more blatantly, because law enforcement officers are unable to enforce the law of the land. Already, when under Muslim pressure, the Arbitration Act was amended in Canada, which had worked well before, this has adversely affected other parts of the population. Canadian Catholics, for example were banned from their ability to annul marriages according to Canon Law, thus avoiding entanglement in civil courts. Similarly, the repeal of religious arbitration annulled the rabbinical courts' quietly settled marriages for Jews, as well as custody and business disputes. That meant that rather than soften the edge between religion and state, the Muslim intervention threatened to eliminate it with the imposition of the *Shari'a*, proving that flexibility can backfire when all parties do not seek to uphold basic precepts of tolerance, concluded Kennedy. He also determined that Muslim enclaves were uniquely perilous because there were few, in any, internal enclaves that adhered to a policy of abrogation of secular law and the imposition of a supreme religious law. For in Islam the concept of *Shari'a* is so fundamental that prominent Muslim jurists argue over whether a Muslim can fully discharge *Shari'a* obligations while residing in non-Muslim territory[57]. Yet, he posits, that Muslims have peacefully resided in non-Muslim lands since the seventh Century. But he is not totally right. IF he knew of the bloody uprisings of Muslim minorities in 19th Century China and in 20th Century Asia, and if he took under consideration the present unrest and trouble-making of Muslim minorities across the globe, he would have avoided this sweeping generalization. All the more so, since Muslim radicals already consider Europe as an "acquired" territory in view of the imminent demise of Western cultures and their substitution by a Universal Islamic order.

---

[57] Kennedy, op. cit.

The North American experience offers some lessons to Europe as far as the penal system is concerned. Radical Muslim chaplains in Western countries, welcomed into their military units and other bureaucratic apparatuses, such as the prison service, to serve Muslim recruits or inmates (a phenomenon that has no parallel in Muslim armies where there are no non-Muslim recruits), who are trained in Islamic ideology, are trying to impose a radical Muslim agenda and often gain a monopoly over religious Islamic activities in American, Federal, State and City prisons, as reported by American historian Stephen Schwartz:

> I and a group of individuals with whom I had worked, began consultations on the problem of radical Islam in prison. We identified change in the prisons as a leading item in the agenda of our nation in defeating the terrorist enemy. Some of us had received letters from American Mulim prison inmates complaining that radical chaplains had harassed and otherwise subjected moderate Muslims in prison to humiliation, discrimination, confiscation of moderate Islamic literature, and even physical threats. Muslim chaplains have established an Islamic regime over Muslim convicts in the American prisons; imagine each prison Islamic community as a little Saudi kingdom behind prison walls, without the amenities. They have effectively induced American authorities to established a form of "state Islam", or "government-certified Islam" in correctional systems[58].

Many prisons in America have been dominated by radical Muslim chaplains[59], but one of the most noteworthy events in that con-

---

[58] Stephen Schwartz, "Islam in the Big House: How Radical Muslims took over the American Prison System", *The Weekly Standard*, 24 April 2006.
[59] Ibid.

text was when in March 2006, Umar abdul-Jalil, Chief Islamic chaplain in the New York City Depatment of Corrections was reported to have said in a speech that "the greatest terrorists in the world occupy the White House", that the Jews controlled the world media and that Muslims were being tortured in Manhattan prisons. New York Mayor, Michael Bloomberg, refused on free speech grounds to dismiss him. In another case, Marwan Othman al-Hindi, a Jordanian born American citizen who had served as an imam in the Toledo Correctional Institution, was charged with recruiting terrorists to fight in Iraq. These were cases of Imams imported to America after being trained in Saudi Arabia, while the US lacked judicial and correctional authorities with the requisite expertise to assess their fitness for those jobs.[60] European prisons were penetrated by imported radical chaplains in the same fashion. Particularly interesting are the insights offered by renowned scholar Efraim Karsh to *Front Page Magazine*, following the publication of his book on *Islamic Imperialism*[61]. He said that the September 11 attacks and their underlying ideology tapped into a deep imperialistic undercurrent that has characterized the political culture of Islam from the beginning. In his book he challenged the traditional narrative by showing that Islamic history has been anything but reactive. Indeed from the Prophet Muhammad to the Ottomans Islamic history has been the story of the rise and fall of an often astonishing imperial aggressiveness and of never quiescent imperial dreams. Even as these dreams have repeatedly frustrated any possibility for the peaceful social and political development of the Arab-Muslim world, they have given rise to no less repeated fantasies of revenge and restoration, and to murderous efforts to transform fantasy into fact. He pursued:

---

[60] Those were remarks made by Stephen Schwartz at the " Domestic Security Preparedness Conference" on 12 April, 2006.

[61] Jamie Glazov, "Islamic Imperialism: Interview with Efraim Karsh", *Front Page Magazine.com*, 5 May, 2006.

… Islam envisages a global political order in which all humankind will live under Muslim rule as either believers or subject communities and obliges all free, male adult Muslims to carry out an uncompromising struggle in the Path of Allah, or Jihad. This concept was developed and amplified until it became the rallying call for world domination. As he famously told his followers on his farewell address: " I was ordered to fight all men until they say "there is no god but Allah". This goal need not necessarily be pursued by the sword; it can be achieved through demographic growth and steady conversion of local populations by an army of preachers and teachers who will present Islam in all languages and in all dialects. But should peaceful means prove insufficient, physical force can readily be brought to bear. This is by no means a vision confined to "Islamists". This we saw in the overwhelming support for the 9/11 attacks throughout the Arab and Islamic worlds, in the admiring evocations of Bin Laden's murderous acts during the crisis of the Danish cartoons, and in such recent findinds as the polls indicating significant reservoirs of sympathy among Muslims in Britain for the feelings and motives of the suicide bombers who attacked London.[62]

There is a pervasive guilt complex among left-wing intellectuals and politicians, which dates back to the early 20th Century and stems from the belief that the West has been the arch-aggressor of modern times, to use the words of Arnold Toynbee, one of the more influential early exponents of this dogma. This has resulted in a highly politicized scholarship, especially under the pretentious title of "post colonial studies", which berates Western imperialism as the

---

[62] Ibid.

source of all evil and absolves local actors, Muslims included, of all blame or responsibility for their own problems and their sometimes murderous reprisals against the West. Thus, Karsh believes that whether or not Europe falls under Muslim domination will depend on whether Europeans awaken to reality and recognize the real nature of the threat confronting them. Mu'ammar Qaddafi the mercurial and unstable Libyan dictator, had predicted the imminent Islamization of Europe. He stated in a public speech aired on *al-Jazeerah* Television: "We have million Muslims in Europe. There are signs that Allah will grant Islam victory in Europe- without swords, without guns. The fifty million Muslims of Europe will turn it into a Muslim continent within a few decades... Allah mobilizes the Muslim nation of Turkey and adds it to the European Union..., that is another fifty million Muslims. There will be one hundred million Muslims in Europe". While this outdated prediction was usually dismissed as delusional gloating of an eccentric leader, to this day many Muslims and Arabs unabashedly pine for the reconquest of Spain and consider their 1492 rout and expulsion from the country as a grave historical injustice waiting to be redressed. Indeed, as immigration, conversion to Islam and higher birthrates have greately increased the number of Muslims in Europe over the past several decades, countries that were never ruled by the Muslim Caliphate have become targets of Muslim imperial ambition. Since the late 1980s, radical Muslims have looked upon the growing population of French Muslims as proof that France too has become part of the expanding *Pax Islamica*. In Britain, even the most moderate elements of the Muslim community, like the late Zaki Badawi, the doyen of interfaith dialogue in the UK, put it succinctly:"Islam is a universal religion. It aims to bring its message to all corners of the globe. It hopes that one day the whole of humanity will be one Muslim community".[63]

---

[63] Ibid.

One of the most used propaganda devices to raise Western public opinion to sympathize with their cause and reduce their opposition to the Muslim subversive moves which undermine the Infidel societies into which they have been penetrating, is to play on the guilty feelings of Europeans and castigate them for their colonial past and haughty attitutes towards their colonized peoples, sins they must expiate today by making concessions to the new immigrants who are in turn expected to exonerate them. The radical Muslims, headed by the likes of Sheikh Qaradawi, who believe it is their right to invade Europe and reconquer it by "peaceful" means, are those who cannot hide their jubilation at the "success" of a major terrorist operation against the West or lend their approval to *Islamikaze* activities, unlike the "moderates" among them who are either afraid of the scourge of Western retaliation or prefer to sedate the fears of the West from Islamic violence by blarney and appeasement. A number of knowledgeable and courageous scholars and columnists like Bernard Lewis, Victor Hansen, Fouad Ajami, Thomas Friedman, Daniel Pipes, Martin Kramer and Sheikh Palazzi, have come out with extensive analyses which defy the stifling political correctness that has paralyzed Western political thinking in our generation and have provided enriching insights to the bewildered public opinion of the post September 11 era. Perhaps the bluntest of them and the most assisduous critique of radical Islam, is Daniel Pipes, who lashed out at the present state of paralysis among the governing elites, which unsuccessfully attempted to disconnet between Islam and the acts of terror. He pointed out that the problem at hand was not the religion of Islam as such but the totalitarian ideology pursued by radical Muslims which prods Muslims to hold power, and when they do to apply their *shari'a* law and to enfore it through the state apparatus.[64] However, beyond the 10-15% of radicals that he

---

[64] Daniel Pipes "Fighting Militant Islam, Without Bias", *City Journal*, Autumn, 2001.

discerned in the Muslim world, with the rest "fearing and loathing them", there was a vast silent portion of Muslims who sympathize, if not with militant Islam, then at least with its horrendous acts of terror, as the profuse statements and demonstrations of jubilation among Muslim intellectuals, professionals, columnists and the masses attested in the aftermath of September 11. These same proportions seem to be reflected among the Muslims diasporas in the West too, where we see a minority of militants who recruit, incite and raise money for building mosques, train Jihadists and launch major (often violent), and attempt to impose Muslim norms around, with intellectuals and other publicists (clerical and others) writing essays and devising the propaganda, launching demonstrations and publicizing appeals, the general mass of Muslims approvingly watching in the aisles.

A dramatic incident in France, followed by many others which terrified the French population and forced it to change course, to place police in its streets on a massive scale, to declare a state of emergency and to induce many of its Jews to emigrate for safety, unfolded in October 2005, when two Muslim youth fled a police identity check and scaled an electric relay station where they were electrocuted. This triggered a Muslim rampage in Paris and its surroundings, under the cries of *Allah Akbar*!!! which reverberated everywhere, and talk circulated about turning the glamorous French capital into Baghdad-sur-Seine. An Islamic site informed its readers that "the cops are petrified of us, everything must burn!!!" and a younf leader of the Arab European League demanded that France allow Arab sections to govern themselves. He said that Arabs rejected integration when it leads to assimilation and emphasized: "We are at home here, and whatever we consider our culture to be, also belongs to our chosen country. I am in my ountry, not the country of the Westerners".[65] While Interior Minister Sarkozi called the rioters "scum", President Chirac imposed a state of emergency, condemned "racism" in public in order to calm tempers, and declared himself to be aware of the discrimination and lack of equal opportunity among Muslim youth. But the government's inability to provide instant remedies triggered the even larger all encompassing and more violent riots of March 2006. The French police seized explosives and firearms from Muslim groups who were said to have links with al-Qa'ida during the riots, something that should have augured ill for the large scale murders in Paris in 2015. The pattern was set and the realization was reached by large sections of the population that France wuld never be what it used to be. Similar gloom was overtaking other parts of Europe as these disturbances, which have grown into full-fledged acts of terror, spread all over the continent as the authorities understood that the combination of a slow and "peaceful" incremental penetration of Islam into European societies, supplemented by sporadic outbursts of violent terrorism, would create havoc in their countries unless stringent counter-measures are adopted.

Particularly poignant and enduring is the condition of the African Americans in the US. This condition is complicated by the fact that in all 50 states of the Union there are black people who are promised equal rights, but whose concentrations in certain towns and slams in larger cities have aggravated the situation, rendering the pledge of one nation under God not only unrealizable, but also given to explosions of violence, rage and manifestations of racism that have become part of American life. A century and a half after the Civil War which had been fought on the noble issue of repealing slavery, though tearing the country the country apart and causing hundreds of thousands of fatalities and injured,

---

[65] Stefan Kanfer, ""France vs France: France's Muslim Prroblem will only get Worse", *City Journal*, Winter, 2006.

racism and resulting discrimination, poverty, joblessness and crime remain a challenging issue in American society. Maybe that other minorities which have more easily fitted into the American melting pot, this was due to the skin stigma that could no be hidden or disregarded. To a great extent, the addition of the Islamic element to the already exacerbated condition of the many Black Americans has further aggravated the situation when the "ethno-religious" element of the "Muslim Nation" was appended to their racial plight. No one can deny the great strides made by the Black population in terms of civil rights, economic advance and climbing the ladder of success in politics and the bureaucracy. But the stain of slavery and residue of bitterness from those centuries of servitude that it took a bloody war to reverse, are apparently stronger than the present trend of goodwill and openness of American society towards further progress.

The sense of discrimination has been has been lagging for centuries prompting disruption in American society and just accusations of racism and police violence that are hurled right and left despite the tremendous leaps forward in human rights and civil equality that have been instituted in American society and political system over the years. Yes, jazz music and basketball teams have been dominated by Black Americans for many years, and there was even a Black American President, but that did not wipe out white supremacists nor eliminate police violence in Ferguson, Charlottesville, and their likes. When a permanent bias, prejudice, grudge or discontent is so deeply ingrained, it can be occasionally overlooked as part of our conventional manners and courtesies so as to make believe that we are civilized, democratically and civil-right inclined, and have learned how to behave in public and to avoid unpleasant suspicions of racism and bigotry. But when the chips are down and individuals are hard pressed, there occur outbursts of rage, hatred and outright racist violence. That is human part of human nature, abhorrent as it may be, but it is an unchanging fact. It is it that we have to address, not the lofty but impractical ideals of equality and harmony between all humans, everywhere and at all times because that simply does not work. You cannot mix oil with water, no matter how hard you try, they will always gravitate each to its sphere and settle there. It is a fact that we observe happy black nations in Liberia and South Africa, Senegal and Tanzania, but much less content in the America's despite their usually superior material wealth and world standing. It seems that what give satisfaction to people is not their prosperity but their sense of sovereignty and their feeling that they are not bossed around, disdained, tolerated and patronized by others, who happen to be white. Maybe, if Blacks could claim their independent territory in America, which they have earned by several centuries of slavery and oppression, perhaps they will feel upgraded and equal to others once they exercize their sovereign rule over their turf. For example, if two or three states in the US where the largest Black population exists were declared as designated to become black states within the Union within a given time frame, people (blacks and whites) could begin to move in or out according to their free choice and at their own pace, with federal aid, so that withing the designated time they would alter their population but remain Americans within the Union. But whites who would elect to stay in under a Black majority rule, or Blacks who prefer to dwell in the rest of the states would of course be free to do so.

A more optimistic prospect was offered by Cat J Zavis on the occasion of the Jewish New Year of 2019, based on the Biblical story of Jonah[66]:

> Jonah is such a complicated story. Jonah's unwillingness to see the humanity of those who commit wrongdoing is something we see regularly today. And I have to

---

[66] Cat Zavis, "Prophet Jonah, Murder of Another Black Man by a White Police Officer, and the Limits of Forgiveness ", co-editor of TIkkun Magazine, magazine@tikkun.org, October, 2019.

say, I have compassion for Jonah sometimes. The level of evil and destruction being perpetrated is overwhelming at times. And yet, moments arise when people are able to engage in individual acts of forgiveness that boggle the mind. A very recent example that many of us are aware of is the almost shocking act of forgiveness by Brandt Jean, the brother of Botham Jean, that was witnessed by so many. Botham Jean was the African American man who was shot dead in his own apartment by a white woman cop (Amber Guyger) as he was watching television, eating ice cream in his underwear. Brandt Jean's act was a stunning act of forgiveness. And it has raised many questions for me and others, questions and explorations that I think are relevant on Yom Kippur — the day of at-one-ment, during this time of repentance and forgiveness. There is a lot of conversation buzzing around on social media and in the general media about the amazing act of forgiveness and grace of Brandt Jean's act of forgiveness. There seems to be some indication that because he forgave her, we as a society should likewise forgive her. I think there are at least two problems with this. First, there is a difference between individual acts of forgiveness and grace, and collective acts of forgiveness and grace. Second, there is an important difference between forgiveness and grace, and repentance and *teshuva* (i.e., returning)... I do not entirely fault the officer because she was caught in a legal system that does not provide opportunities for true repentance and forgiveness. Rather it judges only guilt and innocence. But even in that system, she had a choice. She could have chosen to plead guilty and to take responsibility for her actions. To admit she was wrong. To ask for forgiveness. To genuinely reflect on her own racism and biases. To seek deeper understanding of how systemic racism influences her own thinking and biases. She did none of this. The victim's brother certainly had a choice to forgive her. But his forgiveness does not alleviate her responsibility to do proper repentance and *teshuva*. The Jewish New Year provides all of us, Jewish or not, a wonderful guide for how to engage in proper repentance and *teshuva*. And our tradition requires so much more than to be forgiven by those we harmed. It actually requires a returning to our highest selves – and in that, a return to the Divine. Forgiveness does not absolve us of our own responsibility to repent and do teshuva. And repentance and teshuva requires significantly more than merely tears of regret and sorrow. So how do we engage in *teshuva* and what does it mean to do so when we are so profoundly shaped by the social reality in which we live? What does teshuva actually look like when we participate in, perpetuate, and cause harm not just on an individual level, but also on a collective level? What is the intersection between individual acts of harm and systemic acts of harm? And how might this case, and the story of Jonah help us understand what is called of us? The murder of Botham Jean and Brandt Jean's forgiveness of the murderer also points to the question of how we repair not only on an individual level for harms we've committed, but how we repair for systemic harms, in which we play a role and for which we bear some responsibility.

I respect and honor the brother's actions and am left wondering about the systemic implications of such individual acts of forgiveness, and the intersection of personal forgiveness and collective responsibility and repentance. I watched the officer's testimony where she expressed her regrets, stating, "I feel like a terrible person.

I feel like crap. I hate that I have to live with this every single day of my life." What exactly is she regretting? That she took an innocent man's life or that she has to live with herself having done so. That is not an insignificant difference. When someone repents, they are called upon to repent for the impact of their behavior on others, not on themselves. Perhaps Jonah struggled with these same questions. Maybe he was reluctant to speak to the people of Nineveh because he did not believe their regret would be genuine regret for how their actions impacted others, but rather that it would simply be a perfunctory regret and change of behavior to save themselves...

And these dynamics play out in terms of racism too. Just as women have been taught to defer to and please men, so too African Americans vis-à-vis white people. Just think of the videos of African Americans pulled over by cops who are waving their gun and out of control and the African American person is trying to calm the officer down. This is the reality of being the less powerful in society – you learn to be deferential and to control yourself so as to not offend those with more power and to keep yourself safe. If that is the case, how do we understand individual acts of forgiveness by the less powerful in our society of those with more power? And what do we do about it? To what extent does the forgiveness by the less powerful of those with more power uphold the systems and structures of society and maintain power imbalances and injustice? How do we hold individual people accountable when they too are conditioned in a patriarchal, racist society? What does forgiveness, repentance, and teshuva look like with this understanding? Maimonides says that the first stage is to recognize the harm we have caused. To what extent are we individually and collectively able and willing to do this? In the case of Amber Guyger, that is easier – she murdered someone. There is clearly harm to the person and their loved ones. Yet even she struggled. She focused more on how her actions impacted her – she do not know how she could live with herself – than on how the Jean family will go on living with this huge hole in their hearts and lives. The next stage is to renunciate the harm we caused unequivocally and commit to never do it again. What do we do when the harm we cause not only occurs on a personal level but also a collective level? What might this look like in the case of Amber Guyger? How could she renunciate the harm, not only of her individual act, but of the ongoing harm she created by her racist texts, by her own biases, by those within the Dallas Police Department, and by those of society-at-large? What responsibility does she have to renunciate systemic harm and injustice? The third stage is recitation – publicly confessing and a committing to change. Simply saying I'm sorry is not enough, even if done in public. Maimonides calls for something more – namely, a commitment to change. And that cannot just be words, it must be intentions to act.

In this example, perhaps Amber Guyger could make a public statement committing to educate herself on how her biases and racism played a role in her decision that night. Perhaps it would include her reflecting honestly upon whether she would have felt scared if the person sitting on the couch was a white man (or woman). Publicly grappling with these questions, it seems to me, would be more in alignment with Maimonides' intentions. Reparations is the fourth stage – making amends for the harm caused. There have been more and more calls recently for reparations for slavery and that's great. And, that is not enough in my mind. There has been an ongoing assault financially, physically, psychologically, and spiritually upon the African American community in our country (and they are certainly not the only ones) since the time of slavery to the present time. Reparations requires compensation for that past and also for the ongoing harm and injustice and can and will need to take many forms. Reparations must occur on all the levels mentioned, not just the economic level. One role Amber Guyger could play in this is, once she educates herself and comes to understand how racism played a role in her decisions that night, to commit to speaking with police officers throughout the country about how police have internalized racism and biases. Racism must be weeded out of police departments and officers need to engage in reparations with their local communities. Reconciliation is the next stage of the *teshuva process*. This phase involves an ongoing process of accountability between the individual(s) harmed, the individual(s) who committed the harm, and the larger community to which all the aforementioned parties are accountable. In this stage, perhaps Guyger would call for all police forces to hold listening and reconciliation circles to begin to repair the harm that has been done. This is different from reparations in that the reparations are simply giving something back to the individuals and communities harmed, whereas reconciliation is a recognition that the individuals and communities harmed have important voices that need both to be heard and included in the decision-making process in the future.

And finally, resolution and return. This is the moment when the party who committed harm is confronted with the possibility of recommitting that same harm and chooses a different path. This is critical not only on the individual level but also on a community and society-wide level. This moment will occur again and again and again, thus resolution and return are ongoing processes. This is where the possibility of genuine transformation occurs. This is where the opportunity for individuals in a society (or in a police force) and for institutions within a society and society as a whole to make different choices that rather than cause harm, create goodness, build community, repair past breaks, seek justice, and foster peace and love. Perhaps Jonah did not have faith in the people of Nineveh to do the hard work of *teshuva*. Maybe Jonah was wanting God to be more discerning, to hold the people of Nineveh accountable for their actions. And God's response was, perhaps just as Brandt Jean's was, individuals are to see the best in one other and encourage one another to be their highest selves. And the rest is in God's hands. Amber Guyger will have to live the rest of her days knowing what she did. I hope as she seeks a path to self-acceptance and to self-forgiveness, she chooses to search the depths of her soul and of our society to gain clarity as to how the social reality in which she lives impacted the lens through which she saw Botham Jean and from that heightened awareness she engages in a path of repentance and forgiveness that can help our larger society heal as well.

Chapter Five

Racial and Cultural Hatreds

It seems quite odd that when Western civilization was preponderant in the world and manifested itself by penetrating other cultures of Asia, Africa and the Americas, in the process of colonization, it was accused of having "stifled" the cultural and economic development of the colonized countries and peoples, but now that the reverse trend is happening, of vast movements of Asian and African people to the Western world, the claim of "enrichment" and "cross-fertilization" is emitted to justify the failing policy of multi-culturalism, even as many Europeans have been retreating from it. Indeed, it seems that all civilizations, be they in Asia, like the Chinese, the Indian, the Japanese the Korean or the Javanese; or in Africa like the ancient kingdoms of the Eastern or the Western parts of the continent; or the Aztec, the Inca, the Maya or the native Indians of North America, had all attained their apogee when they developed almost independently of each other, before they were intruded upon by outsiders and their respective and distinctive original cultures were encroached upon, "soiled" by foreign accretions and irretrievably altered.

And yet, we still dig into the ancient archives and excavations, and we developed the sciences of history, anthropology and archaeology in an attempt to discern the ancient civilizations and their distinctive roots before they were stained by others and mixed into alien cultures, and entire areas of scholarship are devoted to differentiated and very specific geographical, cultural, religious, linguistic and ethnic groups, precisely to study their specifity and the characteristics that distinguish them from others. This means that paradoxically, while we are experiencing in the real world this frantic doggedness to mix races, to blurr national and ethnic boundaries and to create bridges over nations, religions and cultures, we are also seeking to deepen our knowledge of every nuance of any culture, tribe or national heritage that ever existed on this earth, so fascinated are we with it. At the same time, we realize that the increased movement of people worldwide, not merely for temporary visit or study, but with the goal of permanent relocation elsewhere, tends to erode these differences and remold them into an entirely new entity. Take small groups of nations, like Serbs or Sikhs or Chaldeans and Inu, especially those among them who do not live on their independent turf, they are bound to be diminished gradually into oblivion and to deprive future generations from the richness and originality of their culture, faith, language and social mores. Is that what we should be aspiring for? Are'nt we aware that not only the immigrants into an alien society will necessarily change in order to assimilate to their new environment, but very often, like in the case of Muslim minorities everywhere, they will endeavor to alter their host societies amidst friction, discomfort, violence and the loss by erosion of the two original cultural systems that were and are no longer. We should just glimpse at what had already happened in the large swaths of territories which were conquered by Islam since its inception, across all continents, on its way the rich Byzantine cultures of Anatolia, the Eastern Christianities of Syria and Iraq, the Berber patrimony of North Africa, the Coptic civilization of Egypt, and the Bengali and Punjabi cultures of the Indian sub-continent, to cite only a few example. Other civilizations too have eliminated and replaced previous cultures, like the local Indians by the Europeans in the Americas, or the aborigines in Australia and New Zealand, but at least, unlike the Muslims, they are not reaffirming their intention to it again in our days, as Muslim thinkers have been stating their adamant goal of overtaking the West.

The Spanish Ministry which oversees religious issues, financed publication of a school textbook, *Discovering Islam*, which it said in 2006 was unlike any other in Europe, a primer for Muslim fifth graders to learn about Islam in Spanish to integrate better into Spanish society. Jose Manuel Lopez, the managing director of The "Pluralism and Harmony Foundation", which was part of the Justice Ministry, said plainly that "Europe had 40 million Muslims, but the governments did not know what to do with them", and that book was a hint in that direction[67]. Even if we overlook the major *faux-pas* of the Spaniards, who pretended to teach Muslims about their own faith, a sure way to have that teaching rejected as patronizing and ignorant, it nonetheless reflected the debate in the West at the time between the politically correct and incorrect, with the former sheltering abusive Muslims who laid demands on their host country out of their sense that they were in their right as the rulers of Andalusia for 800 years before they were repulsed by the *reconquista*; and the incorrect who stood courageously for the old values, invoking the insightful and introspective look at the history and soul of Europe.

Writing in 2004, Matthias Dopfner reduced the worldview of the average German to seven formulaic sentences, starting with "Bush is stupid and evil". He emphasized that only a twin approach would defeat the Muslim radicals: tough resistance from the outside through the Western democracies and clear distancing of the moderates, in the Muslim world, especially among the clerics, from the extremists. He still did not understand then that the differentiation

---

[67] "Spain Publishes Public School Primer on Islam", *AP*, cited by the *Jerusalem Post*, 18 October, 2006.

between Islam and "Islamism" only existed in the minds of Europeans, because for all Muslims there was one Islam, one doctrine with the same Jihad applying to all, with sometimes various degrees of implementation, to be sure, the more "moderate" counseling graduality and longhaul, and the radicals pushing a here and now approach at all costs. Passsion in impatient. Dopfner asked why the non-Islamic world, apart from America and Britain had little willpower to contribute its part in the combat, while only those two nations (and Israel) were protecting themselves and the West in the face of the war declation of Islam on September 11? He also admitted that "those who act also make mistakes", but he praised their tough policy of resistance to the challenge, particularly lauding Bush and Blair for acting upon their convictions against the generally negative spirit of the time, which sometimes prevailed within their own parties, "to be doing that which an international alliance of cowardice is not prepared to do". He courageously pursued:

> It is about weighing the balance as to when tolerance for intolerance has to stop. And when doing nothing is worse than defending the Western system with military means... The illusion that the aggressor could be soothed by good behavior is reminiscent of 1936... Maybe George Bush is not stupid and evil. Maybe one day, look back on the developments that have just begun, we might even be thankful to him because he was one of the few who acted on the maxim:" these things have to be nipped in the bud", a phrase often used in Germany to refer to stopping the re-emergence of Nazism.[68]

---

[68] Matthias Dopfner, "*Bush ist Dumm und Bose*" (Bush is Stupid and Evil), *Die Welt*, 21 April 2004.

Dopfner, apparently inspired by Henryk Broder's mood of retaliation, that had been expressed in his "Europe- your Family Name is Appeasement" in early 2004, responded by his own "Europe, your name in Cowardice", warned the West soon thereafter against capitulation to Islamic pressure, and pleaded for the re-emergence of the good old national European cultures which had accorded that Continent its luster and glorious history and culture. He contended that appeasement had cost millions of Jews and non-Jews, as France and England were negotiating and hesitated long before they noticed that Hitler had to be fought, not bound to agreements. Appeasement had also stabilized communism in the Soviet Union and the Eastern Bloc in that part of Europe where where inhuman suppressive governments were glorified as the ideologically correct alternative to all other possibilities. Appeasement also crippled Europe when genocide ran rampant in Kosovo and European debated until the Americans did their work for them. Appeasement had also allowed Europe to ignore 300,000 victims of Saddam's torture and murder machinery and, motiveated by the self-righteousness of the "peace movement" to issue bad grades to George Bush. He asked what else had to happen before the European public and its political leadership understood what especially perfidious crusade consisting of systematic attacks by fanatic Muslims was underway, focused on civilians and directed against free, open Western societies. That was 2004, but these two courageous and insightful German commentators could not even image how prophetic and accurate were their predictions so lucid had been their analysis. For a decade later, in 2015, the worst wave of terror descended upon stunned Western Europe, after the early warnings of the massive train explosions in Britain and Spain were not enough of a jolt to put every sensible European on his feet.[69]

---

[69] Matthias Dopfner, *Europa deine Name ist Feigheit*, Europe, thy name is Cowardice, *Die Welt*, 20 November, 2004.

Those two wise commentators also predicted that that the conflict would last longer that the great military conflicts of the 20th Century because they were triggered by an enemy who could not be tamed by tolerance and accommodation, but only spurred on by such gestures, which will be mistaken as signs of weakness, as they indeed were over the years. They also praised the two American presidents who had the temerity to more against appeasement: Reagan when he ended the Cold War and Bush, together with Blair, who recognized the danger of the Islamic fight against democracy, which has been in fact a battle against the West and culture and values. Thus, while those Western leaders were risking their economy, the Europeans preferred to defend their social welfare system and listen to their pastors who preached about "reaching out to murderers"[70], a notion that President Obama also extended to reach an "agreement" with the Iranians, which while President Trump has dissociated from, the Europeans still cling to against all logic and long term interest. Apparently in despair of seeing Europe recanting before it is too late, Broder proclaimed in 2006, at the sight of what the Cartoon crisis had done to Europe's pride, "We might as well capitulate since we are already on our way".

In effect, Henryk Broder's *Hurra Wir Kapitulieren* (*Hurrah, we Surrender*), which spent a number of weeks atop the *Der Spiegel* bestseller list was thought at the time to have shaken up public opinion, which it did for a while, was not to evoke again the same numbing sense of helplessness and hopelessness in a European public until until Michel Houellebecq's *Submission* (2015) in France, which created a real panic among the public, when later that year his predictions proved correct and may have caused the French President Macron to dare to voice for the first time an express and public recognition of the Muslim radical danger and his vow to resist it. Submission is a novel that gained immediately translations

---

[70] Ibid.

into other languages, and raised the question why did a "science fiction" novel gain more credibility and won larger audiences that the myriad research books in all European languages. The book instantly became a bestseller in France, Germany and Italy and later in England, since it imagined a horrifying situation in which a Muslim party upholding radical Islamic values is able to win the 2022 presidential elections in France. Did Macron regard that prediction as a threat on his throne? Even the critique on Houellebecq in the New Your Times Review of Books[71] admitted his enduring reluctance to read that book, like all the books of this author, due to his suspicion that he might have to face an excellence of writing that he himself could not match, perhaps hinting that the author was so outstanding, popular and praiseworthy that no one, let alone the non-initiated populace could not resist the authoritative and credible impact of the book.

Coincidence or act of prophecy, *Soumission* was published on the same day as the attack on *Charlie Hebdo*, where 12 people, mostly journalists, were murdered by Muslim terrorists, which of course significantly amplified the event throughout the country and the world, once again paradoxically signaling that the media provide immediacy, and when the media are themselves the news, they become the message rather than the reported news. It is reported that Houellebecq himself was featured on the magazine's front page that week, probably since he had reportedly said in an interview that Islam was the stupidest of religions. It was not difficult to conjecture that since Muslims were the perpetrators of the horror, and Houellebecq featured Islam as the major actor in his book, the two became associated in the people's minds. Even when the Prime Minister took the usually cowardly position that Houellebecq was not France, instead of putting the might of the country behind this

---

[71] Karl Ove Knausgaard, *The New Your Times Review of Books,* November 8, 2015.

potentially hounded intellectual, the way Britain and the US had stood behind persecuted Rushdie. Thus, this courageous author, just like the author of the cartoons which triggered in 2006 the crisis, and also the ravages of the Muslim crowds all over the word, the manhunt of the cartoonist and the shameful apologies of certain Danish and EU officials[72], who disregarded the sacred value of the freedom of speech and only reinforced the perpetrators in the righteousness of their outrage, became the victim of his own culture, and was abandoned to the hounding dogs. What could the terrorists conclude from that? That Europe stood united to surrender to Muslim terrorism even at the price of betraying its own values and the people who upheld them.

The very scary reality confronts the average Frenchman today in this novel when he is faced with the semi-realistic election result won by a Muslim party, in which the left collaborated with it just to block the path before Le Pen's National Front, meaning a death sentence to the French republic and the spectre of an Islamic state rising into the actual world. To make things sound cynically worse, he nonchalantly raises the question whether ultimately it matters at all, since all men are the same, and he even prepares his hero for his own conversion ceremony into Islam to mark his final *Submission* (that is the meaning of the word Islam).However, his conversion is not performed with enthusiasm, like that of real European converts, as attested by the Chief State Prosecutor on the Paris region, Jeanclaude Marin:

> ... The non-Arab French who coverted to Islam are
> sometimes the most zealous because they have to prove
> the authenticity of their conversion, We can find them
> in the networks of fighters in Iraq, Afghanistan and

---

[72] R. Israeli, *Retreating from the Mirage of Multi-Culturalism*, Strategic Books, Tx, 2018, Chapter III- *The Watershed of the Cartoon Affair*, pp. 75-119.

Chechnya. Vey often their knowledge of Islam and thei
political consciousness are non-existent, all they want is
to become *Islamikaze* [self-sacrificing Jihadist, erroneously known as "suicide bombers"] and to shoot. But
they are dangerous because they grow within groups
whose mobility and leadership are constantly in a state
of becoming and they keep circulating between Italy,
Germany and the Netherlands, without belonging to any
one particular group or coming under the financial or
military direction of anybody. Their numbers are hard to
gauge... We only know the numbers of those who are
caught, but not those who are not... There are probably
many dozens of [converted] Frenchmen who are ready to
combat for Jihad[73].

These numbers have multiplied since the rise of ISIS in the 2010s
and the flow of thousands of Muslims youth, including European
converts who gravitated towards the killinkg fields of Syria and Iraq.
In that intermediate decade the Islamization of France had deep-
ened, the number of Muslims and their visibility have increased, so
much so that after Hoellenbecq's hero returns to Paris from a fervent trip to the Virgin of Rocamadour, which was a sort of hidden
farewell to his faith and culture, he converts to Islam as a pragmatic
step short of which he would not regain his appointment to the
Sorbonne, which had converted to an Islamic center of learning, the
definite sign that France had been taken over by Islam and that
French culture and faith had gone with the new wind of Islam, to
be replaced by a new Islamic ambience. What Frenchman would
not quiver and be hysterically startled by this frighteningly realistic
prospect? Especially when as recently as October 2019 the French

---

[73] Denis Demonpion,, "Interview with Jean-Claude Marin", *Le Point*, 20 October, 2005, p. 25.

media reported about the Paris court system (*La Cour d'Assises*)has convicted five Paris women, all converts to Islam, for terrorism. Two of them, Ornella Gilligmann and Inès Madani got 25 to 30 years of solitary incarceration. They were indicted for having intended in the night of 3/4 September 2016 to blow up a car bomb near an historical church in the heart of Paris. And those were French women who should have cared about the culture and the values they had been imbued with. Their alienation from their cultural bedrock once they converted (probably as a result of marriage to Muslims) attests to the deep gap which separates Islam from Western culture.

When Broder published his book which provoked the same kind of jolt in Germany one decade before Hoellenbecq in France, he spoke nostalgingly about the familiar and agreeable "normalcy" of life in his environment before the curse of multiculturalism and foreign immigration diluted and then dissolved that illusion. Those had been the days when intellectuals were debating whether Fukuyama was right in predicting the end of history, and hardly anyone was preoccupied with the differences between "peaceful Islam " and Radical Islam. But since the beginning of the third millennium the world Muslim population, its sensitivities, mores, intentions and intrusion into the Western world had become the focus of talk and of concern. The issue was not merely the change in agenda but raising the question of tolerance, freedom of movement, action and expression, and the desirable approach to deal with other cultures which themselves had no respect or tolerance towards other civilizations which they considered decadent and on their way to wane away. Broder correctly predicted that the Cartoon Affair which unfolded in those days was only a preamble of things to come unless Europe corrected in policy of appeasement, which unfortunately it did not. He saw that continuously faulty policy as replicating the 1930s when small and defenseless Czechoslovakia was sacrificed by the appeasers for the interests of an illusory "peace" under the Munich Agreement which was in fact a capitulation to the thug of the neighborhood. Similarly, the Europeans today, also believed that the Islamic adversary was invincible since it had elected death over life, and therefore only moderation, good behavior, concessions and surrender were likely to appease him. But he predicted that all the Europeans were likely to gain was a temporary reprieve of indeterminate duration.

Broder also contended that those who react to kidnappinps and beheadings, to massacres of people of other faith and to eruptions of collective hysteria with a call to "cultural dialogue", do not deserve any better. Their determination to disregard the facts or to conveniently distort then by referring to Islam as a "religion of peace" emanates, he claims from a natural tendency to avoid conflict and from fear. Mao had famously urged: " strike one to educate one hundred!" an axiom that had helped him solidify his power. The wilder and the more brutal the West's adversaries appear to be, the more likely they are to attract attention and gain recognition[74]. In March, 2004, the Romanian-American author, Norman Manea told the German *Die Welt;*

> Nowadays, acts of terrorism are not done for their own sake, but in the name of an ideology one could call Nazi-Islamic. The difference is that this ideology invokes a religion, whereas the Nazis were mythical without being religious... World War III has already begun, although Europeans are postponing recognition of the conflict that has arrived. The willingness to submit to self-deception is as widespread today as it was in the years leading to W W II. While the Berlin office of the International Physicians for the Prevention of Nuclear War published a paper which predicted two million

---

[74] Henryk Broder, op.cit.

deaths and a million injured if America launched a nuclear strike against Iran, it neither poses nor answers the question of the consequences of an Iranian nuclear attack. No one wants to address this question because no one knows how to prevent an Iranian nuclear attack or even influence Iran's policies. In contrast there is a very small but real possibility that public pressure can be used to influence the American government to move in one direction or another.. For this and similar reasons, one after another concession is demanded of Israel, including the same Palestinian Authority which dispatches *Islamikaze*"Suicide bombers" ito its cities…

Oskar Lafontaine, a one-time Chairman of the Social-Democratic Party of Germany, saw a commonality between leftist policies and the Islamic religion. In an interview to *Neues Deutchland,* he opined:

> … Islam depends on community, which places it in opposition to extreme individualism, which threatens to fail in the West. The second similarity is that the devout Muslim is required to share his wealth with others. The leftist also wants to see the strong help the weak. Finally, the prohibition of interest still plays a role in Islam, much as it once did in Christianity… This is a basis for a dialogue to be conducted between the left and the Islamic world… The West must engage in self-criticism and constantly ask ourselves through which eyes the Muslims see us… we must also understand the indignation of Muslims, for Muslims in Muslims countries have expressed their indignation on many, one of the most recent being the Iraq War. What we are seeing here is resource imperialism …

But Broder plaintively retorted that

If Muslim protests against a few harmless cartoons [during the 2006 Cartoon Crisis], can cause the free world to surrender in the face of violence, how will this free world react to something that is truly relevant? It is already difficult enough to see that Israel is not merely battling a few militants, but is facing a serious threat to its very existence from Iran. All too often it is ignored that Iranian President Ahmadinejad has already taken the first step by calling for a world without Zionism, a call that pro-Israeli Europeans only managed to condemn with a mild "unacceptable". How would they react if Iran were in a position to back up its threats with nuclear weapons?

Defeatist positions among Europeans were not voiced only in Germany, of all places. Back in 1972, a Danish lawyer, and part time politician, Mogens Glistrup, had an idea that brought him instant fame.. To save taxes he proposed that the Danish army be disbanded and an answering machine bet set up in the Defense Ministry that would play the message: " We Capitulate!!". Not only would it save money, but it would also save lives in an emergency. On the strength of this "program", Glistrup's Progress Party managed to become the second most powerful party in the Danish Parliament in 1973, that fateful year in which Israel proved once again, that short of its resourceful reserve military it would have vanished in the face of the combined surprise-attack of Egypt and Syria on the Holy Yom Kippur when all Jews were busy praying in the synagogues. Broder sarcastically added that 1973 was a number of years premature, but when he published his earth-shaking article in 2006 that was the right time to set up the answering machine. In the aftermath of the Cartoon Affair in which Denmark was mortified and humiliated, it is doubtful that any person in her right senses would have repeated that non-sense.[75]

In Britain the battle against terrorism which was entangled with the issue of accommodating Muslims as part of its fervent multiculturalist policy before it relinquished it after a decade of trial and error, was hard to pursue because the government was hampered then, as the government of Israel has been inhibited today by the verdicts of the Supreme Court. In effect, the judicial focus on human rights, in Britain as well as in Israel, would be laudable under normal circumstances, but in times of war, especially on those fought purely on the terrorists' terms, with the choice of timing, arena and style of combat given to their discretion, it is the terrorists who are allowed the benefit of the doubt. This happens in all liberal democracies and hampers the legislation and other arrangements that governments wish to put in place. Regulations were introduced by the Home Office in the UK, for example, to prevent illegal immigrants from using a bogus marriage as a way of staying in Britain, but were declared unlawful by the Appeal Court. But Judges opined that regulations introduced in 2005 to block thousands of alleged marriages of convenience, breached human rights laws. Hundreds of couples who claimed to have been prevented from marrying were able to claim compensations. Under the existing regime, non-EU citizens effectively needed government permission to marry. They had they had to attend designated locations and pay 135 pounds for a certificate of approval. The Appeal Court- upholding an earlier High Court ruling, said this was a "disproportionate interference" in the human right to marry. One Whitehall estimate suggested 10,000 marriages a year were bogus. Liam Byrne, the Immigration Minister, said he was considering an appeal, arguing that:"Since we introduced these checks the number of suspicious marriage reports has collapsed from 3,740 to less than

---

[75] Broder, op.cit.

300 by the end of 2,005[76].

In another case, Mahmoud Baiai, an illegal Immigrant from Algeria, and Izabela Trzcinska from Poland, brought their plight before the English courts which tested Article 12 of the European Convention on Human Rights which protects the right to marry and found a family. They were banned from marrying in England because Baiai was in the country illegally. But if he, a Muslim and his spouse who was a Roman Catholic had been members of the Church of England the government could not have stopped them marrying. Under the rules, by which immigrants wishing to marry must apply for written permission from the Home Office, the Church of England is Exempt. It was excluded because vicars usually meet couples several times before the wedding. Justice Silber, sitting in the High Court, determined that the rules discriminated against those subject to immigration rules on the grounds of religion and nationality. Meanwhile, new marriage guidelines were being drawn up by the Church of England amid fears that its clergy may be unwittingly conducting bogus weddings. Home Office officials noticed a sharp rise in th number of migrants seeking church weddings since the government imposed a crackdown on marriages of convenience at register offices. Because Church of England weddings were exempt, the number of applications for "common licenses" – a legal preliminary for church weddings – increased markedly, particularly in London[77].

Since the Asylum and Immigration Act came into force in February, 2005 the number of marriage applications at some offices dropped by 60% in some areas of London, with Birmingham and Leicester reporting reductions of 25%. Previously, registrars could only report suspicions about marriages of convenience to the Home

---

[76] Philip Johnston," Rules to Stop Sham Marriages", THe *Daily Telegraph*, 24 May, 2007.

[77] Jonathan Petre, "Church Acts to Stem Sham Marriages", *The Daily Telegraph*, 23 April, 2007.

Office, but the new rules have exposed the true number of foreigners marrying to gain citizenship. Karen Knapton, the General Secretary of the Society of Registration Officers, was explicit on this score:

> If people want to get married they will persevere, but the new regulations have highlighted the scale of bogus marriages. Register offices, especially in London, have been very quiet. We have been asking what nationality applicants are for two years and we have been aware that crime rings have been making a lot of money of sham marriages. It has been no fun when we know people have been using marriage to get around immigration laws. It has made a mockery of our job... We had a massive increase in January 2005 – perhaps four or five times the usual number of people rushing to get married before the new regulation came in... It is a relief that the decision has now been taken out of our hands[78].

While the right (and burden) to marry and start a family is unarguably a fundamental right, here the matter is not one of safeguarding civil rights for innocent and well meaning individuals, as doctrinaire jurists would consider it from their narrow angle, but an issue of immigration policy involving large groups of migrants who circumvent the entire legal system and break the immigration limitations, sometimes with the purpose of plotting terrorism or pursuing Muslim demographic growth in Europe, according to their own declarations, or seeking asylum as economic migrants. In such a situation, a democracy is duty bound to protect itself. Just as in W W II, when the home Secretary had the authority to arrest

---

[78] Dancan Gardham, "Tough Rules Expose Scale of Bogus Marriages", *The Daily Telegraph*, 16 May, 2005.

any citizen who was suspected of collaborating with the enemy as an emergengy measure, or when American nationals of Japanese extraction were interned due to the perceived threat they were thought to put to the country, the situation today also presents similar menace to national security, which is the duty of the government to scuttle. Therefore, limitations on sham marriages in Britain are not worse than the trend in Europe since September 11, more so after the Madrid and London, and even imperatively so after 2015 in Paris, to eavesdrop electronically on civilian suspects and aliens by authorities across the continent, by the authorities who are obtaining more powers and meeting less public opposition than President Bush over his post-2001 wiretapping programme. Indeed, as part of the package of EU anti-terrorist measures, the European Parliament approved legislation requiring telecommunications companies to retain phone data and internet logs for a minimum of six months in case they are needed for criminal investigations.[79]

Of course, the European Parliament was still playing "hide and seek" with terrorism when it adopted the law of eavesdropping when a "criminal investigation" required this procedure. But terrorism is not a criminal endeavor, because it is not committed for material gain or for personal vengeance. Quite the reverse, most of the Muslims who venture into a massive orgy of killing of that sort do it with a considerable risk of dying in the operation, or of being crippled or incarcerated for long years, while they themselves only register a pure loss of their family, career,business and very life. Their only ambition is to gain acceptance near the throne of Allah in Paradise as martyrs who have acted on the Qur'anic injunction to "drive terror in the heart of the enemy". In short, ideological terrors cannot be fought by criminal means, because it is not a crime.

---

[79] Victor Simpson, "Europeans see Need for Power to Snoop", *AP*, 11 April, 2006.

And if unconventional means like wiretapping are required to prevent it, then the human rights of those murderers must be relegated to a second plan. In Italy, which is the most wiretapped Western democracy, the number of authorized wiretaps more than tripled, from 32,000 in 2001 to 106,000 in 2005, since it has been accustomed for along time to use that device in its struggle against the *mafia.* It also passed a terrorism law after the 7/7 London bombing that opened the way for intelligence agencies to eavesdrop if an attack is feared to be imminent. Only an approval from a prosecutor, not a judge is required, although the material gleaned cannot be used in court. Similar laws have ben approved in France and the Netherlands, prompting some unjustified complaints from purists of human rights that the terrorist threats have given authorities a pretext to abuse powers.[80]

A parallel process of diminishing the Islamic threat among politicians and some intellectuals, by softening its impact and ignoring its potential damage, has been taking place among Muslims too who began to rewrite their narrative of terrorism by denying their decisive part in it and imputing it to Western "provocations", to the extent that the horrors of New York, Madrid, London, Bali and later Paris and Manchester are minimized when it seems to them that the West is losing its vigilance and lagging behind in educating its public to recognize the roots of terrorism and its motivations. For at the same time that new details are revealed about Muslim terrorist plots worldwide, - something that should galvanize the spirit of resistance, the liberal court system of the West refuses to awaken to the danger and continues to ties the hands of its own governments which try to raise the consciousness of their constituencies and mobilize their support for the harsher measures that may be required against against suspects. Ben Ward, the Associate Director of the European and Asian Division of Human Rights Watch,

---

[80] Ibid.

put it succinctly in terms of: "There is clearly a legitimate role for surveillance. It is the question of what the safeguards are". However, while the use of hidden microphone in criminal investigations is routine in Italy, a Swedish government proposal to allow similar taps has drawn sharp opposition from civil liberties advocates. Maybe the difference between the two countries is due to the density and volume of the threat of the migrants, with Sweden inviting and welcoming them in, and Italy is obliged to rescue them from sinking rubber boats which had perilously crossed the Mediterranean and landed on its shores uninvited.

These complaints by human rights champions are still relatively muted compared with the criticisms that have arisen in the US Congress and among civil liberty groups over the surveillance measures installed under the Bush Administration (2000-2008), and further tightened under Obama (2008-2016). In a 2003 report, the Max Planck Institute for Foreign Criminal Law in Germany put Italy at the top of the wiretapping list, followed by the Netherlands, using figures published by governments or emerging from parliamentary debates. The Dutch Secret Service, known by its acronym AIVD, which gained large powers after September 11, had a hand in lowering in 2004 the threshold for wiretapping and surveillance in the wake of the murder of *cineaste* Theo van Gogh due to the shift in public opinion. Suddenly the public realized that contrary to its naïve expectations, it could not share the values of the Muslim immigrants, one of whom killed in the open a recognized artist and public activivist on the "sin" that he did a film "insulting the Prophet of Islam. That was a precursor of what Muslims would do to Denmark during the Cartoon Affair of 2006. Siebrand Buma, the ruling Christian Democratic Party's spokesman on anti-terrorism and civil rights issues, said that while the Dutch were liberal on drugs and euthanasia policies. "people see the need to combat serious crime as worth the sacrifice of personal privacy". Therefore, disregarding the continuous naivete of viewing terrorism as "criminal" and not "ideological", the new anti-crime law introduced in France in 2004, also made easier wiretapping of suspects, allowing prosecutor to apply for wiretaps while investigations are still in primary stages, rather than wait for an investigating magistrate to take over the case[81]. No liberal civil rights champion in Western societies could deny that Muslim immigrants did force many changes on certain aspects of the lives of Europeans and Americans and deepen the perceived gap between the world of values on both sides of the aisle.

The infamous violent 2006 riots in the Muslim-populated neighborhood *cites* around Paris, prompted the police to seize explosives and firearms from groups who were linked to al-Qa'ida, something that did not bode well for the future, because they meant that those Muslim radicals were no longer just disappointed protesters or frustrated dissidents, but enemies of the Republic, who took up arms against it, in connection with an international terrorist organization, in order to topple the institutions of the state. In other words that signified that it was no longer a question of settling a discord between the state and part of its population, but of taking over the state and altering its political, social and religious system to fit the Muslim *modus operandi*. Not an evolutionary situation of educating people into another mold of thinking and acting, but reversing the state of affairs in a sudden and violent *coup* in the style of the French Revolution of old or the *Fanshen* (upside down) of Mao's Chinese Revolution of our days. At that time, demographic projections predicted that if the current trend continued undisturbed France would become a Muslim state in the 21st Century[82]. The immigrants who regard Europe as their territory and believe it must acquiesce in their culture, language and religion, and not the other way round, will not lay down their arms, and the tremendous pres-

---

[81] Ibid.

[82] Stefen Kanfer, "France vs France: France's Muslim Problem will only Get Worse", *City Journal*, Winter, 2006.

sure of their demography before they see their goal accomplished. The rest of Europe, which is still deluding itself that it would do better than France, and is trying to placate Muslim minorities instead of standing up to them, may wake up totally to reverse these trends after the way of no return had been irreversibly blocked. In other words, the French civilization, as an example, has come to the point that it can neither integrate the Muslims into its cultural sphere nor would the Muslim community seprate from it willingly as it considers it as its pure gain of what was *Les Territoires Perdus de la Republique*[83].

The riots did not change the perception of the French about the Muslim suburbs (*cites*) as different places where things happen independently in what is taking place in the rest of the country, manifesting the deepening gap that was building between the two parts of the population, and the hopelessness of integrating them into one nation. The Muslim youth of the suburb continue to ee their neighborhoods as their own territory, and their sole contact with French society as procceding through its police force. A proposal had arisen out of the riots to the effect that the CV of applicants to new jobs should be evaluated by prospective employers without the names of photographs of the applicants attached so as to avoid discrimination against African and Arab Muslims, in an attempt to sooth the complaints of Muslims about the biases against them, but at the same time in recognition of the scope of the problem. For the personal contacts between elites (*pistons*) that one needs in order to advance in this closed and centralized system is a genuine barrier to the upward mobility of new recruits, to which most immigrants belong. But that is only part of the problem, for over the years, as one integrates into society one can usually overcome this impediment by forming one's own elites, but here

---

[83] This was the title of the book edited by Emmanuel Brenner and published in 2002 (Editions Mille et une Nuits) which described in apocalyptic terms the takeover by Muslim anti-Semitism of the French school system.

instead, the immigrants keep even after many years their name and physiognomy (that is amplified by the skin stigma when they are African) and therefore cannot shed easily their built-in handicaps. For even if they obtain a job anonymously and blindly, the employer who dislikes them will always find enough pretexts to lay them out after they are employed, unless they prove extraordinarily talented, devoted and capable to compete for their position.

The French middle class, eager to preserve its short work week, early pension, paid vacations and job protection, opposes any change in their status and fears that it might be degraded by the mass unskilled laborers of the immigrants whose job demand might lower salaries and labor perks. In addition, Muslim youth are cultivating hatred toward the country which gave them asylum, all right, but also made them dependent on her, though young hard working women among them have learned to struggle out of their state of inferiority in their countries of origin and grown to savor an independence that they had never known before, much to the chagrin of their male siblings who watch them helplessly slipping out of their grip. So, while Muslim suburbs keep to themselves and hardly any Frenchman dares to approach them,it is the French bourgeoisie, like their south-American counterparts in the opulent city centers, who dread the day when the impoverished *cites*, like the *favelas* on the Americn continent, which will launch a decisive assault against the prosperous centers, with no one able to arrest the onslaught.[84] That was reminiscent of the Lin Piao's (one of Mao's associates and the legendary commander of the 8th Army which helped defeat the Japanese and win the Communist Revolution in 1949) theory of the class struggle that he transmuted into a cosmic international struggle, arguing that the all-encompassing general revolution would come about when the proletarian parts of the world, namely

---

[84] Theodore Darymple, "An Update from France", *Wall Street Journal,* 11 February, 2006.

the poor areas of the third world,would assault the wealthy parts of Europe and north America, that is the industrialized world, and take them over.

Ron Geaves, a British professor, contrary to renowned columnist Melanie Phillips[85], preferred to view the Muslim attacks on London as a legitimate demonstration and long-term protest rather than acts of terrorism, bringing to bear the obtuse European preference to hope for the best and rely on the good nature of people, rather than their evil and destructive designs. As part of his research Geaves has looked into the history of demonstrations of British Muslims, and through them he investigated the changing nature of Muslim communities, from the violent demonstrations against Salman Rushdie to the anti-war protests as a result of the Iraq war in which British forces participated actively. He considered the London hostile events as merely extreme cases of demonstrations and asked himself about their significance to the Muslim community, adding that "terrorism is a political word which always seems to be used to demonize people". In his lecture at the University of Chester, which was entitled "Twenty years of fieldwork: reflexions on reflexivity in the study of British Muslims", he admitted that the title referred to the personal transformation that had taken place over the past two decades, in which he had moved from the position of academic neutrality to one of active engagement with the Muslim community[86]. He claimed that he represented what he called "Britain's first Muslim youth programme work degree", while in fact he was typical of the Europeans who were ready to capitulate, and he even hinted that he was preparing to convert and reluctant to resist or fight. He did not ask what legitimized in his eyes the violent demonstrations by Muslim immigrants, who did not seek to understand

---

[85] Melanie Phillips,, *Londonistan: How Britain is Creating a Terror State Within,* Gibson Square, London. 2006.
[86] Andrew Anderson and Chris Hastings, "July 7 Bombs were a Demo, not Terrorism", *The Daily Telegraph*, 9 April 2006.

or at least stay silent while the democratic government which had admitted them into Britain had adopted democratically its policy of landing in Iraq to assist the task of the Ameican forces there. For demonstrators the Islamic issue was paramount, and they could not legitimize the fight of their sponsoring government against any Muslim, whatever the reason. Even a Labor MP from Hendon described Geaves' claims as "absolutely barking", showing when Labor was in government it was much more cautious not to toe the line of the fanatic pacifists who would rather surrender to Islam than fight it. That MP said that "Mealy-mouthed academics trying to justify deaths of innocent people are ludicrous"[87].

But fortunately, on the other side of the Atlantic, just as on the old continent itself, there are other voices of reason, even when the American Congress has been contaminated by the Islamic views of its two radical Muslim members, Rashida T'laib and Ilhan Omar, who have been trying, in concert with the American Islamic associations like CAIR, to persuade Americans that they should also capitulate to the rising wave of Islam in the world. They are trying, one should hope in vain, to demonstrate that thy can be loyal Muslims and at the same time uphold the Americn Constitution, ignoring the contradiction in terms between the two systems which makes their co-habitation virtually impossible.For one thing, Americans hold that faith is the domain of each individual, while Muslims insist that Politics is part of religion. For Americans sovereignty and the right to legislate belong exclusively to the people, but for Muslims those two prerogatives belong exclusively to Allah. How could these two systems dwell under one roof? At some point, when that contradiction becomes manifest, either the Americans will have to yield to the politically correct liberal thought which is fighting against a resilient incumbent president, or rally behind their Republican hardliners and resume his anti-Muslim policy. The

---

[87] Ibid.

problem is that those who resist the Islamic pressure stand on their own and have to face all alone their numerous hostile enemies from within, while the radical Muslims rely on a large and naïve liberal public opinion which naturally tends to protect minorities and other perceived underdogs.

One of the sober minds who refuses to capitulate to the Muslim onslaught is Brigitte Gabriel, who put her courage to the test in a American campus where Muslim influence was most in evidence. She asserted that campuses "are battlegrounds where we must fight to win back the opinion and allegiance of American college students. This is made harder when Islamists in both the college and local communities try to intimidate us and deny our free speech on campuses" What applies to the US certainly applies to many European universities too. Gabriel, a Christian refugee from Lebanon who has shrapnel in her body, (dating from the time when she and her family were targeted by Muslims during the Lebanese civil war), has grown accustomed to negative attitudes on the major east and west coast elite university campuses that harbor Leftists professors and anarchist student and radical Muslims. Yet, she was stunned to find that in the heartland of America, specifically at the University of Memphis, the Muslim community launched a full-scale campaign to stop the lectures which she was invited to present for the Judaic Studies program. They demanded the cancellation of her speech, emails flooded the administration from the Muslim students on campus and Muslims in the community and mosques. Although their comments were largely detached from reality, they provided a sample of troubles to come, when the Muslim portion of the population could not accept the notions of free speech that were sanctified as a a major tenet in the American constitution. In effect, people argued that:

> People like Brigitte are plenty in the world, they are
> the true enemies of Islam. And despite their rubbish talk,

the truth about Islam is spreading like a wildfire across the Americas and across the globe (All praise to Allah). Dr. Patterson's hosting of this lady is in orders of magnitude worse than hosting the Imperial Wizard of the Ku Klux Klan. Do you honestly think the scheduled lecture will serve any useful purpose other than inflaming the Muslims, insulting them and spilling poison in the community?

Gabriel wrote that "if they would put the same energy into condemning the radical element within Islam and join us in saying that slaughtering people in the name of Allah is murder, not Jihad, maybe we wouln't question their loyalty as American citizens." Dr Patterson, who invited Gabriel, into refuse to bow to the Muslim intimidation, and introduced her by telling the audience what an eye opener had become her lecture because of the violent reaction. He stated that he had never realized that in Memphis a speaker's safety could be threatened, necessitating a police presence[88]. This sad state of affairs, when speakers need police officers to protect their freedom of speech, a novel mode that has been imposed by Muslim students thoughout the Americas, applied of course in European universities too. And when police ignore this threat on freedom for the sake of "public safety", it provides the break that Muslim activists are seeking to start the process of disintegration and chaos that would facilitate their takeover of campuses in the West, a key link in impacting to their tune its leadership of the future. At the end of Gabriel's lecture the Muslims swarmed in front of her, questioning and intimidating her. Police officers quickly moved in and took her to the police cars as the emnraged Muslims were shouting at her. Such a behavior has turned univer-

---

[88] Brigitte Gabriel, "Muslims Muzzling Memphis", *American Thinker.com*, 10 April, 2006.

sity campuses in the West into testing grounds where this battle will be waged in the years to come and Western freedom will have to defeat Muslim radicalism. As during the Cartoon the affair, the issue for Muslim activists is not a Muslim value or the honor of the Prophet, but whether the Western-style concept of freedom and open market place of ideas can resist the coercion that Muslims are trying to impose on the West.

A British University was accused of selling out academic freedom, by a German scholar who experienced a similar abhorrent experience to Gabriel's in America. An acknowledged expert in the field, he planned a talk about the link between Nazi and Islamic anti-Semitism, which the university cancelled after receiving emails from Muslims proresting the event. The lecturer, a German political scientist, Matthias Kuntzel, was told by the University of Leeds that a talk and a workshop on: "Hitler's legacy: Islamic Antisemitism in the Middle East", has been annulled due to "security fears". Two academics in the Leeds German Department who had organized the event claimed theat the university had bowed to Muslim protests. Kuntzel said that he had given similar lectures around the world before, without any problem or objection, emphasizing that

> I was told it was for security reasons, they cannot protect any person. But I don't feel in any way threatened… My impression was that they wanted to avoid the issue in order to keep the situation calm. My feeling is that this is a kind of censorship… and the contents of the "threatening" emails described to me did not overtly threaten violence but they were very very strongly worded[89].

---

[89] John Steele, "Freedom of Speech Row as talk on Islamic Extremists is Banned", *The Daily Telegraph*, 15 March, 2007.

The university denied censorship, the way any *dhimmi* under Islam denied being oppressed, saying the organizers had not given it enough notice to arrange for stewards to be on duty at what was bound to be a potentially controversial event. Since when an academic lecture becomes "potentially controversial" in a democratic society? Obviously, the authorities were afraid of a "potentially violent event" and they surrendered to the threat instead of putting what was needed to protect freedom of speech and academic integrity. That was a typically *dhimmi* behavior that the University of Leeds, like many of its counterparts around the world, could be proud of. One of the protest emails, from a student who described himself as "of both Middle Eastern and Islamic background" complained that the title of the event was "profoundly offensive", a comment that no Westerner brought up on democratic notions, would have thought to advance. Is this the kind of enrichment that multi-culturalists had anticipated would cross fertilize the British scene which imported those Muslims? This was exactly the same Muslim outrage that the Cartoon Crisis had caused: a"profoundly offensive " depiction of the Prophet in Western journalism, in the same free spirit that Christ, Moses or Buddha would hve been treated in the free media, but without the hanging threat of violence over their heads. This is the profoundly divisive and unbridgeable gap between the two worlds that no multi-culturalism or *dhimmi* surrender can ever make up.

That student of Islamic background also elaborated, to make himself clear by commenting that "to insinuate that there is a direct link between Islam and anti-Semitism is not only a sweeping generalization but also an erroneous statement that holds no essence of truth[90]. But the said student, contrary to what enlightened Western universities teach the young people given to their upbringing, that assumptions, claims and theses are not to be taken for granted and

---

[90] Ibid.

are to be debated with sckepticism, or decided based on the Islamic eagerness to preserve its reputation intact by denying any wrongdoing, or that it "was an erroneous statement", without suggesting any evidence to his ignorant view and insisting that the evidence that the German scholar wished to present could not be heard. Kuntzel later accused Britain of being the worse country for stifling debate on Muslim extremism. The debate was not about Muslim extremism but about Islam in general, for anti-semitism has been one of the fundamental traits of Islam[91]. The cancellation of his lecture came two weeks after students at Oxford University launched a petition demanding the sacking of David Coleman, a professor of demography, over his links to MigrationWatch, an immigration think tank. Kuntzel said:

> This is a worrying trend, if I say something that is not positive about a particular brand of Islam, the imposition is that I am inciting hatred of every Muslim. I am very concerned about this, it is an attack on academic freedom… There is nothing wrong with holding beliefs but you must be able to challenge and debate them. Academic integrity is all about the exchange of positions and the search for truth. I think this is in danger in the UK[92].

Kuntzel's lecture finally went ahead in Leeds in October, 2007, but more than a decade later the situation on campuses in Britain, Europe and the Americas went worse, with the increasing Muslim

---

[91] Andy Bostom, *Islamic Antisemitism*, Prometheus Books, Amherst NY, 2008; Robert Spencer (ed), *The Myth Of Islamic Tolerance: How Islamic Law Treats Non-Muslims*, Prometheus books, 2005; and Dario Fernandez Morera, *The Myth of the Andalusian Paradise: Muslims, Christians, and Jews under Islamic Rule in Medieval Spain*, ISI Books, Wilmington, 2016.
[92] Graeme Paton, "Academic: Extremism Debate is Being Stifled", *The Daily Telegraph*, 17 March 2007.

immigrant population gathering strength and imposing more limitations on freedom of speech in institutions of higher learning, especially those which came to hinge their financial solvency on Arab finances and Muslim donors. This alarming situation generated hearings in the American Senate which may in the future serve as reference and precedent to future European Palrliamentary inquiries.One of the statements before the inquiring committee referred to the relations between the Department of State and the Muslim Brotherhood, which influences radical Muslim movements worldwide, like CAIR in America. Previously, moderate Muslims and the 9/11 Commission which investigated the events of the Twin Towers and the Pentagon, together with European security experts, had pointed to the Brothers as the forefathers of modern Islamic terrorism.But several years later, the State Department seemed to be willing to flirt with them, even before the Obama Administration shifted to "engaging rather than confronting Islam". Indeed the State Department sent its Head of Counter-terrorism to be the keynote speaker at a conference co-sponsored by the International Institute for Islamic Thought (IIIT), Brotherhood-linked Northern Virginia organization. It was reported that the US Embassy in Rome was planning to co-sponsor a high profile two-day symposium about immigration and integration, with the highly controversial grandson the Brotherhood founder, Swiss scholar Tariq Ramadan as a keynote speaker[93].

Shortly thereafter, it was announced that the conference had been postponed. At the hearing on "Islamic extremism in Europe in" the Senate, various government officials outlined the initiatives to "reach out" to European Muslims. The US Ambassador to Belgium at the time, Tom Korologos, explained how he had been promoting various seemingly laudable initiatives within the State Department, in which American and European Muslim organizations opened a

---

[93] Rachel Ehrenfeld, "When in Rome…" *The New York Sun*, 19 April, 2006.

"dialogue" to "break stereotypes and foster networking opportunities". So, instead of initiating a dialogue with moderate Muslims in order to empower them, the organizations that were chosen represented the Muslim Brother network on both sides of the Atlantic.[94]. Ambassador Korologos' main European partner was FEMYSO, the Youth Branch of the Federation of Islamic Organizations in Europe (FIOE), the umbrella organization for various groups that were closely linked to the Brotherhood. FEMYSO was also the cofounder of WAMY, a Saudi charity that was widely suspected with links with terrorism, before the Saudi establishment had straightened up, detached itself from Bin Laden once it realized he had turned against it, and decided to toe tha American line, a tendency that was accelerated after Iran aligned itself against the Saudi Kingdom as part of the tectonic Sunnite-Shi'ite struggle,and Prince Muhammad Ben Salman ascended to his position of power. The American Muslim partners in the inititive were no less suspects, one of them being CAIR (the American-Islamic Relations, whose unrelenting apology on behalf of radical Islam has become widely known).

Security officials from Europe's largest countries backed a plan to profile mosques on the continent and identify radical Islamic clerics who raise the threat of homegrown terrorism. The project focused on the role of Imams, their training, thir ability to speak and preach in the local language and their sources of funding. This was revealed by the EU Justice and Home Affairs Commissioner, Franco Frattini. The Italian Home minister Giuliano Amato added that Europe already had extensive experience with the "misuse of mosques, which instead of being palces of worship are used for other ends. This is bringing about a situation that involves all our countries and involves the possibility of attacks and the development of networks that use one country to prepare an attack in another". Adel Smith,

---

[94] Lorenzo Vidino, "State Department Flirting with the Muslim Brotherhood",, 20 April, 2006. In the *Islamic Extremism in Europe Hearing,*before the Committee on Foreign Realtions,, US Senate, 5 April 2006.

a well-known Muslim activist in Italy, said that mosques in the country were already extensively monitored, and called the EU plan discriminatory[95]. These revelations which came after the Madrid and London bombings and in the wake of the Cartoon Crisis which shook much of Europe, exposed publicly the facts that public opinion and governments alike had refused until then to acknowledge openly, how hopeless was the gap separating the host countries of Europe and the guest Muslim populations which were supposed to integrate by melting together, with the predominant European culture absorbing the immigrant one. In reality, Europe looked at the immigrant populations with such a deep suspicion as to regard them as hostile enemies, not desirable reinforcements to fill in its demographic deficit. It was puzzling to think that new inhabitants of liberal democracies should be subject to monitoring and profiling, suspected of scheming attacks on their countries of shelter, and that the Muslims should feel that the generous and liberal policies which had permitted their absorption in Europe, were viewed as "discriminatory".

When Muslim intellectuals in the West who confront Islamic radicals, like Wafa Sultan, are receiving death threats[96] and hit-lists of "apostates" are circulated by Islamic groups like the Muslim Brotherhood, in Egypt [97], attitudes of yielding to threats only incite more violent reactions, with Muslims regarding every Western attempt at accommodation as a surrender, something that is not met with gratitude and reciprocity, but with contempt and more outrageous demands. Thus, in view of the inescapable conclusion that matters will grow worse and even out of control, as they indeed

---

[95] Colleen Barry, "EU Proposes Monitoring Radical Mosques", *AP*, 12May, 2007.

[96] Munir al-Mawry, "Arab Intellectual s Receive Death Threats", *Al-Sharq al Awsat*, 10 April, 2006.

[97] Rusty ("John Doe") Shackelford, "Islamists Post Hit-lists of Apostates", the *Jawa Report*, 11 April, 2006.

did in the following decade, even the relatively liberal and accommodating Europeans began to sense the hopelesness of integration due to the build up under their eyes of two separate if not hostile societies side by side on the continent, with little or no prospect for integration into one harmonious community. In consequence, British teachers called for ban on government funding of any faith schools (eying specifically Muslim community schools in Britain, which encouraged the deepening of the gap between Muslim kids and their British counterparts, with government funding). Delegates of the Association of Teachers and Lecturers voted indeed to cut off government money to those schools by 2020, and instead promote integration, to mitigate the fears of scientists who had been warning of the dangers of teaching creationism in those institutions. According to a reliable report, there were 7,000 faith schools (not all of them Muslim, of course) in England, of which 600 were secondary[98]. It was obvious that the initiators of the debate feared Islamic separatism and chose to cloak their language by reference to creationism.

---

[98] Alexandra Blair, "Teachers Demand End to State Cash for Faith Schools ", *The Times*, 12 April, 2006.

CHAPTER SIX

Ethnic, National and Linguistic Competition

What makes the integration of Muslims into European culture a vain enterprise, due to the built-in contradictions explained above, is further aggravated by the general reluctance of people, any people, to countenance the close proximity to, and the tight neighboring relationship with other, different religious, racial, ethnic, linguistic and cultural groups. For one by nature prefers one's own kin on all those grounds, feels comfortable with the familiar and ends up suspecting the different, the dissident, the odd, the alien, despising it, excommunicating and suppressing it as a minority, and finally expressing hostility towards it and fighting it. Anyone who follows the history of the Black people in America, the Rohinga in Mianmar, the Jews in the various Diasporas, the Roma throughout Europe, the Hakka and Muslims in China, the Mauris in New Zealand, the Moros in the Philippines or the Basques and Catalans in Spain, has tasted the malaise of the mixture between cultures, religions, races and ethnicities, especially when it comes suddenly and in great doses, and would prescribe the formula of "separation and good neighborhood" as the recipe for coexistence and harmonious living.

Muslims live in their 57 Islamic countries, that they have admittedly conquered from others, who became oppressed minorities under Islamic rule in their own native turf, like the Copts of Egypt, the Berbers of North Africa, the Christian populations of the Near East and Anatolia and many others. They have created their own morass in their own conquered territories which became their own countries, while Muslim theology had developed the idea that Muslims must live under Islamic rule for only there, under the protection of the Muslim state, can the Believer practice fully the tenets of his faith. And it must be said that though Muslims were dominant in the slave trade of Africa, the dark color has been looked down upon in Muslim tradition, the Islamic faith has elaborated a remarkably multi-racial culture, extending from Black Africa to the fair complexion of the Caucasus, from the brown color of the Indian sub continent to the fair skinned Southern Slavs of Bosnia. And although the tolerance towards non-Muslim minorities knew ups and downs throughout the centuries, the boundaries of Islamdom were recognized as containing a large variety of races and ethnic groups which managed to survive for better of for worse, on the outer boundaries of the rival Christian world in the West and the great cultures of East Asia like the Chinese, the Japanese, the Korean and Vietnamese.

The mobility of populations in the modern era has forced the mixing of populations, some of which went peaceful, when it was Buddhists, Chinese and other Asian cultures which proved docile and adoptable, Jews and various Eastern races and creeds who mixed into existing Christian Europe and the Americas, or when Muslim and Christian Arabs migrated into the Americas as migrants of fortune in small numbers, and in no time became an integral part of their new adoptive countries; but at other times when it was massive Muslim populations knocking on the doors of European and other countries as refugees or labor seekers, there were invariably among them enough radicals who strirred their appetites and incited them to aim for higher and to press for growing demand, taking advantage of the liberal regimes which emphasized human rights in those countries. Those were the watershed years when Islamic doctrine started to develop the ideas of ideo-logical, mission-loaded immigration into Europe with a view of taking it over in the long run, even though if this time "peacefully", and converting it to Islam.

In an article by literary critique Lucette Lagnado[99], she invoked the fact that the Alexandria of the novel *Justine*, of the celebrated writer of the *Alexandria Quartet*, Lawrence Durrell, was an exotic city of constant interactions between cultures and religions which he missed when he was no longer living there, noting that the nov-elist understood Islam's "suffocating beastliness and all it stands for, bigotry, cruelty, and ignorance." He had indeed written about the international city that was Alexandria, prior to the "Free Officers Revolution" of 1952 in the decadent era of King Farouq, when the laxity of the loose bourgeois *bella vita* was impregnated with the tolerance that corruption, nonchalance and easy going life of instant satisfaction permitted, so much so that the Muslim mark within the medley of nations, cultures, languages and faiths which populated that lively city was hardly felt. Come the Nasserite Revo-lution, which tightened the social screws on the free wheeling life model, nationalized foreign firms and caused the departure of many foreigners who had given that city its glamor and cultural variety, and the imposed "Arab Socialism" with its ascetic limitations and puritanical austerity, and the lure of Alexandria was diminished until it almost vanished. Those were the fertile grounds for the reemergence of Islam, especially following the 1967 Six Day War, when the Muslim Brothers started to reassert themselves until they reached full bloom under President Sadat in the 1970s.

This sort of domestic fluctuations which alternately favored or militated against the emergence of Islam or its suffocation as a cen-tral force in society, and marked the nostalgic writings of Durrell

---

[99] Lucette Lagnado,"Lawrence Durrell's Justine: Missing Alexandria", *Wall Street Journal*, October 19, 2019.

and other Western writers, do not characterize the status of Islam in the West, which has been in constant rise there since the second half of the 20th Century, maily due to Muslim migration, legal and illegal, which has been altering the demographic constitution of the European continent. For in the Islamic countries, the rise and fall of radical Islam could be regulated by incumbent rulers in accordance with the threat it posed to their regime, because tyrants or military juntas could always mount a *coup* and shape government to their tune. At any rate, the population remained basically Islamic, traditional, and patriarchal, whether or not Islam was more or less pronounced. In Europe, it is different, because the missionary zeal of the Muslim immigrants to Islamize Europe and take it over necessitates a constant and relentless push towards Islam, without any back sliding, the ultimate stage being the waning of the European state and its replacement by a Muslim entity. Incidentally, the same blueprint is envisaged for Israel by the Islamic Palestinians (Hamas) while the Palestinian "secularists" (PLO) speak of a secular state in Palestine side by side to, or in replacement of, Israel.

The Muslims who arrive to Europan shores and settle there, especially since the 1950s and the establishment of large, self-confident and permanent Muslim communities amounting to millions there, came carrying a heavy luggage of their Muslim culture, tradition, religion, customs and politics. Triggered at first by Arabs from North Africa, who brought in their wake ill-disposition towards Israel and Jews in the Arab-Israeli dispute, and the perceived European sympathy to Jewish and Israeli issues, they were reinforced by more Muslim immigrants of other origins- from the Indian Subcontinent to Britain, from Turkey to Germany, and later Muslim refugees from the entire troubled Muslim world: Iraq, Iran, Somalia, Afghanistan, Kurdistan and parts of Eastern and Western Africa. That negative discourse, which was often violently expressed against Israeli legations in the West and local native Jewish communities, has consolidated the Muslim demonstrations into an amalgam of anti-Israel and anti-Zionism together with a protest against Western countries which supported them, but also gave the Muslim refugees asylum and allowed them public demonstration of displeasure which helped crystallize the anti-Western attitude of the Muslim immigrants against their host societies.

In the Islamic world itself, the anti-Western outbursts on which the Muslim immigrants had been nourished, were typically directed against the US as the arch-representative of Western civilization, and have become practically the norm in all Muslim countries which are for the most part non-democratic, authoritarian, often economically backward, religious, traditional and lacking in freedom and human rights. Western civilization is evoked by them not only to explain their own failures, but to hurl accusations against the "imperialist-colonialist" and "oppressive and exploitative West" which has caused their misfortune. Paradoxically, at the same time that they claim to cherish Western values such as freedom, democracy, secularism, economic prosperity and peace loving, they also give them a twist of their own, making them their own and interpreting them their own way, which amounts to using them to undermine their host societies and stir toubles to destabilize them. For example, democracy for many Islamic countries (and other developing nations for that matter) may also mean a continued authoritarianism (e.g. Erdogan's regime in Ankara), which perhaps derives from and suits best the native traditional systems of those societies, but also will help them transform European societies and impose Islam on them. At the same time, the successful regimes of the West which are feared and admired simultaneously, and on whose doors long lines of visa applicants keep knocking, are also hated, despised, shunned defamed and outrightly blamed for aggression, corruption, terrorism, materialism, degeneration and impending decay.

As the mixture of awe and hatred, contempt and envy is imported to the West with the Muslim immigrants, who also come in contact with the local Jewish communities who had totally acculturated and are often at the forefront of professions, intellectual life, art, commence and politics, as the quintessential representative of the Western culture that they abhor because they fail to integrate into it. As those Jewish communities usually tend to support Zionism and Israel, though always in civilized and non-violent ways, the Muslim immigrants find themselves squeezed between between their envy of the Jews' success and the latters' politics which are also found to coincide with Western values and policies. So we see Muslim immigrants associating with native European anti-Semites from the Right who hate the Jews for their success and with European Leftists who detest Israel's politics or its very existence, dubbing their distate as "anti-Zionism". The ubiquity, simulataneity and uniformity of anti-Jewish and anti-Israeli outbursts have served as a mobilizing anti-establishment instrument for Muslims and opposition movements in Europe and serve well Muslim designs for the longhaul. The newly established Muslim communities in the West are becoming part and parcel of the European societies and are using their incremental political voting power to edge closer to the realization of their goal, first to introduce selected Islamic components into their societies and then to Islamize and take them over. They can count on their exponential demographic growth, the influx of more Muslim refugees, asylum and work seekers, and the growing numbers of European converts to solidify the constant increase in their numbers, especially in view of the negative growth of Western societies.

Unlike the first generation of Muslim immigrants, which was busy searching for livelihood and job opportunities, the new generation of Muslims, more educated and attuned to the local scene, will have less difficulty and more propensity to express itself on affairs of its concern, notably domestic and foreign policy. Thus politicians of all convictions, particularly in areas of large concentrations of immigrants, who realize their growing dependence on the votes of the newcomers, will by necessity be more and more attentive to the needs and demands of their Muslim constituencies, not least with regard to the relations between the countries of shelter and the Islamic world, a trend that is bound to accelerate Europe's merger into Islamdom. This trend has been accelerated in the past decade and already made a long term impact, due to the following:

1. The established Arab/Muslim populations have learned to make use of their numbers and to hinge their political support to candidates for public office on the satisfaction of their demands;

2. Paradoxically, those new immigrants who had been deprived of free expression in their authoritarian countries of origin, can now use their newly acquired democratic rights to exert pressure on their adoptive countries to lend support to the politics and culture of their countries of origin they had left behind;

3. On the national scene, the new immigrants who enjoy equality and tap the resources of their adoptive countries to facilitate their own absorption, end up imposing the ideas and positions they imported with them from the Middle East, not least the cultural and religious among them, on their countries of refuge;

4. As they grow in numbers and influence, and are no longer content to make their voices heard in local politics and to proselytize Islam, the Muslims try to marginalize the much more affluent but much less numerous local Jewish communities, either out of jealousy or a sense of competition. Antagonism between the two communities aggravates as a result in spite of many sincere, but vain, efforts by the Jewish communities to engage in dialogue with their Muslim compatriots. For Muslims it seems evident that only the removal of the successful Jewish communities from the scene can erase the

humiliation built into the comparison in their own disfavor of the success of the Jews to their own backwardness;

5. Thus, the tension between Muslims and Jews in Europe, which has already cost many victims to Islamic terrorism and caused thousands of Jews to relocate to Israel, are not merely socio-economic, emanating from the vast gulf between them, but also political deriving from their diverging views. Add to that the traditional contempt for Jews that every Muslim carries with himself as part of his religious, mental and cultural luggage, and the perception by Muslims of Jews an obstacle to the Islamization of the continent, and you have the recipe for the continual rift and friction between the two, on Middle Eastern terms and in Levantine style, on European soil.

Muslim immigrants to the West were brought up with non-Muslim minorities of all sorts in their countries of origin: Copts in Egypt, Christians of many denominations in Syria and Lebanon, Chaldeans and Assyrians in Iraq, Alawite s in Syria, Druze in the Levant, Jews all over North Africa and the Middle East, Kurds (though Sunni Muslim)in Turkey, Iraq, Syria and Iran and Yazidis in Iraq, etc. All those minorities have been persecuted because despised and looked down upon. Most of them, belonged to the religiously subjugated status of *dhimmis* (protected people) until formally canceled by either the colonial power in North Africa or in the shrinking territories of the Ottoman during the *Tanzimat* reforms of the late 19th Century. But the official cancellation of millennial discriminatory measures against non Muslims could not eliminate overnight the discriminatory practice and certainly not the contemptuous attitudes that had occasioned them. So when Muslim immigrants started to land on European shores in our era, they arrived and settled in with their heavy residue of hatred and contempt, though they had to live with the blatant contradiction between the miserable image of Christians and Jews inherited from

Islamic tradition, and the reality of their success and wealth that superimposed them as the more powerful, influential and prosperous population of Europe.

Muslim cultures, which had, for centuries, been preserving a self-image of "protecting the *dhimmis*" and "living in harmony" with them, as long as they were subjected to their rule, like Chrisians and Jews in the mythical "Paradise"of Andalusia[100], cannot simply face with equanimity a documented scholarly deprecation and denial of their own writings, and of the positive legends they have been weaving for centuries around their treatment of Christians and Jews, whom they had in fact always wished to either Islamize, or at the very least to preserve as humiliated *dhimmis* in accordance with *Shari'a* tenets. Many examples could be cited from the millennial records of that sorry history, from the books of Bat Y'eor,[101] Morera, Israeli[102] and many others and commented upon to illustrate the taste of *dhimmi* treatment under Islam, but we leave the essentially religious description of it to Chapter Seven. Here we shall concern ourselves with the social, economic and cultural aspects of it, which the Muslims settling in Europe were hoping to impose gradually before they could reach their ultimate goal of Islamizing the continent. This contradicts the claim of harmony and tranquility for the Jews and Christians, advanced by Muslims (and also some Jews and Christians admittedly, who have perpetuated their *dhimmi* mentality and are thankful to their oppressors under what is known today as the "Stockholm Syndrome"), and their false assertion that it was only modern Christian colonialism and imperialism and Jewish Zionism which spoiled this idyllic state of affairs.

---

[100] See Dario Fernandez-Morera, *The Myth of the Andalusian Paradise: Muslims, Christians, and Jews under Islamic Rule in Medieval Spain,* Wilmington, 2016.
[101] Bat Ye'or, *Juifs et Chretiens sous l'Islam:Les Dhimmis face au defi Inegriste,* Paris, Berg International, 1994.
[102] See R. Israeli, *Back to Nowhere: Moroccan Jews in Dream and Reality,* Lampert Press, Germany, 2008.

Under the Umayyad rule in Spain, while Christian and Jewish practices were usually tolerated, public ostentatious displays of faith like ringing of bells, or public funerals, or praying loudly in public near the Jerusalem Wailing Wall, and the Tomb of the Patriarchs in Hebron, were prohibited for Jews (as they were also near the Jerusalem Wailing Wall and the Tombs of the Patriarchs in Hebron. Today, Muslims throughout Europe and in Israel not only claim those rights for themselves, but also pretend to be rightful in their imposing them on the general population, by blocking roads for prayers, squatting in front of cathedrals and public buildings for their Friday gatherings, and voicing outloud their calls for prayer from the top of their minarets at odd hours, regardless of the disturbances they pose to the generally polite and law-abiding populations which usually avoid inconveniencing them. For example, in 1438 (quite a few years before the rise of Zionism), the Jews were expelled from the old city of Fez (*Fas al-Bali)* in Morocco, and they built their *mellah* (ghetto). From that time on, at every *inter-regum* when the heir to the departed ruler was struggling against other contenders to the throne, Jews were always the easy prey, with each party demanding extra taxes, ransoms and protection money from them, while committing massacres against them and intimidating them into conforming to the extortion imposed on them. In the years 1553-5, for example, the rulers levied money from the Jews to finance their domestic or internecine wars. When, in 1558, Muslim Turks invaded the *Maghrib*, they killed the incumbent ruler and massacred Jews, raped Jewish girls in the city of Sousse, took many Jewish prisoners back with them, if they remained alive, as slaves, and those were probably converted to Islam. Admittedly, horrors were done by Muslims against other Muslims too, killing them by the thousands and chopping their heads off beyond measure. But those were the accepted norms of action at the time against invaders from the outside, or rebels against the rule from within, and one can claim that there was no other way to repel the enemy or quell a rebellion. But Jews did not belong to either of these categories: They were native and preceded the Arab rulers in place, so they could not "invade " them, and they never rose violently against the ruling dynasty, in spite of the oppression which would have warranted such a rebellion. For one thing, they were too weak, unarmed and unhopeful of success. So, the cruel intimidation, oppression and outright massacres against them were not used by the Muslims in defense from them, but, for some very specific ideological reasons deriving from their *dhimma* status.

In 1606, namely, once again, much prior to any talk about Zionism, the Chronicles of Fez tell us of eight hundred dwellers of the *mellah* who died of starvation after a vain search for food in the public garbage piles; so were they either condemned to starve within the ghetto, or to be massacred if they ventured out of it. In this situation, six hundred Jews had to convert to Islam to escape both starvation and murder. This meant that it was not a state of general starvation which reigned everywhere, but that hunger depended on faith. Namely if, as in the days of Torquemada in Catholic Inquisition Spain, a Jew wanted to live or just to eat, he had to convert, regardless of the Qur'anic verse so often cited to demonstrate "Muslim tolerance", and that Muslims are so fond of repeating, to the effect that "there is no compulsion in religion". Many Jews were led to slaughter, and sometimes their own children had to rescue them from those dilemmas by converting, while others committed suicide and died as martyrs. In 1610 the Jews of Fez were burdened by the ruler with a special tax of ten thousand ounces of silver in payment for the ruler's "rescuing them from pillage by other Arabs", as if the other Arabs were not his subjects or as if he did not owe any measure of protection to the Jews who paid their regular *jizya* poll-tax as part of their *dhimma* obligations. Moreover, since the Jews had no way to collect that enormous sum within the one day which was allotted to them, the sum was doubled. So bad was the situation, and so insistent and cruel the oppressor, that the Jews had to cancel their *Yom Kippur* rituals in order to busy themselves with the collection of money to satisfy the tyrant and save their own lives. That atrocious measure did not sound much like the "harmonious and tolerant" mode of accommodating Jews that Muslims often boast about. However, since that heartless oppressor was removed from power by his brother, the newcomer demanded the same amount, and the Jews were compelled again to violate their Tabernacles festival to busy themselves with the collection of the funds, which included the melting of the precious metals that decorated the synagogue, in order to fill the tax quota imposed on them from high.

Thus, many Jews were dispossessed of all their property and knew the intimidation of starvation. Traders among them, who were on their caravan's way, were also robbed and maltreated. As if man-induced calamities were not sufficient, an epidemic of plague killed another four hundred helpless Jews in Fes. On *Hanukka* of that year, merely a few months after the unfortunate *Yom Kippur* and the Tabernacles festivals were just experienced, another ten ounces of silver were levied on the Jews, who, in order to produce them, had to melt the gold and silver ornaments and embroidered covers of their Torah scrolls, an act of last resort and of ultimate despair. How pitiful and deeply aggravating it was to them to see the Holy Book bare and naked, like the community itself which stood on the verge of bankruptcy, that was added to the humiliation, shame and grief that all its members shared. All these extra exactions came in addition to the ten thousand ounces of silver of regular taxes which were levied on the community annually, and to the wine tax which Jews had to pay in order to be permitted to produce it for their needs. During the festival of *Purim*, a few months later, while the Jews of Fez were busy trying to respond to another exaction of eight thousand ounces of silver, news from the city of Tedla came to cause further despondence and spoil their holiday, to the effect that Arabs had destroyed Jewish homes and burned fifty scrolls of the Torah, and two thousand books of the Pentateuch, followed by three thousand more. Again on Pentecost, the Arabs, having learned by then that the holidays were the most vulnerable days on which to "squeeze" the Jews, struck again. The Arab governor of Fez demanded from the Head of the community another twenty five ounces of silver, and the Jews had no choice but to conform, if they wanted to extricate their president from certain imprisonment and death. Rabbi Saul Serero, the rabbi of the time, who also kept the records of his community, wrote with bitterness:"Had all the skies been parchment, all the lakes full of ink and all the forests pens, they would not have been sufficient to write all our troubles in full". This picturesque and somewhat exaggerated description, which cried out from the depths of despair, was to repeat itself many times later in the Fez Chronicle.

At the same time, many synagogues were robbed and their treasures stolen. The members of the congregation had to stand watch round the clock near their houses of prayer, or pay protection money to thugs, to the point that they were so impoverished that they could do nothing more and decided to throw their lot in the hands of the Creator. This was done by prayer, fasting, and bringing their babies into the synagogues; it was hoped that the cries of the children would generate God's mercy. As a rule, the worst moments for Jews came during the transition from a ruling king to his children, who fought for power; any one of them who emerged victorious could blame his Jewish subjects for not identifying with him from the outset, and exact from them taxes and ransoms as a chastisement. The Fez Chronicles are replete with the reports of the prayers for rain which were heard from every synagogue of the *mellah* in the Fall, for fear that if rains were scarce, the Jews would be blamed and made to pay the damages in consequence. In 1646, local troops were directly involved in the destruction of the Fez synagogues, in spite of all the bribes paid to the governor and his underlings to avert the disaster. The bribes sufficed only to rescue the Torah scrolls, but the houses of prayer were so utterly destroyed that they were found comparable, in the eyes of the local rabbis, to the destruction of the Temple (in AD 70 by the Romans). Therefore, lamentations were read and sung, as on the 9th day of the month of Ab, which commemorated the destruction of the Temple, the holiest place in the history of Judaism. On the next *Yom Kippur*, the two colleges (*Beit Midrash)* of Torah learning were also razed to the ground. These traumas and their likes are deeply incrusted in the hearts and minds of most Jews originating from Islamic countries, who constitute, together with their descendants, about half of modern Israel's population. Thus, in spite of the prevailing mood among some intellectuals in Israel today, including scholars in the fields of Islam and Jewish history, who preach leniency towards Muslims in general, and emphasize the mythical "golden age and harmonious existence of the Jews under Islam", those who had experienced that "coexistence" continue to be terrified by Islamic persecutors and hate mongers knocking at their gates to this day.

What was amazing, and may have attested to Jewish survivability and durability even under the most calamitous duress, was the expression "due to our sins", which usually accompanied the descriptions of those calamities, as if turning the guilt inwards would somewhat mitigate the disaster once the blame was not directed to others but reflected on oneself. The Chronicle did not call for vengeance or retribution, for such were considered impractical and unfeasible against the powerful rulers and their incited and hate-seething crowds. In return for the houses of prayer which were destroyed and the desecration of Jewish holidays by the Arab hosts, the oppressed Jews believed in full reliance on God who would "take our vengeance". Indeed, the praises of God for having preserved the Jewish communities from total annihilation, were the prevailing themes in that register of sad events. Accommodation with those horrible events, in recognition that they could be worse, was due not only to a fatalistic acceptance of one's lot for the misfortunes that occurred; there was also in them an element of hope and optimism that not everything was lost and that renewal and consolation, redemption and better days, could be seen looming ahead beyond the murderous present. Indeed, in 1672, during the first prosperous years of the Alawite Dynasty which rules until our days, such words of comfort and faith in the future were recorded in the Chronicle; this was done under the relatively generous and benevolent kingship of Mulai Rashid and Mulai Isma'il, who alternated between their ancient capital of Fes and the newly established one in nearby Meknes. Jews were exuberant and attached great hopes to the future, teaching us that in the long series of massacres and forced conversions, robberies, and destruction, there were also occasional intervals when the Jews saw the light. Even faint stars looked bright to them against the backdrop of the very dark skies they had grown accustomed to contemplate.

Either way, it became evident once and again, that Jews depended for their very existence on their sycophancy towards absolute and corrupt rulers, who legislated, enforced their cruel laws and punished ruthlessly, all at once. Christians who had thrived under ethe Visigots were totally extirpated from the land by Islamic rule. But Jews, who had nowhere else to go, became unfailingly aware, every day anew, of their misery under this kind of oppressive rule and of the hazards of sitting atop a bubbling volcano which could burst at any time, without warning or transition. In the year 1680, for example, while everyone was asleep, the king decreed that all the inhabitants of the Fez *mellah* had to be pulled out of their beds and sent to the surrounding fields, the very same fields which, on happier days, hosted their *mimouna* picnics which followed the *Pesach* festival. The reason was that a sword set with precious stones had been stolen from his palace. The horrified Jews, with their praying elderly, yelling infants and helpless sick, lay on the cold and barren earth, not understanding either of what they were guilty, or when that collective punishment would be terminated. Only when the Jews were permitted to go back to their homes, and when they realized that nothing was stolen from their property in their absence, did they burst into celebration of the "miracle" which was done to them, for they were able to remain alive, while the torment, the terror and the menaces heaped on them in the middle of the night were considered "normal". Moreover, that inhuman ruling king, Mulai Isma'il, was considered "benevolent", and when one day, the news was released that he had just escaped from falling prey to lions, they celebrated the happy occasion in great pomp and ceremony, abstained from work, decorated the streets of the *mellah* with silk materials, and donned their most festive outfits. On that day they could even visit the royal palaces and enter the mosques with their shoes on, as they jubilantly reported in their records of 1699. But, in the same breath, they reported of Mulai Zaydan from the royal house in Tefilalt, who stormed the *mellah*, taking as booty anything he and his underlings found of worth, and imposed a fine of two hundred and fifty gold coins on that impoverished community. These were the two poles of Jewish existence, which implied that the more the helpless Jews submitted and bent their heads down, the more mistreated and humiliated they were bound to be at the hands of their rulers. Just for the "privilege" of remaining alive, they would hold themselves grateful to their oppressors for the "generosity" from which they had benefited. That was, in essence, the status of "*dhimma*" which we will have to elaborate upon.

From the onset of Islam in the 7th Century AD, as the new religion was expanding rapidly through quick conquest of the entire Mediterranean basin and beyond, where ancient and exhausted nations were disintegrating, Islam divided humanity into three categories and the earth into two kinds of territory. At the center, of course, stood the Muslims, the humans closest to the ideal, due to their submission (*Islam*) to the will of Allah. The second category were the Scriptuaries (*ahl-al-Kitab*), namely people like Christians and Jews, who possessed a holy scripture, which was recognized by Islam until it was "distorted" and "forged" by its holders, and subsequently "amended and updated" by the revelations of Allah to the Prophet Muhammad. As the years wore on, and as the conquests were expanded further afield, other people too, like the Manicheans and the Hindus, were recognized as Scriptuaries. The outermost circle included the pagans who did not know one God. The lands where those people dwelt were differentiated as either the Islamic Dominion (*Dar al-Islam)*, or *Pax Islamica*, that is the territory ruled by Islam, regardless of the composition of its population (for instance, the lands still populated by a majority of non-Muslims, like Andalusia, were still part of this category, as long as they were ruled by Islam); and the Dominion of War (*Dar al-Harb)*, namely the land that was yet to fall under Islamic rule. Evidently, for practical reasons, these categories are not effectively operational these days, for otherwise the entire system of international relations, and international rules of conduct would be chaotic, if every nation determined for itself its attitude towards others as it pleased. But in pre-modern Islamic countries, there was no public opinion, and the rules of conduct were determined by *Shari'a* law, exactly the way some revolutionary Islamic movements are attempting to revive them today. That law is immutable and not open to reform, pressure or whim of the ruler, even as some of those same rulers have occasionally deviated from those severe rules, depending upon whether they were personally more fanatic puritans or more open-minded and benevolent beings. Under the more puritanical Hanbalite and Malikite Schools of Law, when *shari'a* implementation was the strictest, the suffering of the Scriptuaries reached its peak.

According to Islamic political theory, following the Jihad wars which generated the expansive conquests and the enlargement of *Dar al-Islam*, the Muslim ruler found himself managing the lives of three sorts of people: the Muslims who occupied the masters' position, the submitted Scriptuaries who were merely tolerated under certain conditions, and the pagans who were compelled to Islamize, or run away for their lives until they would be subjugated in the next round of conquests, or be killed. According to this theory, which has been revived today in ISIS lands or in other territories managed by radical Muslim groups, only the first two categories could dwell in the Muslim Caliphate, while the pagans had to expeditiously determine their choices. They were converted to Islam in their majority, as were many Jews and Christians who could not bear their "tolerated" status. The pace of conquest was so dizzying that the occupied pagan peoples had little time to ponder the new situation, and in general had to adapt to the new rulers. But the People of the Book, whose scriptures were recognized, had only to recognize Islam's superiority by submitting to it, and were otherwise permitted to observe their religion under the status of *dhimmitude*, and to pay a special and demeaning poll tax (the *jizya*) in return for their "protection". On the face of it, Muslim societies in the Middle Ages were thus much more tolerant and open to Jews than was Christendom. This has created the myth of tolerance and of the "Golden Age"[103] of the Jews (and Christians) under Islam, as if they had enjoyed total freedom (that even the Muslims did not have), or total equality in the Muslim medieval world.

The status of *dhimma* (protection or *dhimmitude*) has gained considerable treatment in the Muslim judicial treatises of the Middle Ages. To be a *dhimmi* not only signified the inferior class of the tolerated peoples, in contrast with the privileged Muslim subjects of the Caliphate, but meant also a lesser judicial stature (e.g. the evidence provided by a *dhimmi* was worth half of the Muslim's, and the *dhimmi* was legally incapacitated to bear witness against a Muslim; an inferior economic and social position (certain dirty jobs and occupations were reserved to the *dhimmi*s); a submissive political

---

[103] This myth has been completely debunked in the recent study of Fernandez-Morera, Dario, The Myth of the Andalusian Paradise: Muslims, Christians and Jews under Islamic Rule in Medieval Spain, ISIS Books, Wilmington, 2016.

rank (Jews and Christians had no political rights and could not be trusted to serve in the government or the military); and a cultural handicap (Jews were always suspected of plotting schemes or mirroring Satan). When Muslim children were disciplined by their parents for their misconduct, the "threat" that the Jews would be brought upon them was often used. That was understandable because the Qur'an instilled the idea that they were "the descendants of monkeys and pigs", and discouraged any amicable relations with them or with Christians. Many of the limitations imposed on Jews (and Christians) were crystallized in what came to be known as the 'Umar regulations, which expressed the ambivalent attitude of Muslims to the Scriptuaries: On the one hand they were supposed to be tolerated and protected due to their holy scriptures and to their payment of the humiliating *jizya*; but on the other hand, they were to be humiliated and tormented due to their "forgery of the Word of Allah", unless they complied and converted to Islam, as most conquered peoples did. But one has to emphasize that those regulations were often violated, for the better or the worse. In Muslim Spain, where Jews attained temporary grandeur, served among the highest bureaucracy of the state, and distinguished themselves as professionals and intellectuals of the first degree, their actual stature was a huge improvement on their official status of *dhimmi*; but in Almohad North Africa and Mamluk Egypt, Jews knew worse periods of genocide of entire communities, massacres and extortions, even after they paid their poll tax and filled their obligations under the *dhimma*.

There is no doubt that, compared to medieval Christianity which did not tolerate any non-Catholics in its midst, and activated its infamous Inquisition to enforce conversions to Christianity, or to eliminate or expel Cathars, Jews and other dissidents in the West, and committed horrible pogroms and expulsions against Jews in Western and Eastern Europe, the Muslim world was much more open and tolerant. It absorbed Jewish refugees expelled from Christendom, and generally did not persecute Scriptuaries in any systematic and constant way. This was possible, because while Christian society was uni-compartmental and supposedly homogeneous, allowing no diversity in its midst, the Islamic Caliphate was bi-compartmental which recognized, like under the Roman Empire, a place for others, though in a secondary or subordinate position to be sure (like the slaves in Rome), but a protected and tolerated class (*dhimmi*s) within Muslim society. Evidently, Jews of the time felt better protected under Islam than under Christianity. But to jump to a hasty and incorrect conclusion that they "always lived in equality, harmony and peace", as Muslim propaganda would have us believe, is, unfortunately a gross hyperbole. The fact is, that the moment the Jews of Islam could leave their land, some sought shelter in the Western world, which had, in the meantime undergone emancipation, liberty and modernity, while Islamdom, as a whole, did not experience such developments; and some decided to migrate to the newly established state of Israel. It is true that most Muslim countries, mainly under the impetus of the colonial powers, had formally canceled the *dhimma* in the 20th Century or slightly before, but the built-in hatred and contempt toward the Jews did not relent. The continuing Arab-Israeli dispute, and the revival of Islam and its norms, have contributed immensely to the renewal of the traditional Islamic political thought concerning Jews, even though they have all practically left Islamic lands. All one has to do is to read the platforms of Hamas, al-Qa'ida or Hizbullah, to realize the full-fledged retrieval from almost oblivion of the anti-Jewish ideology and vocabulary, and their euphemistic demand to "return the Jews (and Christians) to their former state (of *dhimmi*s)". This has in fact been implemented in areas controlled by Hamas, ISIS and other radical Islamic movements.

The most insidious aspect of *dhimma*, however, beyond the humiliation and institutionalization of discrimination in the judicial, social, political, economic and cultural domains, has been the state of mind of the fatalism and submission of the *dhimmis*, born out of centuries of inescapable persecution and oppression, on the one hand, and the mood of sycophancy and identification with the oppressor, which has turned this state of affairs into a "natural and immutable" situation, on the other. In other words while it has been possible to extricate Jews and Christians from the *dhimma*, it is next to impossible to extricate the *dhimma* mentality out of some of those who had suffered it. We have already described the mood of submission and sycophancy that had characterized Jewish and Christian conduct during the dark ages of their existence in the various *mellahs* (Jewish ghettos) of Morocco. For even after their exodus from that backward society, and their rootedness in the modern and advanced societies which absorbed them, where liberty and safety are guaranteed, there is among some of them a lingering habit of praising the Muslim rulers for their "benevolence" towards the *dhimmis*; it is as if the Jews owed their right to exist to those absolute and corrupt rulers who held thousands of political prisoners in jail without trial. This typically Jewish parochial outlook of judging rulers only based on their conduct towards Jews, and not on the basis of their universal and human rights records, is what distorts the thinking of those Jews today, who erect monuments in Israel to Moroccan kings, or praise Moroccan monarchs, and participate in their funerals, only because they were thought to be "pro-Jewish", or accepted bribes to let Jews leave their bondage there, or had otherwise collaborated with Israel. Furthermore, the *dhimmi* outlook has insidiously penetrated the domain of international relations, inasmuch as the political correctness cultivated by the media, academics and diplomats, has imposed rules of conduct which prohibit criticizing anything Islamic, including their repressive regimes, their backward societies, their corrupt leaderships, or their aggressive and discriminatory policies. We have been surrounded by a sub-culture of legends and lies, which holds Islam as "the religion of peace", in the face of the rampages of *Jihadi* Islam across the world, while it is the more militant trends of Islam which prevail today. The Rushdie syndrome, the hiding of European politicians in their own lands from the wrath of Muslim attackers, the kowtowing of European countries before the masses of Muslims who threaten to submerge them and to change Europe to their tune, the violence used by Muslims across the world, the fear of western media and publishers to give vent to anything critical of Islam, and the wimpy supplications of the West for Iran to desist from its nuclear program, are all manifestations of this malaise. And if one dares to resist this *dhimmi* doctrine, one is dubbed "racist" or "Islamophobe".

The hypocrisy and sycophancy surrounding Jewish existence under those conditions, must be, in the final analysis, the main reason for their eagerness to relinquish all their past and heritage behind and venture into a new life abroad. The same Jew, Habib Toledano, who reported, in the Fez Chronicle of the year of 1699, the celebration of the rescue of Mulai Isma'il from the claws of lions, also whimpered in 1701 about "the troubles we experienced under Mulai Isma'il, who exacted from Moroccan Jews one hundred silver pounds for the conduct of his wars". Of that, the Jews of Fez were to pay twenty two pounds, such an enormous sum that "our hearts melted, our knees trembled, our hands weakened, our eyes blurred, our bones broke… and the joy of *Pesach* turned into disaster. Many households did not read the *haggadah,* and those who did intoned it like a lamentation". Following all those levies, pains, and whimpers, the Jewish community dispatched a delegation to the Court, with gifts to express gratitude, and to appease the ruler, who might be influenced to alleviate some of that burden. But it was all in vain, and they had to "cry and pay". To collect that money, the Jewish leadership imposed on the wealthy between six and ten thousand silver ounces each; the rabbis, who generally were penniless, had to pay "only" two thousand each. To get that sum, Jews again had to melt the silver decorations of the Torah scrolls, but felt that this act was so demeaning to the honor of the Torah, that they refrained from reading from those naked scrolls during the following feast of Pentecost. In the 1704 Chronicle, more reports of robbery, taxes and acts of cruelty against the Jews were reported. One Jew, who had hardly been married for a month, was abducted and burned alive. The local governor who ordered the murder also sent his underlings to exact a "ransom" for the dead Jew. Others of his underlings visited the *mellah* every day to demand more taxes and gifts, or to collect cones of sugar, silk materials, food stuffs, and clothing, as if the Jewish pockets were bottomless, and anyone who had any authority or wielded any power saw himself entitled to dip his hand and grab as much as he could. But when there was no other source from which to pay, delegations of Jewish notables went to the Court in Meknes to complain about this endless procession of exactions. The king ordered them flogged with lead-garnered whips, until two of them died, and the rest of them were ordered burned alive in the lime furnace. But he reconsidered and elected to hold them hostage until their community in Fez redeemed them with another twenty pounds of silver. Jews who could not pay were arrested, and they either died under torture or announced their conversion to Islam in order to escape that hell. After all these horrors, the chronicler sang the praise of Mulai Isma'il at his death (1727), perhaps to signify that the other leaders were worse. He was specifically lauded for the security of trade in his times, due to his ruthless security forces, and for his "wisdom and intelligence". And on the circumstances of his death, it was mentioned that "due to our sins, he fell ill and died", as if the Jews' sins caused his death, or that they should regret the passing away of the despot. Maybe they sensed that the successors might turn out even worse.

Nothing could better illustrate the *dhimmi* state of mind than these dismaying reports. They were founded on the miracle of the permanently flimsy and threatened existence of the Jews, where the oppressed, who hardly maintained their breathing, were overly grateful to their persecutors and to God for their survival. They thanked the Lord that they were not compelled to convert from their faith, and that they could withstand the tortures, the hunger, the fears, and the threats which accompanied their survival. They thought that things could always get worse. Sometimes they did indeed. In the *inter-regnum* year of 1790-1, for example, the Jews were compelled to leave the Fez *mellah* for twenty two months, and upon their return from their shelters in the mountains or in other cities, or from their hiding places in town, they began to build the ruins anew, to refurbish the walls which were breached, and to rebuild their private as well as communal lives. After all this, the great luminary, Rabbi Yehuda Ben-Attar, sang the praise of the Lord for "all the miracles He performed for us, to our benefit. Let us sing in gratitude to the Lord, for we should not be ungrateful. We have seen with our own eyes and heard with our own ears, the miracles done to us, just like the exodus from Egypt". Shortly thereafter, in 1793, during the years immediately following the French Revolution, the rule again revolved, and new persecutions were imposed, on *Pesach* at first, in the town of Tetouan - whose Jews were robbed of all the provisions they had accumulated for the holiday, and many of them were killed, raped, burned and despoiled. These rampages spread to other cities and lasted until Pentecost, seven weeks later, when nothing was left to be despoiled, not even the honor of deflowered Jewish women who tried to cover their nudity with extant pieces of burnt Torah scrolls. In the city of Oujda, the Jews who came out in festive Arab dress to welcome the new ruler, instead raised his wrath because they were indistinguishable from the Arabs in the crowd, so he ordered the right ear of all Jews present, old and young, men and women, to be cut off in order to tell who was who. Rabbi Shriki, a great scholar in Torah in that generation, to whom a high position had been promised by the king if he converted to Islam, but he refused, was burnt alive while the cruel ruler watched and sang. Other Jews were hanged alive by their feet at the entrance to the *mellah,* for all to see and be struck by terror. That king, Yazid Ibn Muhammed, was known in Jewish sources as "arrogant and Jew hater, like Haman from the Book of Esther", who delighted in chopping off the heads of Jews and hanging them at the city entrance. When his brother, Suleiman, took over the reign, the Jews regarded him as "savior and redeemer".

And so the lives of the Jews proceeded from one ruler to the next, one more or less greedy, cruel and evil than his predecessor or his successor, to the point that periods of slightly less duress (there were no good periods) looked like a golden age. Namely, a king who did not indulge in massive massacres, or in frequently despoiling the Jews, was adulated as "benefactor" and "benevolent". The next century was not any better. In 1811, a large scale pogrom plagued the Jews of nearby Meknes, many synagogues were burned, with their books and scrolls inside, and so many houses were destroyed that families were compelled to spend the nights in the streets. The Jews were afraid to decry the ruin of their community or to eulogize the dead in public, lest the authorities suspect that they identified with them. Despite the discretion of the mourning, reports were passed to the rulers that Jews had built new synagogues, something strictly prohibited under the Umar Regulations. That prompted the authorities to destroy the new buildings and impose fines for the violation of the rules. Only now, when one looks back at the past, but now better equipped by the learning, experience and an historical perspective, can one understand the significance of the deep sighs so often sounded by the resigned old generation of fathers and grandfathers, accompanied by the prayer:" May God pronounce our suffering plentiful!". When they repeated that prayer, their voices were shaky and painful, as if the entire weight of the universe rested on their shoulders. At the time, one could never fathom their individual and communal agony which was imprinted, generation after generation, on their flesh, and not only on their recollection, in spite of the atmosphere of quiet, serenity and normalcy which they tried to weave around the younger generation they wished to raise. That saga of suffering not only was recorded by the Jewish victims, but was also confirmed in the writings of their oppressors, who saw no wrong in their doings; that was what the prevailing rule of the Muslim masters, was supposed to mete out to the inferior *dhimmis.*

That treatment of the *dhimmis* was enshrined not only in ancient Muslim judicial theory but also in modern practice. A 15th century Moroccan scholar, al-Maghili, described the day of payment of the poll-tax which was levied on Jews individually and on their community collectively:

> On payment day, they [the *dhimmis]* shall be assembled in a public place like the *suq* (market place). They should be standing there waiting in the lowest and dirtiest place. The acting officials representing the law shall be placed above them and shall adopt a threatening attitude so that it seems to them, as well as to others, that our object is to degrade them by pretending to take their possessions. They will realize that we are doing them a favor (again) in accepting from them the *jizya,* and letting them thus go free. Then they shall be dragged one by one (to the official responsible) for the exacting of payment. When paying, the *dhimmi* will receive a blow and will be thrust aside so that he will think that he has escaped the sword through this (insult). This is the way that the Friends of the Lord, of the first and last generations, will act towards their infidel enemies, for might belongs to Allah, to His Messenger, and to the Believers.[104]

---

[104] Bat Ye'or, *Islam and Dhimmitude*, Fairleigh Dickinson University Press, Madison, 2002, p. 70.

Four hundred years later, at the end of the 19th century, an Italian Jew, visiting Marrakesh, personally watched this similar scene at the gate of the *mellah:*

> The Governor and the Judge planted their tents at the entrance to the *mellah* and urged the Jews to proceed to the payment of the *jizya* which they collected for the sultan… I was also summoned, and since I inquired whether strangers who enjoyed European patronage were also obliged to pay their part, I was told that others had already paid, therefore I agreed to conform too. After I paid the tax to the officials, I was beaten on my shoulder by the guards of the Judge [the act of payment, which is a religious duty, is overseen by the Judges, but the law enforcement is assured by the Governor]. I addressed the two officials and told them that I was under the protection of the Italians. Thereupon, the Judge ordered the guards: "remove the kerchief from his head and beat him forcefully, and let him complain to whomever he wishes!" The guards obeyed and beat me energetically. This kind of attitude to a protected European subject only shows the local Arabs that they can mistreat Jews without any fear of punishment.[105]

When one examines the spread of Islam into Europe in recent decades, one must come to the conclusion that it is not enough to account for Muslim immigration into the old continent and its transformation at their hands, but one must also account for the European counter-measures after major acts of terror occurred there, and of the Muslim worldview, which regards those Western defensive measures as aggression, persecution, racism, Islamophobia, and

---

[105] Ibid.

discrimination against the ever-docile and always poor, helpless, innocent, and victimized Muslims who had just come to seek work. When Britain or Germany idolized multiculturalism as a way to enrich European culture and celebrate the fake difference between moderate Islam of the mainstream and the few violent radicals, Muslims regarded that as an attempt to dilute Islam in order to dominate and eliminate it. As far as they were concerned, only their unrestricted violent activity in Europe, in favor of the recognition of their own mores and norms, such as wearing the veil, forcing marriage on their women, or pursuing "honor killings," would be acceptable as fair behavior of the host countries toward them. In other words, not satisfied with full equality of opportunity and freedom of speech and of religious cult, Muslims of the new era begin to demand special privileges for themselves, like the prerogative to train terrorists or incite violence against other citizens. When they burned down a Jewish synagogue in Berlin or Paris or blew up trains in London and Madrid, they expected their adopted countries to accept that as a matter of course, and they were often aided in that belief by the local European extreme-left and extreme-right organizations that boosted Muslim demands due to their common anti-Semitism, or in order to appear as progressive multiculturalists, or as a tool to increase their own ranks by luring Muslim immigrants into their political organizations.

The 1990s were the preparatory years for 2006, the year of the Cartoon Affair when, like in the Rushdie antecedent, the values of Islam clashed violently with the West once again. But now the Muslims were much more experienced and battle-hardened, after blowing up the London and Madrid railways, causing hundreds of Western casualties, and forcing the Spaniards, under threats, to dismiss the Aznar government in favor of a socialist leader who was to become more docile to Muslim causes. This time, the Muslim militants were even more daring and vociferous, more militant and aggressive, than in the Rushdie case, for they had acquired the knowledge that the West would cave in. The underlying triggers were the same, all focusing on "insults" to Islam. In 1989 it was the *Satanic Verses*, which was claimed to have inexcusably mocked the Word of Allah, and in 2006 it was the Prophet of Islam who was unforgivably ridiculed in the cartoons which triggered the crisis. In both cases the flimsy self-confidence and paranoia of the Muslims was so deeply shaken that they had to resort to violence, threats, and mayhem to rescue their desecrated honor, as if a movie or article criticizing Moses or Jesus should have provoked such reactions in the West. Muslims revealed the uncertain grounds of their convictions by signaling that any rock pelted at their idols risked to totter them completely. This conduct is the sort that puts a total ban on foreign missionaries in Muslim lands and is intolerant of non-Muslims in their midst, as the persecution of Christians (and Jews in history) in Egypt, Nigeria, Syria, North Africa, and other Muslim countries attests today.

The idea of an open market of ideas is foreign to them, for they are not sure enough of their convictions to let them compete on equal grounds in the public square. Saudis and Kuwaitis build mosques and Islamic centers all over the globe, but woe to any Christian who would attempt to act similarly in their lands. In a Muslim rally in Los Angeles on February 18, 2006, one of the slogans waved by furious demonstrators was "Islam shall dominate!" In other words, they were not seeking accommodation as the Cartoon Affair raged on but victory; not calming their tempers but seeking vindication of their fanatic positions. Many movies and slogans had been produced in the West that could be interpreted as injurious to other faiths, but in no case had such a violent uproar exploded in which other people were attacked as in this alleged "harm" done to the Prophet of Islam by mere cartoons published by the European free press. Nothing that the West can do will ever match the volume of abuse Muslims heap on Christianity and Judaism, or their violent attacks against the followers of other faiths. It is both Muslims and non-Muslims under Muslim regimes who flee for their lives to Western societies, and it is to Western consulates that long lines of visa-seeking Muslims form up, not the other way around—an indication in itself of where persecuted individuals feel safer. The cartoon controversy, which transcended the boundaries of a religious row, initially looked like a repetition of the Rushdie Affair, with a prize promised to whomever killed the blasphemous cartoonists who were seen as insulting the Prophet of Islam. There were also many clamors of vengeance resounding from one end of the Muslim world to the other. Western journalists were dismissed for supporting freedom of the press, politicians resigned or were castigated by a frightened Europe, and large-scale violence was used by Muslims against European national symbols, including flags and embassies. Only a clear death sentence by a cleric (a *fatwa*) was missing to make the comparison complete. There was nevertheless a world of difference between the two: the Rushdie Affair was directed at a Muslim individual who had apostatized in Muslim eyes, and therefore deserved death, whereas the cartoon explosion was directed at a country (Denmark) and expanded into an anti-Western campaign of abuse and violence. Also, in the age of naiveté and candor, when the West wrongly differentiated between the vast majority of peaceful Muslims and a few extremists, political correctness assumed that if one could understand the offense done to Islam and apologize for it, even if that entailed sacrificing one individual (Rushdie) to appease Islam, then peace and tranquility would prevail. The Cartoon Affair taught the West that the more apologies and understandings (which are unfailingly directed unilaterally from Christendom to Islamdom, never the other way round), the more violent the explosions of anti-Western fury, because Muslims have convinced themselves that the infidels aspire to undermine Islam, and their courteous apologies are proof of that admission.

Chapter Seven
Religious Confrontations

Islam regards the entire community of Muslims, the *umma*, as one nation (*umma islamiyya*), which gave rise to "Muslim nationalism", a seemingly odd designation of a religious entity as a political one, without distinctions between various races, ethnicities, nationalities or linguistic groups. That is the reason why it always appears strange when Muslims in Europe complain about "racism" against them, since their demography is all-inclusive, from the black Muslims of the US and Africa, to the fair-complexion blonds of Bosnia, the lower Volga and the Caucasus. That explains why the Mulims who endeavor to Islamize Europe, care little about their nationality, because once converted, the French of the Germans cease belonging to those nations which are expected to merge into the universal *umma*. In other words, while the West had innovated the idea of nationalism which defined national character, language and boundaries, Islam has followed in its footsteps when it divided Islamdom into 57 modern Islamic nations at the same time that it is striving to merge the non-Muslim Europeans into the universal Islamic Caliphate. And when in 1960, Tito decided to grant the Muslims of Bosnia recognition as a "nation", equal to the Orthodox Serbs, and the Catholic Croats and the rest of the Yugoslavians who were defined by territory, ethnicity and faith, they were ready to fight for their own identity as "Bosniaks" in the tragic war of the 1990s, though they differed in nothing ethnically from the other southern Slavs of former Yugoslavia.

To illustrate the Muslim dislike, if not outright contempt towards non-Muslims on ethnic and national/political grounds (apart from the predominant religious scorn towards others), Fernandez-Morera brings many examples of dubbing Christians under Islamic rule in medieval Spain in derogatory terms, such as *agemis* (barbarians), *muahid* (one under subjugation agreement), or *dhimmis* (beneficiaries of the pact of protection). But in popular speech they used the insulting attribute of *khanzir* (pig) a particularly abhorred animal which Christians ate but Muslims were prohibited to due to its distasteful stigma[106]. Incidentally, Jews who are also banned from consuming pork were even further debased when accused in the Qur'an of having been accursed as the "descendants of pigs and monkeys" due to their sins. This is far more serious than a popular attribute in occasional use for Christians, because depending on the mood of its users, it could be skipped or emphasized in accordance with the fortunes of the passing relationships between Muslims and Christians. Conversely, the sacred encrusted Words of Allah in the Holy Book referring to Jews, are eternal and cited daily by Imams in sermons, which lend them an immutable and incontrovertible quality.

Christian *dhimmis* under Islamic rule in Spain were also called *Mozarab* when they began to escape from their life under the ruling Umayyad Dynasty to the norther Christian kingdoms. They had been partly acculturated into Arab/Muslim culture, spoke an archaic Romance dialect and had acquired Arabic sounding names. Northern Christians who absorbed them in their midst, also called them *muzarabs* which derived from the Arabic *musta'rib*, just like the Jews of Spain who had grown to acquire also Arabic or Arabized names (for instance the *Ibn* prefix to the famous names of Ibn Gavi-

---

[106] Fernandez-Morera, op. cit. p. 206.

rol, or Ibn Ezra, which means the son of…), and to write philosophical and religious works in Arabic, so overwhelming was the Arab/Muslim cultural impact on their lives under Muslim rule. But eventually, scholars adopted the word *Mozarab,* not only to designate the Christian *Dhimmis* who fled into Christian territories but also to those who remained, like the Jews (who had nowhere to flee) under the Islamic Dynasty. Nonetheless, the Christian *Mozarab*s, again just like their Jewish counterparts, tried to keep they religion, language and customs for many centuries, until the Christians were rescued in the process of the *reconquista,* while the Jews were expelled in 1492 and compelled to seek refuge in other lands of Islam, like North Africa and the Ottoman Empire, since Christendom mistreated them even worse than Islamdom and banned both of them from Christian territory. Morera elaborates:

> As late as 9th Century Eulogius of Cordova had a large library where he produced a copy of Saint Isidore's *De Natura Rerum.* As they watched the decay and sometimes the destruction of their churches and monastries, *dhimmis* preserved the memory of their lost Christian kingdom. Thus, the *Chronica Mozarabica,* [just like the Fez Chronicle mentioned above], still makes reference to those happy times when Visigoth Toledo was a royal city…[107]

Inevitably, as Morera tells us, the *dhimmi* Christians, (just as their Jewish counterparts) yielded to the hegemonic culture and adopted the language and many customs of the dominant Muslims, and the only option for the conquered Hispano-Visigoths (as for the Jews) if they did not become submitted *dhimmis* and pay the *jizyah* poll tax, was to flee for their lives, or to convert to Islam,

---

[107] Cited by Morera, op. cit. p. 207.

despite the (in)famous verse in the Qur'an that Muslims like to cite to prove their "tolerance", that "there is no compulsion in religion". The stark choice between Islamization or death was reported, for example under the Almohad fanatic rulers who dominated both North Africa and Spain in the time of King Abd an-Mun'im (1130-63), as related by his Secretary, Ibn Atiya, when he was asked: "How is it that in these lands [of the *Maghrib*], not even a a single *dhimmi* was to be found, nor sysnagogues or churches"? His answer was:

> The Dynasty came to power through extreme ruthlessness. The Mahdi [Ibn Tumart, the founder, d. in 1130] had told his companions: "these *Mulaththamun* [the preceding Almoravids who were *veiled* to survive the desert sands], are champions of innovation (*bid'a*)[a big sin in the conservative tradition of Islam] who attribute a human body to Divinity, being anthropomorphists and infidels whom it is permitted to kill or reduce to slavery for opposing the true faith. This policy having been pursued by them, and [the Almohads] having won the upper hand, after conquering Morocco, Abd al Min'im summoned the Jews and Christians of Morocco and said to them: "Is it not so that you [meaning your ancestors] had repudiated Prophet [Muhammad]' mission and had refused to believe that he was the herauld announced in your scriptures? Did you not say:"He who will perforce come will only do so in order to strengthen our law and to consolidate our religion?"? "Yes", they answered. "So", he retorted,"Where is the one that you await? Moreover you claimed that he would not tarry more than five hundred years. Our religion has fulfilled its 500 years, yet no apostle or preacher has emerged from amongst you. Therefore, we cannot allow you to persist in your disbelief, for we have no use for your tribute (*jizyah*). It is

either Islam or death!".

He then set for them a time limit to dispose of objects that were difficult to transport and to leave his states. Most of the Jews immediately decided to to outwardly adopt the Muslim religion and they retained their belongings. As for the Christians, they immigrated to Spain while just a small number of them embraced Islam. Monasteries and synagogues were destroyed throughout the kingdom and up to the year 600 [*hijri*] ((1203), that is to say at the time I left the Maghreb, there were no polytheists [Christians) to be seen, nor any other Infidel who would have dared to outwardly demonstrate his unbelief[108].

As already mentioned, the status of *dhimma,* was designed to diminish, humiliate and oppress Christianity and Judaism under Islamic rule and because *Shari'a* upheld, found considerable elaborations in Islamic jurisprudence, naturally on religious ground, like everything else in Islam. In the next Chapter, we shall elaborate more on the overwhelmingly predominant facet of Islamic law as championed by one of the greatest Malikite jurists of North Africa in the 15th Century. Here, to complete this sequence of the social and cultural discrimination against Christian and Jews, let us cite some of the limitations nd restrictions imposed on them. Most of wht he wrote referred to Jews but was applicable to Christians too. His obsession with Jewish (and Christian) impurity, which turned him into a fanatic maniac, did not nonetheless diminish one iota of his aythority and holiness in the eyes of his disciples and adepts. Al-Maghili's scholarship went as far as not only knowing the

---

[108] Translation of Muhammad al Dhahabi, *Ta'rikh al islam* (the History of Islam), Vol 50, Beirut, Dar al-Kitab al Arabi,, 1997, pp. 222-3. Cited in Paul Fenton and David Littman *Exile in the Maghreb*: Jews under Islam, Fairleigh Dickinson University Press, Madison, 2016

thoughts, the sentiments and the most intimate mechanics of the Infidels' beings, but also presumed that their foods were of three categories, something they themselves never knew.:

1. <u>Food of nourishment</u> is what they cook for their own consumption. This category is lawful for Muslims to eat, though Mālik [ibn Anas, the founder of the Malikites] disapproved of its consumption by a Muslim, regardless of whether [the said food was prepared by] Jews resident in Muslim or in enemy territory. Another scholar, Sahnūn, was cited as adding: 'Such food should not be eaten in their utensils, unless they have been washed'.

   a. <u>The food of Unbelief</u> is that which they prepare for their synagogues and festivals and other such like perverted celebrations. This is not part of the food of nourishment but that of their unbelief. It is unfit for Muslim consumption because, at the moment it was slaughtered, a divinity other than Allah was invoked, intending thereby to glorify disbelief in the messenger of Allah.

   b. <u>As for the food of their deceit</u>, it is that prepared by Jews for Muslims. It does not therefore come under the category of food for nourishment but that of food of deceit. Consequently, it is unlawful for a Muslim to eat, especially if it contains meat because they are known to be a people of deceit, trickery and outright hostility. How can one trust them to prepare food for Muslims, and how can one be sure that they have properly performed the slaughtering in accordance to all the necessary prescriptions?[So much more so for Christians who eat pork and do not perform any *kosher/halal* animal slaughtering]. For this reason it is not lawful for a Muslim to delegate an Unbeliever over any act of brokerage, or purchase, or exchange, because the divine [law] has regulations which the Muslims are obliged to observe and an Unbeliever cannot be trusted to carry them out. Thus, any animal they claim to have slaughtered on Muslim behalf is but carrion, just as the money they claim to have exchanged on Muslim behalf is usurious. It was for this reason that 'Umar b. al-Khattāb forbade them to practice the professions of butcher or money-changer and excluded them from all Muslim markets, stating: 'Indeed, Allah has bestowed upon the Muslims sufficiency for their fellow-Muslims; so do not employ an Unbeliever in your services'. Al-Maghili emphasized that even part of what he stated will suffice for those whom Allah has granted previous guidance, 'yet only the discerning will take heed' (Qur. 2, 269).

Concerning the Obligatory Capitation[*Jizyah*] and humiliation devolving upon *dhimmi*s, determined al-Maghili, that Allah declared: 'Fight those who believe neither in Allah, nor the Last Day, nor hold as unlawful what Allah and His messenger have forbidden—such men as practice not the religion of truth, being of those who have been given the Book—until they pay the tribute out of hand and have been humbled' (Qur. 9, 29). Fighting and slaying Jews and Christians are an obligation imposed by Allah. The sword should constantly be brandished over their necks unless they pay tribute and are humbled. How could it be fitting to allow an enemy of the Master of the first and last generations [Muhammad] to persist among the Believers, in the land of Muslims, were he not submitted to that which is more painful than burning fire—i.e. the payment of the poll-tax amidst humiliation? [Only] then can he be left unmolested with his property and family, because humiliating him by these means is more appeasing to Muslim hearts than slaying him and confiscating his property. Indeed, it is not lawful to allow an enemy of the chosen Prophet in the least hamlet, region or province, except on condition of paying poll-tax and accepting humiliation. The *jizya* (poll-tax) is the sum that is liable to be paid by every free *dhimmi* male adult, sound of mind and able-bodied, who cohabits with Muslims. It is due at the close of every year in the way prescribed by the *sharī'a*. The amount of (*jizya*) to be paid by those Jews and their like in accordance with the prescription of 'Umar b. Khattāb, is about eight *mithqals*, four of which constitute the basic poll-tax. The additional four *mithqals* are an allowance for the military and similar contributions. These should be paid in full by the individual Unbeliever who can afford to pay without difficulty. Whoever is in difficulty must pay the basic capitation and can be exempted from the supplementary tax on condition that he did not break any of the conditions to which the *dhimmi*s are subjected[109]. If, on the contrary, violation has taken place, then no exemption will be granted on account of this violation, and he must fulfill all the obligations appertaining to his condition. A person who is destitute can benefit from a reduction applied in accordance with his situation, there being no limit to the lowest amount of poll-tax allowed to be paid. Whoever converts to Islam shall be exonerated from payment, as well as a person unable to pay even a portion of it. On the day of payment, the *dhimmis* are to assemble in a public place, such as the market. They should present themselves standing up and gather at the foulest and lowest place. The executors of the Muslim law should stand over them, in a threatening pose, in such a way that they will fear for the safety of their lives, so that it is clear to them and others that our intention is to humiliate them by taking their property. Thus they will realize that we do them a favor by accepting the poll-tax from them and letting them go. Then they should be dragged forward one by one for payment. While paying, each individual will receive a slap on his neck

---

[109] In later times the *Jizyah* was imposed communally on communities according to their numbers and wealth, and the heads of the communities apportioned its distribution among the congregations members according to their known personal wealth.

and then be pushed away in such a fashion that he will realize that he has escaped the sword thanks to this [affront]. This is how the lovers of the Lord [Muhammad] in the past and present should act towards his enemies—the Unbelievers. Verily, glory is to Allah, His Messenger and the believers. In order to be valid, the poll-tax must be collected by a person of authority or a man of good standing, so that its collection and distribution are carried out by the same person, and not by numerous intermediaries. The sums which tribal chiefs collect directly from their Jewish subjects, are in no way to be considered as poll-tax but bribery for obtaining appointments.

Al-Maghili stressed that the levying of the *jizya* and the humbling of the [*dhimmis*] is imperative at all times, even if they are oppressed and their oppressors appropriate the poll-tax. Allah has declared: 'Allah charges no soul save to its capacity' (Qur. 2, 286). The Prophet also said: 'If I command you to do a thing, do only that of which you are capable'.[110] That is why Allah has not subjected the levying of the poll-tax to any condition except that it should be received from their hands while they are in a position of humiliation. The [provision] of humiliation is intended to keep them in a state of abasement and degradation in their manner of speech, deed and outward appearance in all circumstances, so that in this way they come under the heel of every Muslim man and woman, freeborn or slave or maidservant. Pains will we taken primarily to humiliate them in their religious practices so that they conceal all that is offensive to Muslim law, even if it exists in Jewish law, in order to avoid any public exhibition in the presence of Muslims of any aspect of their worship, their prayers, and their books. Likewise they should be forbidden to extol any of their scholars in the presence of a Muslim. Indeed, the prophetic message [*risāla*]

---

[110] The capitation tax was initially levied individually. But in latter times it was imposed communally according to the size and wealth of the community and to the economic fortunes of that special year. The Jewish community collected the tax progressively, according to one, income.

and the religious mission/struggle [*jihād*] are a cause for confrontation and are a cause for our domination over them, as is stated in the verse: 'It is He who has sent His Messenger with the guidance and the religion of truth, that He may uplift it above every religion' (Qur. 9, 33). For if Islam triumphs over them concerning their religious practices, by forcing them to conceal and dissimulate their outward signs, then they will be humiliated, however prosperous they may be. So if Islam defeated them on that, it will have certainly saved itself from humiliation in religion and the like. Verily, if Islam triumphs over them in this respect, it will be easy to succeed in humiliating them by imposing upon them discriminatory garments. But if this were not the case, and the banner of their disbelief remained hoisted, then their humiliation would diminish in proportion to the degree to which they are able to practice their religion, even if they were to give in return infinite quantities of gold and silver. Indeed, the acceptance from them of such sums would contradict the very principle of their humiliation. It is for this reason that they should not be authorized to build synagogues in any Muslim land, even if they were to give all the gold on earth. How can a Believer sell part of the honor of Islam to the enemies of Allah and His messenger in return for these worldly vanities? 'Yet unto Allah belong the treasures of heaven and earth, but the hypocrites do not understand' (Qur. 63, 7). 'Warn the hypocrites that a painful chastisement awaits them. As for those who take Unbelievers for their friends rather than believers—do they seek honor in their company? Nay, they will not obtain any honor from them because all honor belongs to Allah' (Qur. 4, 138).[111].

The author concluded his long and seminal *fatwa* by urging his coreligionists to rise up and kill the Jews since they are indeed the bitterest enemies, who rejected Muhammad, as they were killed in

---

[111] Maghili, Sheikh al- *Risala fil-Yahud* (Treatise Against the Jews) (ca 1495), ed. and published in Rabat, 2005, Cited in Fenton nd Littman, Doc A-12, pp. 71-85.

Khaybar at the sword of Muhammad. Besides that general incitement to kill the Jews for what they are, the honorable Sheikh
addressed specifically the "intolerable infractions committed by
contemporary Jews in regard to the Islamic legal provisions that
concern them, whereby they are employed by people of authority";
he used his authority as a Muslim jurist to declare that:

> By Allah and with His assistance, do I with certainty
> declare lawful the blood of the Jews, their infants and
> their wives, to which we have referred, i.e. those of
> Tuwat, Tighurarayn, Tafilalt, Dar'a and many regions of
> Ifriqiyya, and Tlemcen. Likewise it is permissible to con-
> fiscate their property, for they have forgone their right to
> protection. Indeed, the protection which deflects the
> sword from their bodies was established by Islamic law
> and not one ordained in pre-Islamic times. Now the pro-
> tection afforded by Islamic law is conditional upon the
> poll-tax which they must pay with their hands in a
> humiliating manner.

Finally, the Mufti quotes the list of the obligations the Christian
leadership in Syria had taken upon themselves as *dhimmis* when
they submitted to Caliph 'Umar's conquest and his imposed rules
of dhimmitude:

> —not to build in our cities and surroundings either a convent,
> church, chapel or hermitage.
> —Nor to repair such buildings that became dilapidated
> —Not to debar any Muslim from sojourning in our churches by
> night or by day.
> —We shall open its doors to wayfarers and travelers.
> —We shall accommodate Muslim wayfarers for three nights dur-
> ing which we shall provide them with food.

—We shall not harbor any spy either in our churches or dwellings

—We shall not conceal a traitor to the Muslims

—We shall not teach our children the Qur'an.

—We shall neither display our religion nor induce any to embrace it.

—We shall not prevent any of our relations from embracing Islam if he so wishes.

—We shall honor Muslims and rise for them from our places if they wish to sit.

—We shall not imitate the Muslims in their dress, nor in their headgear, turbans nor shoes, nor imitate their parting of the hair.

—We shall not use their speech

—nor be called by their titles.

—We shall not ride on saddles

—nor gird swords, nor wear or carry any weapon.
  We shall not engrave our rings with Arabic.

—We shall not sell wine.

—We shall also cut our forelocks.

—We shall perpetuate our dress wherever we are.

—We shall gird belts on our waists.

—We shall not parade our crosses or our scriptures anywhere in the streets or markets frequented by Muslims.

—We shall not ring our bells in our churches except unnoticeably.

—We shall not raise our voices when chanting in our churches in the least presence of Muslims.

—We shall not display palms at Easter nor on Palm Sunday.

—Nor shall we raise our voices at our funeral processions

—nor display candles on Muslim streets and markets.

—We shall not bury our dead next to the Muslims.

—We shall not acquire slaves who have been the property of Muslims.

When this letter reached 'Umar he added these words: "we shall not harm any Muslim". And they added: "We impose these terms on ourselves while being accountable with our persons and those of our coreligionists, in exchange for security and protection. If we dishonor any of these clauses, we forgo the right of protection. It will be lawful for you to inflict upon us that which is permitted for you to inflict upon insubordinate and rebellious subjects". In his reply, 'Umar invited the Christians to carry out that which they had requested, it having been accepted that two clauses 'should be rightfully added to which they must commit themselves, i.e.: —They shall never purchase any Muslim captives. —Whoever willfully strikes a Muslim has forfeited his rights". (Here ends the letter). The theologians of all the schools rely upon this document regarding the regulations relating to the *dhimmis*, except that they differ among themselves as to what constitutes a breach of the covenant. Concerning the types of consensus (*ijmā'*), the opinion of Ibn Hazm is given in the *Dhakhira* according to which the theologians are divided about what constitutes the breach of covenant by a *dhimmi* to be sanctioned by capital punishment, the seizure of his property and family, in the case of failure to comply with one of the aforesaid articles, and a pledge that they shall not contract an unlawful marriage.[112] There is a debate amongst the jurists as to whether an infraction against any one of the stipulations on the part of a *dhimmi,* constitutes a breach of covenant and incurs their being put to death or reduced to slavery. The jurists differ on the question of whether the violation of a single clause by a *dhimmi* constitutes a breach of the covenant, and consequently entails his being put to death and the seizure of his relatives! What must then be said about Jews who do not uphold even one of these clauses?. They have in fact rebelled against Islamic law, firstly by residing in areas not sub-

---

[112] That is of a Non-Muslim man to a Muslims woman. The reverse is permitted, since the non-Muslim woman married to a Muslim man becomes *ipso-facto* a Muslim woman bearing her Muslim husband's Muslim children.

jected [to legitimate government]. Secondly, they consort with the rulers and employ their wealth to oppose the jurists who seek to [restore] the humiliation [of the Jews]. Surely, there can be no difference of opinion concerning their breach of covenant or about the obligation to inflict them with capital punishment and the seizure of their relatives. Indeed, the afore-mentioned difference of opinion only applies to a Jew remiss in the observance of one of these clauses, without persistence and relapse. But if a Jew were to persistently commit the offence with obstinacy, there would be no disagreement [among the jurists] concerning his breach of covenant, and the obligation to put him to death and confiscate his property since his action is really a rebellion against Islamic law. Consequently, any Jew, who attaches himself to the service of a king or a vizier or a judge or a member of the ruling class, commits a breach of contract, whereby he forfeits his blood and property. For the mere consorting with persons of the ruling class is inconsistent with the condition of humiliation and abasement attending to *dhimmi* status. The gravest possible rebellion against the rules of Islamic law is taking place in our times.

A final warning from the hells of fire, not a moral or ethical constraint to respect the Divine Law, was what al-Maghili, like the Qur'an itself, used to deter the Believers from transgressing upon his verdict:

> Woe betide the protectors of the Jews! It is they who aid them in transgressing the limits of the law. 'These are the ones who deny their Lord: around their necks there shall be fetters. They are the inheritors of the Fire, and shall abide therein forever' (Qur. 13, 5)...For the sake of the beloved Lord, I freed myself from the intimacy of the Jews' abettors. Folk who despise their own religion and honor that of the Jews, it is enough to pronounce judgment on their dishonor and the lowness of the origin of

their substance that they be detached from their faith and exalt that of the Jews. Let them reconsider their affairs and repair their position and ask for forgiveness! Let them conceal their clear support of the triumph of a band of Jews. Do they not consider how the Lord of mankind acted in the past? How can he with whom the Jews are pleased obtain Allah's pleasure? Verily the truth is like a light in every public place. It will not fail. The patient Lord will lend it triumph over the Christians and the Jews. O Lord, (I pray you) through your Prophet, the chosen, the pure guide, and through every Pole (i.e. a great saint) and Saint, he who delights over the downfall of the Jews, who pours calamity upon them and annihilates the remains of their subsistence. And open for them, to exterminate them the door to the infernal fire. Except those who repent and mend what they have broken, and confessed that which they kept secret, so that rigorous penalties can be reinstated.

Thereupon forgive them their past and sign on their behalf your reprieve. And speed on to eternal paradise, those to whom it has been granted. O believers, repent before Allah so that you may escape [punishment] 'Obey Allah and the Messenger so that you may prosper' (Qur. 24, 31). 'Let there be a group among of you who call others to good, and enjoin what is right, and forbid what is wrong: those who do this shall be successful. Do not be like those who, after they had been given clear evidence, split into factions and differed among themselves: a terrible punishment awaits such people. On the day when some faces are bright and some faces are dark, it will be said to those with darkened faces, "Did you reject faith after you had believed? Taste, then, this punishment for having denied the truth!" But as for those with shining faces, they shall abide forever in Allah's grace' (Qur. 3, 104–107). May Allah benefit me along with you from the glorious Qur'an. May Allah grant me and grant you His blessing with the signs and wise discourse it contains. I beseech Allah's forgiveness for me and for you and for the rest of the Muslims. Implore His forgiveness because He is compassionate and merciful. The best formula for asking forgiveness is this: 'You are my Lord, there is no god but You. You have created me and I am Your servant. I undertake and promise to serve You according to my ability. I seek refuge with You against the evil which I perpetrated. I acknowledge Your bounty towards me and confess my sins, so forgive me for none forgives sin except You'. O, Allah, bless the illiterate[113] Prophet, as well as his wives—the mothers of the believers. Bless his offspring, the people of his house, as you have blessed Abraham and his family in the universe. Verily you deserve to be extolled and exalted. Grant him abundant, goodly and blessed peace. May peace be upon the messengers and praise unto Allah, Master of the universe.[114]

The continued invocation of 'Umar's authority (second only to the Prophet's) was due to his central role in the expansion of Islam and his having to make unprecedented decisions as Islam began its process of conquests and had to deal with the rising issues how to treat the newly occupied peoples who dwelt in the newly taken over

---

[113] While in other cultures illiteracy may seem as a liability for the operation of a super-intellectual like a prophet, in Islam it enhances, on the contrary, the miracle of Muhammed's prophecy, proving that since he could not have written the Qur'an himself, it must have been the Word of Allah that was transmitted throught him.

[114] Translation of excerpts from Al-Maghīlī, *Risāla fi l-yahūd* ('Treatise against the Jews'), (ca. 1495), ed. Abderrahim Benhada and Omar Benmira (Rabat: Bou Regreg, 2005), 53–89. Cited by Fenton and Littman, Doc.A-12, pp. 71-85.

territories, of which North Africa was only a part. For example, in a letter that 'Umar dispatched to Sa'd ibn Waqqas after the conquest of the Sawad in Iraq, he wrote:

> I have received your letter in which you stated that your men have asked you to divide among them whatever spoils Allah has assigned them. At the receipt of my letter, find out what possessions and horses the mounted troops "on horses and camels" (Qur'an 59:6) have acquired and divide that among them, after taking away one fifth. As for the land and camels, leave them in the hands of those men who work them, so that they may be included in the stipends of the Muslims. If you divide them among those present, nothing will be left for those who come after them…

> Al Hussain [reported on the authority of] Abdallah ibn Hazim: I once asked Mujahid regarding the land of al Sawad and he answered: it can neither be bought nor sold. This is because it was taken by force and was not divided. It belongs to all Muslims. Al Walid ibn Saleh, on the authority of Suleiman ibn Yasser, that 'Umar left al-Sawad for those who were still in men's loins and mothers' wombs, considering the inhabitants *dhimmis* from whom the *jizya* tax should be taken on their person and *kharaj* (land tax) on their land. They are therefore *dhimmis* and cannot be sold as slaves…

> 'Umar, desiring to divide al-Sawad among the Muslims ordered that [the inhabitants] should be counted. Each Muslim had three peasants for his share. 'Umar took the advice of the Prophet's Companions, and Ali said:"leave them that they become a source of revenue

and aid to the Muslims…[115]

The plight of North African *dhimmis* under Islam in general, was the result of not only the imposition of *Shari'a* law on them as *dhimmis*, which was harsh enough, but also of the added sadism of officials, sometimes backed by the highest authorities who were themselves fanatic and paranoid, and expressed their fears, frustrations and greed by projecting on the weak and defenseless *dhimmis*, who were in theory protected but in practice despised and persecuted, their own deficiencies and often their mental derangements. Few examples will illustrate the point:

a. The matter of forced conversions, in spite of the Qur'anic injunction that "there is no compulsion in religion", only shows how uncertain Muslims felt about competing with other faiths in the open market of ideas. As early as 1148, a poignant letter was sent by a Jewish notable, complaining against this practice in North Africa in the waning years of the Almoravids. It said among others that during the fighting between 'Abd al-Mu'min of Sūs, who was to become the first Almohad sultan (1130–1163), and the Emir Tāshfīn at Oran, the former stormed the city, slaughtered the Almoravid troops, put to death the Emir Tāshfīn and crucified his body. Thereafter, he captured Tlemcen and massacred all the [Jewish] inhabitants of the city, except those who embraced Islam. When word of these events reached the population of Sijilmāsa, they rebelled against their governor, and, in demonstration of their opposition to the Almoravids, expelled them from the city. They then rallied

---

[115] Al-Baladhuri, *Kitab Futuh al-Buldan* (The Book of the Conquest of Countries), translated by Philip Hitti, Columbia, NY, 1916, cited by Bay Ye'or, *The Decline of Eastern Christianity Under Islam: From Islam to Dhimmitude*, Fairleigh Dickinson University Press, Madison, 1996, pp.272-3.

to 'Abd al-Mu'min and delivered the city to him. When he made his entrance into the city, he gathered the Jews and proposed that they convert to Islam. After having held disputations with him for a period of seven months, during which they fasted and prayed, one of his commanders came and summoned them to abjure their faith, which they refused to do. Thereupon he slaughtered one hundred and fifty Jews who perished as martyrs. Resorting to the old notion of Jewish self indictment, which imputed the torments of Jews, including the destruction of the Temple, to "our own sins"[116]-the letter concluded: 'The Rock is perfect in his action' (Deut. 32, 4). Blessed is the true Judge, who judges with righteousness and truth. 'The King's word is sovereign' (Eccl. 8, 4). It remarked with consternation that the remainder [of the Jews] reneged and the first to apostatize was Joseph the son of 'Amran, the rabbinical judge of Sijilmāsa!:

On account of this will I mourn and cry. Now prior to 'Abd al-Mu'min's entry into the city, at the time when the population rose up against the Almoravids, some 200 Jews managed to flee to al-Qasba, among whom were Jacob and 'Abūd, my paternal uncles, as well as Master Judah ben Farhūn and his brothers. After having been robbed of all their possessions, they found refuge in Dar'a but we do not know what fate has befallen them since. In all the Almoravid territories, besides the tribal regions, only Dar'a and Meknes have not yet surrendered. On account of our sins, all the Jewish communities of the Maghreb have been wiped out, and from Bajāya [Bougie] to Bāb Zill there remains

---

[116] See R. Israeli, *Defeat, Trauma, Lesson*, Strategic Books, Texas, 2012.

not one Jewish soul, some having been killed, and
others having apostatized. On the day this letter
was written, news reached us of the capture of
Bajāya. May Almighty God crush their strength
and may the hope that they lose these possessions
be not far off! Indeed, he has conquered the entire
coast from the gate of Seville to the gate of Tortosa.
A terrible calamity [...]. The Andalusians have now
surrendered to him and have given him possession
of all the provinces. The Almoravids have no longer
any allies in the Maghreb, either in Cordoba or
Grenada. [...] They captured [...] the inhabitants
of Fez [...]. However, at the time of the capture of
Fez 100,000 souls were slaughtered, and in Marrakesh 100,000. The news I break is not just hearsay, but I have reported it to you from a direct
witness.[117]

Another case of the same, after the Almohads took over from the
Almoravids, was narrated in detail in a letter of Joseph ibn Aqnin,
around 1190, appropriately connected to the "Hygene of the
Souls"of both the oppressors and their victims. Typical of the Jewish
self-indicting guilt-feeling, which took responsibility for what happened, instead of throwing the blame of others, It said:

...On account of our numerous sins, it was prophesied concerning us: 'And among these nations shalt thou
find no ease, neither shall the sole of thy foot have rest:
but the Lord shall give thee a trembling heart, and failing
of eyes, and sorrow of mind: And thy life shall hang in

---

[117] Translation from an extract from a Judeo-Arabic letter By Solomon al-Sijil-
masi of January 1148, published by Hirschberg and reproduced by Fenton and
Littman, Document A3, pp. 50-1.

doubt before thee; and thou shalt fear day and night'
(Deut. 28, 65–66). …Past persecutions and former
decrees were directed against those who remained faithful to the Law of Israel and kept it so tenaciously that
they would even have forfeited their lives for the sake of
Heaven, following the examples of Daniel, Hananiah,
Mishal, Azariya and the ten martyrs. As for those who
yielded to their demands, forsaking the community of
Israel, [our enemies] would extol and honor them, as is
already related in the Talmud. However, in the present
persecutions, on the contrary, the more we obey their
instructions and comply with their doctrines and forsake
our own, the more they burden our yoke and increase
our travail. In reality, this fact is a manifestation of divine
mercy that we should not be beguiled by them into completely abandoning the community bringing about the
effacement of Israel's memory.

The proof can be seen in the afflictions suffered by the
apostates of our land who, on account of these persecutions, have utterly forsaken the faith and changed their
attire. Yet their conversion has been of absolutely no avail
to them, for they are subjected to the same vexations as
those who have remained faithful to their creed. To be
sure, even the conversion of their fathers or grandfathers
a century ago has been of no advantage to them, in ful-
fillment of the threat announced in the verse: 'He visits
the iniquity of the fathers upon the children, and upon
the children's children' (Ex. 34, 7). Was it not written
'But in the fourth generation they shall come hither
again' (Gen. 15,16)? Indeed, this treatment has induced
many converts to return to their former faith, for 'Lo,
thou trustest in the staff of this broken reed, whereon if
a man lean, it will go into his hand' (Is. 36, 6) […]. All

this confirms the words of the prophet: 'And that which comes into your mind shall not be at all, that you say, We will be as the nations, as the families of the countries' (Ezek. 20, 32). Know that despite all these tribulations, we have continued to bear the yoke of the covenant. Indeed, we cannot cast it off nor make it disappear. Had the Lord not provided first a healing before the blow of adversity, then we would surely have perished and our eyes would have become dim in trying to comprehend the gravity of the great misfortune that had befallen us. Indeed, we would speedily have waned away with no care for survival or descendants.

We would have ceased to have offspring and remained childless, since we would have become as fools and drunkards unaware of their condition. God's healing has prevented us from relinquishing our religion on account of our great fear and anxiety [...]. When we consider the persecutions that have befallen us in recent years, we are unable to find anything comparable recorded in the chronicles handed down to us by our ancestors. We are made the object of inquisitions in which both great and small testify against us. Their slightest statements render lawful the shedding of our blood, the confiscation of our property, and the dishonoring of our wives. But by the grace of God, who has taken pity on the faithful remnant, their testimonies have proven contradictory, for the nobles pleaded in our favor whilst the common folk testified against us. Now the custom of the land did not allow the testimony of the vulgar[*dhimmi*] to supersede that of the [Muslim] gentry. Thus though these measures were repeatedly renewed, God continuously took pity. Then a new decree was issued, bitterer than the first, which revoked our right to inheritance and to the custody of our children. The latter were placed in the hands of Muslims, fulfilling that which is written: 'Thy sons and thy daughters shall be given unto another people' (Deut. 28, 32). They intended thereby to liquidate our resources and force us to assimilate with the Muslims. For the [Muslim] guardians are able to dispose of our young children and their estate as they see fit. When confided to a devout individual, he endeavors to educate these children in his religion, for one of their principles is that all children are originally born as Muslims and only their parents bring them up as Jews, Christians, or Magians.

Thus, by rearing them in [what they claim is] their original religion [i.e., Islam] and not leaving the children with those [i.e., the Jews] that abduct them therefrom, Allah will grant him a considerable reward. If confided to a wicked tutor whose only concern is to extort money, then God will show mercy [i.e., in permitting the minors to be cared for by their own families], just as He had been merciful towards our ancestors, as it is said: 'And the Eternal gave the people favor in the sight of the Egyptians, so that they gave unto them such things as they required' (Ex. 12, 36) [...]. 'Then another misfortune and terrible trial fell to our lot, such as never was since there was a nation even to that same time' (Dan. 12, 1). They took away our livelihood by prohibiting us to practice commerce, which is the very substance of life, for there is no life without sustenance for our bodies and garments to protect them from the heat and cold. This is obvious from nature's rule, for these commodities can only be obtained through trade, their source and cause, without which its effect, namely our existence, disappears. In so doing, their design was to weaken our strong and annihilate our weak. If you consider these persecutions, you will find them to be much worse than those suffered during our bondage in Egypt, for there we were able to retain our possessions, none of which were confiscated [...]. Subsequently, we were ordered to dismiss our servants and were forbidden to employ others in accordance with the divine prophecy: 'Secretly in the siege and distress, wherewith thine enemy shall distress thee in thy gates' (Deut. 28, 57), for he who is deprived of help is likened to one caught in a siege. Then they changed our outward appearance by imposing upon us distinctive garments, as foretold in the Holy Scriptures: 'And thou shalt become an astonishment [a repulsion], a proverb, and a byword, among all nations whither the Lord shall lead thee' (Deut. 28, 37). The word 'repulsion' [employed in this verse] is another term for 'desolation' on account of the scorn and repulsion felt by the nations at our state of humiliation, abasement, and contempt. For no other nation can be compared unto us, no matter how persecuted they be. Indeed, our self-scorn is greater than that of the nations toward us.

We have become an abhorrence and a byword to such a point that when a [Muslim] wishes to exaggerate a state of contempt or humiliation which had befallen him or his fellows, he exclaims: 'My shame was like that of the Jews'. Similarly, if they seek to offend or insult a neighbor, after having exhausted all other insults, or if they are angered at a son or a slave, they will say, 'what a Jew!' Likewise, if they want to curse someone in the most offensive manner possible, they say, 'May Allah make you like them and count you among their number'[118]. If

---

[118] Even today, almost one millennium later, during the bitter battle that goes on between the majority Sunni world and the minority Sh'ites, the former deprecates the latter by dubbing them as "worse than the Jews".

they want to describe a distasteful deed or a blemish they say: 'Even the meanest Jew would not be content with such a thing'. Thus we have become a proverb wherefrom they derive instruction and reproach [...]. As for the term 'byword' [used in the aforementioned verse], it refers to our outward appearance, which is distinguishable from members of other groups. The Hebrew word is a diminutive meaning 'dishonor', for the garments that have been imposed upon us are the vilest, the most degrading, and the most humiliating attire. The prediction uses a general term without providing details. These were specified by the Prophet Ezekiel who foretold that we would become a subject of repulsion for the surrounding nations: 'So it shall be a reproach and a taunt, an instruction and an astonishment unto the nations that are round about thee, when I shall execute judgments in thee in anger and in fury and in furious rebukes' (Ezek. 5, 15).

Such is the case that should a [Muslim] possess a female Jewish captive and have a child by her, he is belittled by them for so doing. Moreover, his children are despised and it is not easy for him to marry them off, for they are spurned and even the meanest [Muslim] will not contract an alliance with him, as it says in the verse: 'Those that be near and those that be far from thee shall mock thee, which art infamous and much vexed' (Ezek. 22, 5). The expression: 'Remove the diadem and take off the crown' (Ezek. 21, 26) refers to the decree enforced against our wearing turbans. As for the obligation for us to wear black, it is on account of its being the color of mourning, as it was prophesied: 'Feign thyself to be a mourner and put on now mourning apparel'(2 Sam. 14, 2) [...]. As for the decree enforcing the wearing of long sleeves, its purpose was to make us resemble the inferior state of women, who are defenseless. They were intended by their length to make us unsightly, whereas their color was to make us loathsome [...]. The ugly bonnets they have placed upon our heads are meant to contradict the verse: 'you shall make for them bonnets, for glory and for beauty' (Ex. 28, 40) [...]. The purpose of these distinctive garments is to differentiate us from among them so that we should be unmistakably recognized in our dealings with them, in order that they might treat us with disparagement and humiliation. This is a form of servitude which results in our blood being spilled with impunity. For whenever we travel on the road between towns, we are waylaid by robbers and brigands and are murdered secretly at night or killed in broad daylight, as it is said, 'Let not mine hand be upon him, but let the hand of the Philistines be upon him' (1 Sam. 18, 17).12 Thus we are exposed to danger and to the insolence of the population [...].

On account of these garments we bemoan our fate, saying: 'And the leper in whom the plague is unclean, unclean' (Lev. 13, 15); but there is no plague worse than the sins on account of which these persecutions have befallen us. As already mentioned, we are both exposed to these economic sanctions and to verbal abuse. The latter are worse than the former, as our Sages have already explained in the *Talmud*. Indeed, throughout the day we hear disgraceful insults: 'My confusion is continually before me, and the shame of my face hath overwhelmed me at the taunts of those who reproach and revile me, because of the enemy, who is bent on revenge' (Ps. 44, 15–16), and yet we remain silent, as it is said: 'But I am as a deaf man, I hear not, and as a dumb man that openeth not his mouth' (Ps. 38, 14). This attitude is alluded to in the explanation of the names of the ancestors of this nation which has reduced us to slavery: 'Mishma, Dumah and Massa—we hear, and yet we keep silent and endure'. Because of our sins, the following prophecy has been fulfilled in our generation: 'His children are far from safety, and they are crushed in the gate, neither is there any to deliver them' (Job 5, 4). This is because they mistreat us. Even their slaves, beggars, and lepers have dominion over us and whosoever can lift his hand against us, afflicts us as best they can. On account of our iniquities, the following prediction has been fulfilled through us: 'Depart ye; it is unclean; depart, depart, touch not (Lam. 4, 15), for they treat us as unclean. It is clear from what I have explained that we have deserved all these persecutions that we have suffered. Moreover, they barely reflect a fraction of the sins that we have committed against God, and the great punishment we deserve for having sinned, whether deliberately or unwittingly, when we were forced to forsake our faith and our community. For of a truth, we should have suffered martyrdom rather than convert. Indeed, if someone compels us to transgress one of the precepts of the Torah, our law requires us to consider his intention. Whenever he obliges a Jew to carry out a task forbidden on the Sabbath by ordering him, for instance, to load his beast with fodder, or when he forcibly abuses a woman, if his intention thereby is to gain some benefit, then one is permitted to sin [to save one's life]. However, if his purpose was solely to convert us, without his benefiting therefrom, then we must suffer death rather than transgress by obeying. However, the latter case is only obligatory when it takes place in public, i.e. perpetrated in the presence of ten Jews. On the other hand, if the coercion takes place in private, it is permitted to perform the sin in order to escape death. The Sages derived this principle from the verse: 'Ye shall therefore keep my statutes, and my judgments: which if a man do, he shall live by them' (Lev. 18, 5) which they interpret according to tradition as meaning: 'he shall live by them—and not die by them!' All this is applicable at times of tolerance, but at times of similar persecutions such as those of Nebuchadnezzar, the Greeks and the Romans, it was obligatory to choose martyrdom so as not to infringe the least commandment. Now, the purpose of Muslim persecution, whether they require us to renounce our religion in public or in private, is only to annihilate the faith of Israel and, consequently, one is bound to accept death rather than commit the slightest sin [...].

Since the intention of the present rule is to force us to forsake our community, it is binding upon us to accept death, as did the martyrs of Fez, Sijilmāsa, and Dar'a, and likewise Rabbi Aqība and his ten companions. But since we have remained alive in a state of sin, having taken pity upon ourselves, and have disobeyed the verse: 'and ye shall love the Eternal thy God with all thine heart, with all thy soul, and with all thy might' (Deut. 6, 4) and we have willfully profaned the Name of the Eternal, our God though not purposely [...], these terrible calamities have befallen us. [119]

---

[119] Translation of Joseph Ibn 'Aqnīn, *Tibb al-nufūs* ('Hygiene of the Souls'), chap. 4, Ms Oxford, Bodl. Neubauer 1273, fols. 143–46. Pp. 52-55 in Fenton and Littman.

Chapter Seven
Religious Confrontations

Numerous were the Muslim Jurists treatises which dealt with the religious aspects of *dhimma*, which are immutable and inescapable, due to being the eternal word of Allah not given to change by human legislation ir fiat. That Qur'anic precept prescribed by Allah in the Qur'an since the early centuries of Islam, could not be bent to modern progress, the best proof being that when radical Islam took over any territory to establish its rule over it, like ISIS or the Taliban, it reinstituted that ancient regime. That means that the liberation from *dhimma* that was enforced by colonial powers or imposed by them through the exercize of influence and pressure that they exerted on the Ottomans to install reforms, was from the Islamic point of view a *force majeure* that it could not resist and would be hard pressed to revive if and when it regains the power of enforcement, as it did in Raqqa, the Capitall of ISI, during its brief domination there in 2016-8[120]. This is all an ominous sign that when Islam has the opportunity to dominate and is free of threatening outside pressures, it is bound to re-enforce these laws whenever it can, certainly in Islamized Europe in the future.

The Prophet Muhammad himself had exercized his rule in

---

[120] R. Israeli, The Internationalization of ISIS: The Islamic State in Iraq and Syria, Transaction, NJ, 2016, expcially, Ch. Three, The Islamic State in the Making.

Medina by relating every decision of his as a ruler, to the Will of Allah. His harshest rulings, for example the murder of the Jewish Banu Quraiza tribe, or his urging of his followers to launch a Jihad against other tribes, or to take over Mecca, his native city turned his bitter rival, were taken to satisfy Allah's Will. Thus, they not only convinced his audiences that omnipotent and omniscient Allah's verdicts, that were revealed to him in his prophecies, could not but be obeyed without question; but also that the ultimate responsibility for his acts and decisions rested with Allah, who had ordered them. Therefore, the Prophet could remain absolved of any responsibility, and infallible beyond reproach. The result is, that we notice in the religious *fatwas*, issued by eminent jurists of Islam in North Africa and elsewhere, a consistent reference to what Allah himself had ordered in the Qur'an, and/or to what the Prophet had done or said, as recorded in the *Hadith*. There are certainly contradictory statements in both holy sources. In the Qur'an they were settled in the formula of "*the nasikh wal-mansukh*" (the abrogating and the abrogated), meaning that what was revealed later annulcd what was revealed earlier. Allah can change his mind, as He is the Almighty, and believers cannot question the logic of His commands, their duty being to observe to the letter what they were told. The power to discern the late from the early commands of Allah, was left to the '*ulama*' (the Doctors of the Holy Law – the *Shari'a*), the *fuqaha*' (jurists), the *quda'*(judges) and the *muftis* who had the authority of issuing religious opinions/verdicts – the famous *fatwas*- hence their centrality in enforcing the regulations of the *dhimma,* as crystallized in the medieval legal compendia based on the rules of 'Umar, the second and foremost Caliph of Islam, whose authority is second only to the Prophet's himself.

The second fundament of the Shar'ia, the *Hadith*, namely the sayings and deeds of the Prophet, were summarized in several "true" (*sahih*) compendia, that were verified for their contents, as well as for their belt of transmission (*silsila),* which ultimately singled out

Bukhari's and Muslim's as the most reliable. The four Schools of Law (*madhhab*) differ slightly from each other in their leniency with regard to whether to adhere exclusively to Allah's commands and Muhammad's set precedents, or also to rely on human judgment, with the strictest among them resorting almost exclusively to Allah's word in the Qur'an and Muhammad's tradition (*Sunna*), and the more lenient having recourse also to the human reasoning that is inherent in the consensus *(ijma')*, analogy *(qiyas)* or sometimes local custom ('*urf, 'ada*). In Morocco, for example, and by extension also in Spain when ruled by puritanical dynasties, it was the Malekite School which prevailed, second in severity only to the Hanbalites-Wahhabis, therefore we will see in the opinions and verdicts of the Moroccan clerics almost only references to the Qur'an and the *Hadith*, resulting in an uncompromising application of the *Shari'a* on the rules of the *dhimma* towards Jews and Christians under Islamic rule.

Unlike Buddhism which shuns enforcement of its convictions on others, though it has engaged in peaceful propagation of the faith, or Judaism that avoids both practices, Islam regards it as its duty (and right) to show the light even nilly to whomever does not see it willy, despite the repeated citation from the Qur'an that "there is no compulsion in religion". In present day Europe and America, it has been the vast networks of *da'wa*, sustained by intricate Islamic school systems, which have undertaken this task, which has achieved some remarkable success, judging from the tens of thousants of Europeans who have converted to Islam and from the thousands of converts who have volunteered to fight in the killing fields of Islam with no return. For not only were Muslim apostates condemned to capital punishment by burning alive, like in medieval Christianity too; but, again like in medieval Christianity, converting to the dominant faith was often imposed on Jews (Christians as shown above) as their only escape from death. Many Christians and Jews indeed chose life and converted, at least to satisfy appearances, but many others died as "martyrs" who elected death over forced conversion. Moreover, if a Jew or a Christian pronounced the *shahadah*[121] (the rite of passage into Islam for native non-Muslims), even in jest, or was falsely declared by two Muslim witnesses, that he or she had done so, even if he or she had not, they were punished as heretics, because denying the faith, once adopted (truly or falsely) is offensive to Allah and the Prophet, and merits death.

For this reason, the history of Christians and Jews under Islam is replete with cases of death penalty intentionally, or beating to death incidentally, in cases connected to religious conversions, true of imagined, or with starving entire *dhimmi* populations in order to force them to Islamize. In addition, horrible punishments were meted out to them if they failed to do so, or they were lured with attractive temptations, or Jewish and Christian girls and children were kidnapped in order to Islamize them and raise them as Muslims. In this way, the prevalence of Islam was shown, as the dominant faith of the Muslim masters, in contrast with the inherent inferiority of the *dhimmis*. Christians, and more so Jews were usually depicted as enemies of Allah and of the Prophet, greedy and misers, hating humanity and especially Muslims, thieves, cheaters, traitors, unreliable, weaving plots and conspiracies constantly, seeking to enslave others and exploit them, inhuman, cruel and what have you, mostly a projection of their own deficiencies onto the unbelievers. Since they were *Shari'a*-based, and their violations and alleged transgressions were *shari'a*-court-adjucated, most of the *dhimma*-connected accusations and indictments against the *dhimmis* for transgressing the *shari'a,* if they did not emanate from the greed or the whims, or the simple wickedness of the Muslim ruler, or of one of his local governors, or were instigated by the indoctrinated and incited mob, they were handled by the Muslim clerics

---

[121] The formula, which is part of the Muslim prayers states: There is no God but Allah and Muhammad is the Messenger of Allah.

who were constrained by the puritanical precedents of the Malikite rite to adjucate them severely. Maybe the most influential of all of them was the 15th century, scholar Muhammad b. ʿAbd al-Karīm al-Māghīlī (1440–1504), a Muslim cleric from Tlemcen in North Africa. His relentless hate of infidels and Jews in particular, led to one of the most tragic chapters of Jewish history in North Africa. Upon his arrival in the region of Tuʾāt to propagate Islam, he was scandalized to discover the prosperity of the local Jews, who had won the favor of the Muslim leadership. Considering this situation to be an intolerable breach of their obligatory status of humiliation, he consequently annulled their right to protection (*dhimma*) and incited the local Muslim population to rise up and destroy their synagogues and kill them. A slaughter ensued. In view of the of his prevailing authority, which made him a venerated saint, his tomb in Tuʾat has become the site of popular pilgrimage. Due to the fact that he is still cited as a precedent and a master, lengthy excerpts from his writings are cited here to explain why they became the foundation of the laws of *dhimma* in North Africa throughout generations.

Dhimma laws were not canceled under colonial rule out of the Muslims' free will, and are still enforced today in territories taken over by radical Muslims such as ISIS and Hamas, areas in Yemen, Afghanistan, and Somalia, where hardly any *dhimmis* are left. In other areas of resurgent Islam, like in Syria, Iraq, Libya and West Africa, where strong *dhimmi* populations had been implanted for centuries, the renewed enforcement of those rules has caused large-scale abuses and massacres, especially of Christians, since most Jews had long ago evacuated Islamic territories. As alread mentioned above, the crumbling Ottoman Empire had abrogated these laws as part of the major reforms of the 1860s (the *Tanzimat)* under the Powers' urgings. In the rest of the Islamic world, it was only foreign Western occupation which annulled that rule, in North Africa by the French, first in the 19th Century in Algeria, and then at the beginning of the 20th in Morocco. Abrogation of the *dhimma* was not easily taken by the concerned Muslims, whose hatred towards the Jews and Christians only increased, though it remained compressed in their hearts, yearning for the opportunity to renew it when possible.

In al-Maghili's treatise against the Jews (ca 1491) we find the following main points, which are for the most applicable against Christians as well, whenever they have the bad fortune as falling within Islamic rule in terrorories that had been previously Chrisan, of various denominations, but were Islamized since then.

1. That the Jews are indeed the bitterest enemies of Islam, who reject Muhammad. Therefore, Muslims are urged to rise up and enslave or kill them as they had been killed in Khaybar[122], at the sword of Muhammad.

2. It is incumbent upon Muslims to avoid contact with Infidels, and necessary for *dhimmi*s to adopt a humiliating posture even when paying the poll-tax.

3. Most Jews[and Christians] are in the state of violation and rebellion in respect to Islamic law, by reason of their being in the employment of Muslims, who hold authority, and in the service of the Sultan.

4. Al-Maghili cited the Qur'an where Allah said: 'O believers, take not Jews and Christians as friends; they are friends of each other. Whosoever of you makes them his friends is one of them' (Qur. 5, 51). He emphasized that only a person deprived of religion, of common sense and of dignity would admit an Infidel into his intimate circle, or entrust to him a portion of his wealth. The rationale is that Allah cannot be pleased with those who associate with an enemy of His, or shun someone who loves Him, whereas no Believer would ever

---

[122] That was a Jewish oasis in Arabia where the persecuted Jewish tribes of Medina found shelter after Muhammad's take over there. Then they were attacked by Muslims and either elimintated or the first rules of *dhimma* applied to the,.

tolerate such behavior on the part of his own servants. Moreover, no Muslim would accept such behavior from any relative, and if one were to perceive that one of his friends was intimate with one's enemy, he would resent, and his mind and heart abhor it, and he would not accept anything short of his dissociating himself from him.

5. He dubs as false the claim that certain [Muslim] individuals believe in the Prophet and love him while, at the same time, they and their families consort with the enemies of the Prophet. Furthermore, they afford protection to his most hostile enemies and on account of this, distance themselves from his friends, going to such lengths as to give refuge to Jews and to oppose the Muslim scholars. 'These are the ones that deny their Lord: around their necks are fetters. They are the inheritors of the Fire, and shall abide therein forever' (Qur. 13, 5). Allah, declared in the following verses: 'O believers! Do not seek the friendship of Jews and Christians as allies. They are allies with one another. Whoever of you takes them as an ally shall become one of them. God does not guide the wrongdoers' (Qur. 5, 56). 'Warn the hypocrites that for them there is a painful punishment. As for those who take the deniers of truth for their allies rather than the believers—do they seek honor in their company? Surely all honor belongs Allah' (Qur. 4, 138). '

6. The Jews have incurred the wrath of Allah and shall suffer eternal punishment. Had they believed in Allah and the Prophet and what was revealed to him, they would not have taken those who deny the truth as their allies, but many of them are disobedient' (Qur. 5, 83–84). 'And you will find no believers in Allah and the Last Day consorting with those who oppose Allah and His messenger, even though they be their fathers, their sons, their brothers, or their close kin' (Qur. 58, 22). 'O believers! Do not take your fathers and your brothers

as allies if they choose denial of truth in preference to faith. Those among you who ally themselves with them are wrong-doers' (Qur. 9, 23). 'Do not take deniers of the truth for your allies in preference to believers. Would you give Allah a clear proof against yourselves?' (Qur. 4, 144). 'Let not the Believers take those who deny the truth for their allies in preference to the believers—anyone who does that will isolate himself completely from Allah—unless it be to protect yourselves against them in this way. Allah admonishes you to fear Him: for, to Allah shall all return' (Qur. 3, 27). There are many other verses that [deal with this theme].

7. Love of the Prophet implies hate of the Jews, claimed this master jurist. He admonished to regret what has passed, but do not repeat it. How can one draw near to the enemies of the Prophet? In the tomb, at the hour of resurrection, until the infernal fire, none will be there to save him when the flames approach his face with which he showed favor to the Jews.

8. Al-Maghili also further cited what Allah, the Most High, said, 'Thou wilt surely find the most hostile of men to the believers are the Jews and idolaters' (Qur. 5, 82). 'Many of the People of the Book wish they might restore you as unbelievers, after you have believed, in the jealousy of their souls, after the truth has become clear to them' (Qur. 2, 109). 'O believers, if you obey a sect of those who have been given the Book, they will turn you, after you have believed, into unbelievers' (Qur. 3, 100)

9. The unbelievers' defamatory calumnies about Muslims and their religion are well known, especially those of the 'ape-like' people—the Jews, whose enmity towards Islam and its Prophet is the most hostile. How mean-minded is he who feels no natural, physical and mental aversion towards them! How lowly and vile is he who tolerates them to come near to him, for none of them can look at us without expressing inside a

hateful, abusive and slanderous thought towards Muslims and their religion. They even go to the extent of abstaining from eating the cattle Muslims slaughter and the food they prepare. Similarly, they will not cook in Muslim pots or eat from Muslim utensils. Worst of all is that they slander Islam, mock its prayers and raise objections to its master and intercessor Muhammad, peace and blessing of Allah be upon him. That is why Allah stated: 'O believers, take not My enemy and your enemy for friends offering them love, though they have disbelieved in the truth that has come to you' (Qur. 60, 1). 'O believers, take not as friends those of them who were given the Book before you, and the unbelievers, who take your religion in mockery and as a sport—and fear Allah if you are believers' (Qur. 5, 8).

10. Consequently, every Believer, whose faith is steadfast, should consider that every Jew is but the devil incarnate [*Iblīs*]. For the sake of his faith, he should flee him so that on account of their intimacy, the [Jew] may not snare him unaware by his deceit. One of the most frequent snares occurs when a Muslim becomes so infatuated with a possession or the manners of a Jew that affection steals into his heart, a state which inevitably incurs divine anger. Another trick is that the Jew may feed him forbidden meat, or wine, or carrion, or involve him in some usurious transaction to his profit.

The foundation for the continued humiliation of the Jews and Christians is also found in those early days when destruction of synagogues(and churches) was found imperative for the sanity of the Muslim soul. Indeed, the Almohad ruler Abu Yussuf al Mansur found it necessary to invoke the *Shari'a* to destroy Jewish places of worship, and even ordered the [Muslims] of Jewish origin residing in the Maghreb to distinguish themselves from the rest of the population by wearing a particular attire. This consisted of a dark blue robe with sleeves that were so wide that they fell to their feet and, instead of a turban, a skull-cap (*qalansawa*) reaching past their ears and which was of such misshapen form that it could have been mistaken for a pack-saddle. This dress became that of all the Jews of the Maghreb and remained so right up until the end of the reign of the said prince and the early part of that of his son Abū ʿAbd Allah [the Just, r. 1224–1227]. Upon the multiple entreaties of the Jews who resorted to the intercession of anyone deemed useful to them, the latter sovereign consented to modify this attire. Abū ʿAbd Allah had them wear yellow robes and turbans and this is how they dress to the present day in the year 1224. The reason why Abū Yūsuf compelled the [new Muslims] to resort to wear distinctive clothing was the doubt he harbored as to the sincerity of their belief: 'Were I sure that they were true Muslims, he would say, I would allow them to merge with the Muslims through marriage or otherwise; if, however, I were sure that they were Infidels, I should have the men slain, their children enslaved and their belongings confiscated and distributed among the faithful. But I have swayed in their favor'. Ever since the Masmūda came to power, neither protection was afforded to Jews nor Christians and neither synagogue nor church was to be found throughout all the Muslim lands of the Maghreb. But the Jews in our parts externally profess to Islam; they pray in the mosques and teach the Qurʾan to their children, complying with our religion and our law. God alone knows what is concealed in their hearts and what they harbor in their homes.[123]

Muslims having found themselves humiliated if and when adjoining Jewish (or Christian) houses were offensive to them when taller that their own, and were determined that no Jews should evince that sort of haughtiness, and should be treated accordingly.

---

[123] Translation of Abd al Wahid al Marrakushi, *Kitab al-Muʾjib fi takhlis akhbar al-Maghrib* (A summary of Maghribi History, 1224, edt. By R. Dozy, Leiden 1881. Document A 5 in Fenton and Littman, p. 55.

A *fatwa* was issued in Tlemcen in 1430 that should have pleased the most sickening anti-Jewish hatred of Maghili, the great master of Judeophobia, and of the promotion of the paranoia of the Muslims being constantly spied on by the Jews, as if they had nothing else to do. It said:

> I questioned our master and lord Abû l-Fadl al-'Uqbânî concerning some Jews who had built a house opposite a *madrasa*. They had elevated the structure to a such a height that a person ascending to the roof would observe what was going on in the ground-floor of the *madrasa* and would stand facing the people in the mosque. Because of its height the building was overlooking all of this. Should the [Jews] be ordered to build a wall on the [terrace] to prevent all visibility, or should they be ordered to demolish the building if they refuse such a modification, or are they allowed to do as they please on their property?
>
> This is his reply to me: Praise be to Allah! As for the *dhimmi*s overlooking the *madrasa*s of the Believers, as you described, this is totally forbidden to them. For such an act, after giving them warning, they should be severely punished. They are to be obliged to take upon themselves to build on the roof that overlooks [the *madrasa* and mosque, a construction] which prevents a person standing on the roof from peering down. An appropriate delay should be fixed according to the importance of the work involved. If they do not carry this out, then the part of the building which enables them to overlook [the *madrasa* and the mosque] is to be demolished. I am unsure about the question of whether they are to be prohibited from building their dwellings higher than those of the Muslims amongst whom they reside. I cannot for

the moment recall any [ruling]. I am however aware of a certain number of restrictions enforcing their humiliation, such as attaching leaden seals upon the necks of those who have paid the poll-tax (jizya), their wearing of distinctive belts, the cutting of their forelocks, and their riding sideways on their pack-saddles, but I recall nothing relating to their constructions. If I happen upon anything I shall send you news, Allah willing. Thereafter, he wrote me, may Allah be pleased with him, the following text: My son, you had questioned me concerning the building of a Jew whose height exceeded that of a *madrasa*. I have since been apprised of the answer. The reply is that such a situation is totally forbidden and the Infidels' building cannot be left in such a state.[124]

The style of dress was another external fashion imposed on the Jews to make their constant humiliation evident to every Muslim, from whom they were compelled to differentiate, lest Allah Forbid, they may be considered Muslims by others when their dress was not distinctly differentiated. Another judgment by the *Shari'a* court of Tlemcen (around 1450)) gave the religious justification for this discrimination.

It is fitting to impose [upon the Jews] a distinctive sign by which they can be identified in order to humiliate them and distinguish them from the Muslims. [The Caliph] 'Umar had decreed that a lead seal be tied to their necks. It can be asked whether it could be considered an offence on their part to disobey this [measure] by omitting to wear a distinctive sign on their clothes and

---

[124] Translation of *Nawāzil azūna* ('Collection of Legal Consultations') (Rabat: Bibliothèque Générale), Ms 521Q, fol.29b–30a. P. 58 in Fenton and Litman.

moreover whether the latter is restricted to males to the exclusion of females, or if it is imposed on both.

It could also be asked if the edict [of 'Umar] authorizing the Jews to ride a saddled animal, but only side-saddle included all mounts or if it was limited to certain types. I would reply that if they ignore the sign that distinguishes them from the Muslims while persisting in associating with them and imitating their dress they should be severely punished. The *Jawāhir* and the *Rules of the Market* report the case of a Jew who adopted Muslim garb and discarded his distinctive mark whereas he was transporting an outrageous quantity of wine. He was punished with a beating and imprisoned and then he was paraded through the Jewish and the Christian quarters so that his case would serve as a warning and a deterrent. Ibn Tālib had written to one of his Qadis requesting him to oblige the Jews and the Christians to wear wide belts (*zunnār*) over their garments so that they could be recognized. Whoever disobeyed thereafter was simply punished with twenty lashes of the whip before being thrown into prison. In the case of a second offence, the offender was brutally beaten and thrown into prison indefinitely. Yahyā b. 'Umar adds that their wives must wear a distinctive badge that would prominently set them apart from Muslim women, while previous authorities have left nothing on the subject. In his *Jāmi' al-ahkām* (a Collection of Judgments) [Al-Māzarī] deduces this obligation incumbent upon women from what is reported in [Muhammad Ibn Rushd's, the grand father of Ibn Rushd- Averroes, the philosopher] '*Utbiyya* concerning [the caliph] 'Umar. The latter would beat his servants to force them to uncover their heads in order to tell them apart. Now, if there is reason to punish servants though

Muslim, because they lack a sign distinguishing them from free women, then there is even more reason to distinguish female infidels from Muslim women. A <u>question</u> was put to the Imām Al-Māzarī regarding the way to appropriately modify the outward appearance of the Jews as compared to the Muslims and whether the Qadi should force them to dye their coat-tails, and if the Qadi had not dealt with this, would a simple Muslim have the duty to see that this was done? His <u>answer</u> was that, quite to the contrary, the Jews should be ordered to modify their coat-tails and adopt a sign which would enable them to be set apart [from the Muslims]. This involves a usage in vigor since olden times down till today. It was imposed since olden times in the large cities. This obligation consists of several details which would take too long to expound. Sheikh al-Burzulī adds that it is obvious that this obligation includes men and women. It is fitting to impose this usage when Jewish women mingle constantly with Muslim women and they go out frequently, excepting if this is not the case. The practice in Tunis is that, more often than not, most Christian women cover themselves like the Muslim women without distinctive signs while others keep to Christian attire. What distinguishes the Jewish women is that they wear *qurq* (coarse clogs) or walk barefoot. The Jewish men wear a distinguishing sign in the form of a length of yellow fabric [*shikla*] over rather than under their outer clothing without which their identity could have been unclear when the person is seen from the rear. [...] Most of the Jews adopt the appearance of the tribes of these provinces whereas in actual fact there is a need for absolute distinction considering that they inevitably associate with the Muslims amongst whom they live. I will add that here [in the

Maghreb] the distinctive sign of the native Jews whose ancestors hail from this country is a length of yellow fabric [*shikla*] worn over their outer garment as is the case in Ifriqiya (North Africa). The dress of the Jewish women consists of a length of filālī(from the southern region of Tafilalt) fabric in which they wrap themselves, with no veil [*niqāb*] either of linen or any other cloth. Instead they cover their faces with the hem of the fabric itself that they hold in their hands. As to the [Jews] originally from Christian countries, or whose ancestors came from there, they distinguish themselves by means of a skull-cap in a thick woolen fabric [*kabbūs min malf*] topped with a tassel [*dhuwāba*] that falls to the nape, and a belt [zunnār], most commonly made of the same cloth. Regarding the Caliph 'Umar b. al-Khattāb's rescript on the obligation of the Jews to ride their animals side-ways—this pertains to donkeys and camels for, according to the *Jawāhir*, they were prohibited to ride horses and mules, even simply fitted with pack-saddles. May Allah extinguish their pomp and confirm the word of Islam through their debasement and humiliation![125]

Another wanton demolition of a Jewish house of prayer in the southern Tu'at region, under the justification of the *Shari'a* Law, was described in 1492, the year of the Jewish expulsion from Spain, in terms of questions and answers, like the Jewish *responsa,* namely a *fatwa*:

<u>Question</u>: 'What do you state on the question of Tamantīt the [chief] town of Tu'at, whose land the

---

[125] Translation of Muhammad al-'Uqbānī, *Tuhfat al- Nazir*, edited by Ali Chenoufi, 1966, A 8, pp. 57-59 in Fenton and Littman.

Muslims reclaimed by irrigation, and by planting date palms and building fortified villages (*quṣūr*) over a period of time, whereupon they were rejoined by Jews, who settled with them in the aforementioned town, and established therein a new synagogue to practice their religion. This has been the situation over time until the present day. Should this synagogue be demolished, even if they had owned the land on which it was built before it was constructed, having obtained it by purchase, or other means, from the Muslims? Or should it not be demolished? Reply to us on this with an unambiguous *fatwā* and may you be rewarded, for the Muslims are in a state of perplexity over this matter. If destruction of it is rightful, they will demolish it without strife or discord. If it is rightful to be left standing, they will leave it so without strife. God it is who brings success. Peace and God's mercy be upon you!

<u>Answer</u>: Know—may God illuminate your spiritual vision and purify your inner essences of the pursuit of base inclination—that ever since its sun shone forth, and its decisive proofs appeared, the *sharīʿa* of Muhammad has abrogated every other religious law and healed ailing hearts of every illness. Learned scholars undertook to preserve it, committing themselves to its defense throughout the ages. Over the centuries, since the time of the Companions [of Muhammad], they have dealt with the explanation of the appropriate judgment to the problem contained in this question. We shall quote from their statements, so as to leave no room for doubt. The basic principles are *hadiths* in the name of the supreme messenger [Muhammad], and subsequent traditions transmitted on the authority of the Companions and Followers, and confirmed by the early and latter day

Muslim scholars. Anas [b. Mālik] related that Allah's messenger declared: 'Demolish monasteries and destroy churches'. [The caliph] 'Umar b. al-Khattāb [d. 644] reported that [Muhammad] said: 'No synagogue (*kanīsa*) should be newly established in Islamdom, nor should any that have been demolished be restored'". [...] Mālik reported that the Prophet made the following prediction: 'Neither Jewess nor Christian should be elevated in your midst', meaning thereby a synagogue or a church. All these traditions constitute proofs of [Muhammad's] prophecy since he predicted them and they came true). It is prohibited to build a synagogue in the territory of Islam, regardless whether [the land] was acquired through a gift or by purchase. The reason for this absolute restriction is to manifest the eminence of Islam by having no other religion appear beside it. An allusion to this occurs in the *hadīth* quoted by Ibn Rushd: 'Neither Jewess nor Christian should be elevated in your midst', for Islam must dominate and not be dominated. When asked the following question: 'Should one demolish a synagogue [*shanūga*], which had been shown to have been newly established?', the Judicial Council of Cordova gave the following reply: 'It is obligatory to demolish it, after giving a warning to its owners for Islamic law does not permit Jews or Christians to establish new synagogues or churches in the towns of Islam, or amongst Muslims'. [So much for the Golden Age of Spain. Here follow the names of the signatories [...]. The Shaykh Abū l-Fadl Qāsim b. Sa'īd al-'Uqbānī was asked whether the Jews of Tu'āt had forfeited their right to hospitality and maintenance provided by [the pact] of 'Umar, since they had not fulfilled their liabilities. He replied that since the Jews had overstepped the limit of humiliation incumbent upon them, all obligations to provide them with hospitality and maintenance were no longer applicable. He predicted terrible punishment for them on the Day of Resurrection and Requital [...]. Furthermore here is an analogous question submitted to the jurist Abū l-Qāsim al'Abdūsi, a resident of Tunis, who confirms our opinion.

<u>Question</u>: Concerning a newly built village in Muslim territory in which Jews—may Allah degrade them!—erected a new synagogue, where they were wont to perform their polytheistic worship. This endured until Allah inspired a certain eminent Muslim endowed with knowledge and religion, to order the outright demolition of this synagogue, thus in eradicating such an enormous infamy and obliterating such an unlawful innovation. Now the Jews—may Allah confound them!—wish to reconstruct their synagogue and re-establish their worship, though no provision for this was afforded in the pact relating to the dhimma and jizya imposed upon them. Should their request be acceded to?

<u>Answer</u>: The Jews may neither establish nor restore any [place of worship] on Muslim territory. So stated Ibn al-Qāsimon the authority of Mālik, in the chapter on 'Pay and protection' in the *Mudawwana*. Doing so in defiance of the prohibition, constitutes a breaking of the covenant, for according to unanimous opinion no Jew is authorized to build or repair a place of worship upon Muslim territory. Consequently, Muslims are allowed to seize their possessions, their children and women, just as they would in the case of enemies on enemy territory. [After having asserted that Mālikite, Shāfite, Hanbalite, Hanafite and Zahirite practice were in agreement with this ruling, Tamansi concludes]:

All able Muslims must exert themselves to their utmost capacity in demolishing the synagogue of Tamantīt. They should make every effort to do so for this is the most meritorious act of holy war (*jihād*). Whosoever endeavors to prevent this demolition falls under the condemnation issued by the Imām of the Maghreb, Abū l-Qāsim al-'Abdūsī, who declares him to be an infidel (*kāfir*) or at the least a sinner (*fāsiq*), incurring the curse of Allah, His angels, and all mankind. The Jews cannot use the argument of their prolonged possession [of the land on which the synagogue was built], for at the most this could only show that they had a right of enjoyment to it. Now, even if they had ownership of it, whether by virtue of a valid gift or purchase, this would not of itself permit them to build a synagogue, in consideration of the rights of Islam. How then is it possible to acknowledge this right in the case where they only occupy [the property] without actual ownership? All the more so since the authoritative texts are in agreement in denying that simple possession has any effect whatsoever in the case of properties subject to the right of Allah, such as pious foundations (*habūs*). Rather, according to these texts, the latter right is indefeasible, even if a judge issues a judgment to the contrary. Neither can the Jews draw proof from the existence of numerous synagogues in numerous towns, for the protracted existence or the extensiveness of an illegal phenomenon do not alter its prohibition. To be sure, there is nothing more objectionable than the neglect of worship, which is punishable by death. Now, the fact that numerous individuals in the East and West are amiss in their prayers has not changed the legal ruling on this, since scholars continue to uphold the death sentence in such cases and take no account of the great number of transgressors. Similarly, they continue to prohibit the construction of synagogues and order the demolition of those that have been erected, regardless of the practice being widespread, or its protracted duration. The texts which oppose such action can only be by someone who denies the validity of the shari'a and strives to destroy it. May Allah preserve us from abandoning or renouncing the religion of him who was sent [...] with guidance and the religion of Truth, that it might triumph over all other religions[126].

Not only Jews realized their state of misery and persecution, but even non-Jewish foreign observers lamented their situation, as the following report from Algiers from 1793, some 40 years prior to the French occupation:

Such is the gross indignation the Mahometans bear toward the Jewish religion, that a Turk may with impunity (if he flees to a Marabout Mosque, or pay a small penalty) murder ten of them. If he kills the eleventh, he is then strangled, no Mosque or penalty will excuse him, Nothing will save his life, except he is pardoned by the Dey (the local ruling King), whose word is absolute. A slave may with the same impunity beat and abuse them in the streets as he passes. While the poor Israelites are not allowed to lift their hands in their own defense on penalty of having it cut off. All the consolation they will have in such cases from Mahometans is encouragement for the slaves to continue their abuse. I have known fifty

---

[126] Translated extracts from the fatwā by Muhammad b. 'Abdallah 'Abd al-Jalīl al-Tanasī, Chief Qādi of Tlemcen, in Ahmad b. Yahyā al-Wansharīsī (1430–1508), al-Mi'yār ('*The Touchstone*'), vol. 2 (Bayrūt: Dār al-Gharb al-islāmī, 1981), 232–49. Pp 85-89 in Fenton-Littman.

in one day, to receive five hundred bastinadoes each for being found with red sash about their waists. As they are not allowed to wear any color except black.A Jew having being apprehended inside the door of one of them (the Marabout Mosques) would be immediately burned or crucified. So the poor Israelites have no protection for their crimes, and must submit to the absolute word of a despotic prince. At Meireja, 12 Miles from Algiers, there are three hot bathes. The water is quite hot, and when it has filled the largest basin, it runs through into a smaller one, where the Jews bathe, as they are not permitted to use the same bath as Mahometans. People of any denomination whatever (except the Jews) are allowed to dress in this habit. The Jews are obliged to dress entirely in black, and wear shoes without any quarters[127]

---

[127] John Foss (d. 1800), *A Journal of the Captivity and sufferings of John Foss, Several Years a Prisoner at Algiers: together with some Account of the Treatment of Christian slaves,* 2nd ed. (Newburyport, MA: Angier March, 1789). A 20, P. 98 in Fenton and Littman.

Conclusions and Summary

Particularly remarkable is the infamous *fatwa* that was pronounced by Khomeini in 1989, condemning Salman Rushdie to death for his *Satanic Verses* bestseller, a theme that became central in Islamic discourse during the years that followed in both Islamic domestic contexts and the international terror it sowed, in the clash of values it revealed between Islam and the West, and sadly in the sometimes capitulating *dhimmi*-like attitudes of Western individuals, institutions, and countries. The Rushdie Affair has served as a watershed nonetheless in bringing the western world to realize that Islamic radicalism had been born, not only as a talk show but as a *modus operandi* of the world of Islam in its growing confrontation with the West. For before, controversies and differences between Islam n the West had been ironed out peacefully, in an open and civilized manner, and the intellectually superior seemed likely to win. Thus, some naïve minds in the West had come to believe that negotiations with Muslim radicals could alter their fanatic attitudes and lead to coexistence between Muslims and their rivals. The problem was that dialogue was treated in the West as policy, whereas it was in fact a non-policy, designed only to fill an awkward vacuum and to make legislators and other talking heads feel virtuous for "doing something." But while

Europeans had regularly entered such dialogues with Muslims in good faith, fully intending to find common ground with their often unruly Muslim interlocutors, for Muslims "dialogue" meant something else entirely. For them it meant the submission of the lesser cultures and religions of the West to their own superior one, hoping to inspire conversion to an Islamic worldview. Anything short of that was considered an abject "failure of dialogue."

Muslim negotiators between Islam and the West were practiced in both cultures, whereas the Westerners have literally become pushovers at this stage in their history. Except for the contemporaries of the pre-Obama United States, Westerners hardly believed that anything was worth fighting for. Nor did they have the stomach for a fight of unlimited duration. They would rather capitulate than investigate in-depth the meaning of tolerance, understanding, dialogue, and peace to radical Muslims of the post Khomeini era. The problem lies in the juxtaposition of a resurgent militant Islam on one hand and a self-deprecating West on the other, unsure of itself or its values. Its people have made a virtue of instant self-gratification, and therefore they invest next to nothing in the future—hence they have stopped rearing children. Their preferred way of life amounts to a "credit card culture." They want everything, and they want it instantly. Never mind that their governments no longer raise sufficient funds to cover exorbitant welfare entitlements, which partly goes to pacify the Muslims that have settled in their midst, or that a bleak financial future awaits tomorrow's pensioners. In short, the West has become a disgrace to its own heritage, in sharp reversal of its fortunes when at the turn of the twentieth century the Muslim Ottoman Empire was considered the "sick man of Europe" and was therefore no match for a self-confident West. US defense secretary Donald Rumsfeld was onto something when he distinguished between the "old" and "new" Europe—except that in their eagerness to grab some (necessarily short-term) economic benefits after emerging from Soviet control, the headlong rush of "new Europe" to join the European Union will inevitably contaminate them with the prevailing Western disease.

There is another drawback to this constant resort to dialogue with Muslim radicals. It lulls the Western populations into believing that their governments are doing something constructive to avert violence or threats of violence in the future. In reality, nothing could be further from the truth, for this non-policy serves to embolden and empower those Muslims whom Western governments have chosen to act as intermediaries with the wider Muslim communities. Invariably, Western governments have elected these Muslims because they are prominent activists in the community, while the governments comfort themselves with the injudicious belief that these figures represent "moderate" Islam. However, these Muslims are familiar enough with the West to have learned to tailor their vocabulary precisely to whom they are facing across the table. They speak the language of peace, reconciliation, and goodwill to Westerners and reserve their true beliefs for fellow Muslims, in what we have often characterized as "double talk"—one for their domestic constituencies and another for their foreign interlocutors; one for their politics at home and another for their interviews with the foreign press. In other words, they have learned to work the system, and admirably so. In effect, these "moderate" Muslim leaders gradually extract one concession after another from Western policy makers, rendering dialogue a one-way street. They enter each session with the full intention of testing the limits of the concessions they can extract, and it is a rare Western negotiator who would risk disappointing them—or else the headlines in the papers the following day would be sure to inflame the Muslim public. Herein lies the value of the worldwide Muslim penchant for overreacting to every perceived slight by demonstrating their outrage loudly and violently. Temperament comes into play here too, for unlike other peoples who experience anger or humiliation, many radical Muslims are either unable or unwilling to contain those sentiments. One has only to recall the orchestrated "Days of Rage" in Gaza, Tehran, or Islamabad, in which Western flags and effigies are burned, foreign embassies and consulates are destroyed, and foreign diplomats and journalists are assaulted, to understand that, in sharp contrast to Westerners, Muslims make a fetish of celebrating their anger. Such an uncontrolled behavior is unthinkable in the West, but not because of lack of provocation. Funerals are also manipulatedby Muslim radicals to vent wrath and fury, emotion, general mayhem, and impromptu rifle shooting. The total and shameless lack of dignity, even at what should be a somber occasion, is jarring to Western eyes. Bodies are held aloft and bounced along the funeral route in a manner that would be regarded as disrespectful to the deceased in other cultures. Bodies have been known to fall off the stretcher amid the melee, and other processions turn chaotic, as was recorded for posterity in the case of Khomeini's own funeral in 1989.

As against the repeated boasting in the Islamic world of its tolerance towards other faiths, which is "supported" by the "evidence " of the "Andalusian Paradise"; by the Qur'anic saying about "no compulsion in religion"; and by the fact that the expelled Jews from Spain and Portugal at the turn of the 16th Century found refuge in the Muslim Ottoman Empire and other Muslim countries in North Africa and elsewhere, there is enough real history and verified testimony to suggest that one of the darkest periods of Jewish existence was the millennium they spent under the Muslim boot. As explained above, the Andalusian myth has been torn to pieces in the marvelous and authoritative work of Dario Fernandez Morera; the tales of tolerance towards Jews (and Christians) have been contradicted by the established fact that Christianity has been waning in the Islamic world since the take-over of its territories by nascent Islam to this very day[128], while the one million strong Jewish com-

---

[128] See e.g. Raphael Israeli, *Christianophobia: the Persecution of Christian Minorities under Islam,* WIPF and Stock, Oregon, 2016.

munity in Islamic countries has dwindled to a few thousand since 1948 when the state of Israel was established; and the reality of forced Jewish migration from Christian lands to Muslim countries at the dawn of the modern era, which must be taken in relative terms, for if the fate of Jews in Christian Europe was much worse than in Islamdom, that in itself did not mean that the Jewish lot was good under Islam.

What can be verified by reality which debunks the myths, is usually denied and rejected in Muslim historiography not always out of malice, but more often as a result of the tradition of self-victimization which has been the best tool to avoid responsibility and to project all the blame on others, while creating a web of delusions and fantasies which overtake reality and replace it. And that delusionary web which has nothing to do with facts or reality is woven into such a strong "narrative" of their own making, that they end up believing in it and turning it into a cause they are willing, even eager, to defend and fight for. The most striking example is their "replacement theory" of Jewish history, which denies and rejects the latter, documentation, scientific evidence and archaeology notwithstanding, all leading to the manufacturing of an alternative history, which when publicly supported by other ignorant nations and interest –oriented governments, provides definitive "evidence" to the veracity of their fabrications. The sequence of events in UNESCO in October, 2016, when an invented history by Arabs was backed by a majority of countries which have either never excelled in science nor cared about historical truth, led to the denial of established and verified history of the Holy Land, and to the adoption first of trumped up Muslim holy places that either never were, or came in second to add to, not to replace existing history. It is significant that all western nations who respect science and history, either voted against this patently false "history" or abstained in order to avoid staining themselves with support for a political lie.

It remains to clarify the tremendous gap between what Islamic theory, as embedded in the Qur'an and the *Hadith*, tells us about the People of the Book, and their mistreatment by the rapacious Muslim authorities in their countries of dwelling. We have already pointed out to the many contradictions in the Holy Book, for example the injunction not to trust the Scriptuaries or befriend them, and the obligation to fight them wherever they are found, which stands in stark opposition to the "no compulsion" slogan. But no less important is the delusion played out by paranoids, who are so haunted by their fears of persecution and conspiracy woven against them, that they often disregard the growing gap between their professed beliefs and propaganda slogans on the one hand, which are geared to improve their self-image in their own eyes and the image they project to the world, and the reality of bigotry, cruelty and tyranny that their societies practice not only towards Scriptuaries, who fare the worst, but against their own citizenry too. A document of the 12th Century analyzes the situation admirably:

> [...] As for the tidings of the Maghreb of which you desired to be informed, you would not believe your ears! Some individuals and groups have arrived, among whom Jews are to be found, who went through the fighting. They relate that 'Abd al-Mu'min of Sūs [Almohad sultan, r. 1130–1163] waged war against the Emir Tāshfīn at Oran. He stormed the city, slaughtered his troops, put to death the Emir Tāshfīn and crucified his body. Thereafter, he captured Tlemcen and massacred all the [Jewish] inhabitants of the city, except those who embraced Islam. When word of these events reached the population of Sijilmāsa, they rebelled against their governor, and, in demonstration of their opposition to the Almoravids, expelled them from the city. They then rallied to 'Abd al-Mu'min and delivered the city to him. When he made his entrance into the city, he gathered

the Jews and proposed that they convert to Islam. After having held disputations with him for a period of seven months, during which they fasted and prayed, one of his commanders came and summoned them to abjure their faith, which they refused to do. Thereupon he slaughtered one hundred and fifty Jews who perished as martyrs. 'The Rock is perfect in his action' (Deut. 32, 4). Blessed is the true Judge, who judges with righteousness and truth. 'The King's word is sovereign' (Eccl. 8, 4). The remainder reneged and the first to apostatize was Joseph the son of 'Amran, the rabbinical judge of Sijilmāsa! On account of this will I will mourn and cry. Now prior to 'Abd al-Mu'min's entry into the city, at the time when the population rose up against the Almoravids, some 200 Jews managed to flee to al-Qasba, among whom were Jacob and 'Abūd, my paternal uncles, as well as Master Judah ben Farhūn and his brothers. After having been robbed of all their possessions, they found refuge in Dar'a but we do not know what fate has befallen them since. In all the Almoravid territories, besides the tribal regions, only Dar'a and Meknes have not yet surrendered. On account of our sins, all the Jewish communities of the Maghreb have been wiped out, and from Bajāya [Bougie] to Bāb Zill there remains not one Jewish soul, some having been killed, and others having apostatized. On the day this letter was written, news reached us of the capture of Bajāya. May Almighty God crush their strength and may the hope that they lose these possessions be not far off! Indeed, he has conquered the entire coast from the gate of Seville to the gate of Tortosa. A terrible calamity [...]. The Andalusians have now surrendered to him and have given him possession of all the provinces. The Almoravids have no

longer any allies in the Maghreb, either in Cordoba or
Grenada. […] They captured […] the inhabitants of Fez
[…]. However, at the time of the capture of Fez 100,000
souls were slaughtered, and in Marrakesh 100,000. The
news I break is not just hearsay, but I have reported it to
you from direct witnesses.[129]

What is the significance of the extreme cases of pogroms, atroci-
ties, torments and other sadistic manifestations by both the Moroccan authorities towards their inhumanly oppressed Jewish minority,
and the incessantly incited mobs that were always on the verge of
exploding and channeling their rage against the Jews? The mobs
certainly did not know the constraints of the *Shari'a*, which itself
cultivated atrocious mistreatment of the Jews, as it transpired in the
clerical incitement and verdicts in the form of explosive *fatwas*; so
what motivated them apart from hatred towards the Jews, envy of
their sometimes economic successes, and simple bigotry? And the
mid-level local governors, who often ignored or contradicted the
highest reaches of government by implementing their own policy
of hatred and greed, at times even in excess of what the degrading
and ruthless monarchs would have warranted; what made them
tick? A few examples will illustrate the point:

a. In a report of 1669 by a foreign observer, he noticed the
   whimsical conducts of the authorities:
   The Jews are to be seen everywhere in this country, they are
   very serviceable to the inhabitants, for they furnish them
   for the most part with foreign commodities, and make

---

[129] Translation of an extract from a Judeo-Arabic letter by Solomon b. Judah
al-Sijilmāsī, dated January 1148, published by H. Z. Hirschberg in Yitzchak F.
Baer Jubilee Volume, on the Occasion of his 70th Birthday, ed. S. W. Baron, B.
Dinur, S. Ettinger and I. Halpern (Jerusalem: Historical Society of Israel, 1960),
142. Pp.51-2 in Fenton and Littman.

those things that are necessary for them. They never grow rich, but the Mahumetans do accuse them of some crime, to have a pretence to seize upon their Treasure, as it happened lately to a Jew, who was grown a petty Prince. He commanded a place strong by situation and art, called Darbinmeshaal [Dār Ibn Mash'al], there was but one ascent, and that so difficult, that without his leave all the Moors of Barbary might have spent their days in the Siege of it. For besides that it is impregnable, it contains so much ground within the Mountain as might very well nourish a thousand head of Cattle, and supply them with Corn and Fodder. This Jew had won the esteem and favor of the Grandees round about by his courteous behavior and good hospitality; for it was his custom to invite all the Persons of Note in his City, and there entertain them very kindly: This dealing made every one, especially the Arabs, to love him, and got him a great Name. When Muley Archeid, otherwise called Taffaletta[130]. found one Point in the Law of Mahomet to justify the Murder, which was approved of, and applauded by the ignorant Multitude. Another Jew named Joseph Ben-Simon, a very great Trader, and one that had Correspondents in many Places, did run the same Fortune. He supplied the Moors with many Commodities, especially with Powder and Shot Guns and other Weapons, which he conveyed out of Spain by stealth. At last his Wealth made him guilty of Death, for he was accused of Adultery, and although common report pronounced him innocent, he lost his Life, and his Estate seized for the Kings Use. Thus all the Princes of these Countries do treat this miserable Nation. When they have occasion for Money, they force it

---

[130] Reference is made to Mulay Rashid, the founder of the ruling ALawite Dynasty, who originated in Tafilalt in the south of Morocco.

from the Jews, either by right or wrong. Gayland[131] as I am informed, did entertain Jews in Arzilla, for no other end but to have some on whom he might prey. He raised a considerable Sum of Money from them on this occasion. About thirty or forty Families of the Jews managed all the Trade of that part of the Country, and were grown rich. Gayland consults his Cadi, and asks from this deceitful Oracle whether it was lawful to suffer Jews, Infidels, to dwell amongst the Musulmans? He answered that it was not lawful, but that if they would not turn Mahometans, he was commanded by the Law of Mahomet to punish that contempt with present Death. This sad News frightened the Jews, especially when they hear that the day was appointed for their Execution. In the mean whiles they Petition the Sultan, and make their Peace by offering a large sum of Money, all they had gathered in many years. This satisfied Gayland's weak Conscience, concerning the bloody clause of Mahomet's Law, and made him free them from the great danger that threatened them. You see by that what favor strangers may expect from this treacherous people. [132]

Intolerance Built into the Culture

Bernard Lewis has made the point that unlike other civilizations, which are essentially regional, Islam and Christianity have, by their very pattern of expansion, become both universal and exclusive in the sense that they consider themselves the "fortunate recipients of God's final revelation to mankind, and therefore it is their duty to bring it to the rest of humanity"; and so, the clash between them

---

[131] The British Envoy to the King of Morocco.
[132] A Letter from a Gentleman of the Lord Ambassador Howard's Retinue to His Friend in London, dated at Fes, 1st November, 1669 (London: Moses Pitt, 1670). Pp. 152-3 in Fenton and Littman.

became inevitable[133].However, while Western culture has forsaken the use of violence to spread its message, and pursues it by ways that the Muslims regard as devious (i.e. through the pop culture of jeans, fast food, music and Coca Cola, television, cinema, alcohol, dance etc), militant Islam and its supporters do not shun violence, as the *Islamikaze* phenomenon dramatically demonstrates. In other words, the humanistic idea of tolerance of the other in Western culture, which has come to mean that the other is accepted as is, without value judgment, has become predominant and has paved the way to the free market of ideas that prevails in the West today. This thinking has not only permitted the renouncing of the use of force in imposing one's ideas on the other for spreading Christianity, democracy, free trade, free expression and organization and other such Western ideas,, but has also allowed Islam and other creeds to compete freely on Western turf, without Christians ever suspecting that the competition would ultimately concern the turf itself. Moreover, since the West accepted to separate church from the modern secular state, faith has become the domain of the individual, while the public square has been made impervious to it.

In the Islamic world, by contrast, all the formally "secular" governments, which for the most part lack legitimacy, must pay a lip service to the Islamic trends in their countries, at times by even including them in their governments, to gain some semblance of legitimacy, since Islam remains, as it had been in the medieval world, the undisputed source of legitimacy for any rule in Islamdom. Even so, Islamic spokesmen, whether clerical or their supporters, appear to be the most popular claimants on power, whether they hold it in practice or aspire for it from the opposition benches. Thus, when they are allowed to operate as political parties, they often show their mettle if and when free elections are held, and they often win access to government. Therefore, no Muslim country or

---

[133] Bernard Lewis, "How did the Infidels Win?", *National Post,* 1 June, 2002.

territory can be made neutral towards other faiths, and the frequent use of violence against them, or even against other variants of Islam that do not conform to the rulers', as the frequent and horrific use of violence day in and day out, proves simultaneously in several lands of Islam (just observe the Shi'ites pitted against Sunnites (in Pakistan, Yemen, Syria, Iraq for example) and the unrelenting persecution of Christians minorities in the lands of Islam, then and now. Only the Jewish minority who survived under Islam for more than a millennium, has escaped its fate by abandoning that land of oppression and moving to Israel, where Jews continue to be persecuted, hated and pursued, only this time under the guise of "Zionists" or "Israelis".

Muslim radicals regard today the defeat of their own illegitimate governments as a prelude and prerequisite to the restoration of the universal caliphate of all Muslims, and therefore treat the western governments who protect, aid and sponsor the dictators in place as the direct enemy of the Muslims. From their point of view, then, not only is western culture despicable for its own sake, for its permissiveness, indecency and nihilism, but it invaded their turf in order to subvert it from within and destroy it. It is the West who came to them, they claim, not then to it. This creates a paradox nevertheless, for while Muslim radicals decry the Western cultural invasion, which is worse, in their eyes than the medieval territorial invasions of the Crusaders, they and their less radical coreligionists at the same time fill the long lines in front of the American, Australian and other western embassies across the world, in order to gain entry visas into those bastions of western values that they love to hate. Some explain their quest as a simple desire to study in the West, especially value-free technical professions which are not "soiled" by western thinking, ignoring the fact that western leaning and protracted sojourns in the West by necessity will have an impact on them, to the point that they are liable to elect to stay there and become a hated westerner themselves. Others wish from the start to improve their economic lot by immigrating to the West, but once they get there, they congregate around their kin and provide fertile grounds for Muslim radicalism, which often produces also Muslim terrorism, and spreads around Muslim *da'wa* as well. Others, like sheikhs Bakri and al-Masri in Britain, has migrated to the West as "refugees", because there was no other safe haven left to shelter them in their countries of origin, and the West was generous and unsuspecting enough to accommodate them. But once they settled down, they made clear their intentions to Islamize the West, not to be westernized by it.

It is the latter who often place themselves at the forefront of Muslim militants in the West and who, benefitting from the hospitality and social welfare arrangements in their host countries, recruit local converts or already naturalized Muslim migrants for training abroad, for indoctrination at home and for Jihadi activities. It is they, who are tolerated by the societies against whom they operate ideologically, who are the least tolerant towards their hosts. Their objective is loud and clear: to Islamize their host societies and let Islam take them over. If so far it was the integrationists- namely those who wished to assimilate into society and fit into the political, economic and social system, and become part of it culturally, if not religiously,- who were the main part of the Muslim immigrants, today it is the penetration of the radicals into the west and their rapid growth, which has begun to turn these trends around. For more and more Muslims, gathering self confidence from their growing numbers and the seeming capitulation of the western political correctness in the face of their "peaceful" invasion, "rebel" against their host countries and demand, as full-fledged citizens that their culture be recognized as a component of the local national make –up. For example, that they be recognized as a collective partner-identity in the land, that the state symbols (e.g. the cross in the Scandinavian national colors be replaced by a more accommodating symbol), and that mosques, foreign Muslim languages and Muslim education should be subsidized by the state. In France, following the scandal aroused by Francois Bayrou, the education Minister in the 1970s, when he refused to allow veiled Muslim women into the secular education system (*l'affaire du foulard*), young French Muslims, the sons of Muslim immigrants from North Africa, frequently boo the *Marseillaise* when it is played on football fields prior to the matches. In the meantime, the ban on the veil was generalized in France in the 2010s, while in Switzerland mosques must yield to the prohibition of erecting minarets at their side, which are considered as a thorn in the eye of the hosts.

All this emanates not only from the absolute conviction of the Muslims that Allah's message to them, being the most recent is also the most updated as it were, and therefore their way to Allah is the most valid. However, in contrast with Christianity, the other universal monotheistic religion which lays similar claims to humanity, the Muslims do not preclude the use of force to enforce their beliefs and to save the infidels from themselves by their own choice if possible, by violence if necessary. As David Bukay has put it:

> Since everything in Islam is so perfect, it is clear that everything out of Islam is so unclean and denied, that the doctrine of *al-Wala' wal-Bara'* (loyalty and disavowal) has emerged to signify that Muslims owe total loyalty and devotion to Islam, and evince total enmity to the other. This princiople has become one of Islam's main foundations and of paramount importance. Total allegiance and love are only to be given within the Muslim Umma, and rejection, hate and hostility against the other is commanded based upon Qur'anic sources[134].

Therefore, when Muslims speak of tolerance, they mean some

---

[134] David Bukay, *Islam and the Infidels: the Politics of Jihad, Da'wah and Hijrah*, Transaction NJ, 2016, p. 61.

sort of temporary measure of accommodation towards the Infidel, who clearly follows an inferior creed in their eyes, until Islam is strong enough to prevail. The miscalculation of al-Qa'ida on September 11, and before that and after that of the Hamas, ISIS and the rest of the Jihadi groups, was that western societies, including Israel, were so ripe for their demise that a shocking trauma' or a series of smaller but frequent and consistently growing blows, would ultimately overwhelm the enemy. Therefore, every time the West responds to Muslim terrorism more forcefully and refuses to capitulate, like the US in Afghanistan and Iraq or the Western allies in Syria and Iraq, or Israel in Gaza, Muslims cry: "foul!, foul play!". For this is not how the rivals of Islam are supposed to behave, and their very resistance to their subjugation by Islam is regarded as "blasphemous" for its failure to recognize the Will of Allah, and its retaliatory strikes against Islam are signs of distress and despair, which augur its approaching demise. Hence the stepped-up activities of the terrorists to speed up that process and bring it to its conclusion. This point of view does not recognize the right of the attacked "for the sake of Allah" to self-defense, as the *dhimmis* under Islam have never been allowed the instinctive response of self-defense when attacked, humiliated and beaten. The Muslims can expand, kill, conquer, enslave, dominate, rule and oppress, for the entire universe is ultimately theirs to be included in *Dar al-Islam*, but woe to those who resist that "noble" and Allah-decreed process.; those who do are decried as "aggressors", "killers of civilians and children", "arrogant" and "perpetrators of massacres"

Thus, any hideous Muslim attack against Western enemies, even when innocent victims are involved, as in the case of the employees of the Twin Towers, the *Charlie Hebdo* journalists, the bus or aircraft passengers, the restaurant and café goers, or the pacific audience of theaters, I "blessed" and "well-deserved" "successes" in the eyes of the Muslim massacre perpetrators, and cause masses to jubilate, and song writers to praise them in their lyrics throughout the

Muslim world, even when the official governments of those land state their embarrassment and try in vain to prevent or to cover up those stories. At the same time, every western retaliation is lamented, condemned and blasted as "unjustified aggression", "disproportionate", "cruel and inhuman" "wanton massacre"; and as proof, if proof is needed of the enemy's inherent evil, and what have you. The idea of fair play, of attack and counter-attack, each reflecting the interest and concern of its perpetrator, and of casualties inflicted on both parties in consequence, is misunderstood in Muslim circles, for only Muslims can inflict losses on the others who are destined to lose and submit; conversely, being afflicted by losses and fatalities, is out of the ordinary and should not be envisaged. In any case, the Muslim casualties are *shahids* (martyrs), earmarked for eternal and blissful existence in Paradise under the throne of Allah. Even the issue of aggressive and defensive warfare is foreign to Muslims, because Muslim definitions of warfare do not follow the accepted objective norms prevailing in the West, but abide strictly by the subjective rules thought out by Muslim jurists, who have formulated Muslim political theory and international relations[135].

Islamic intolerance has also been expressed in their totally exclusive attitude towards other religions and their refusal to contemplate sharing or accommodating others in caseof disagreement. For, the Qur'an itself, the Word of Allah that suffers no contradiction or questioning, prescribes the killing of the Infidels (*kuffar*), or being harsh to them, for they have no rights and should not be treated in the same way as Muslims are. They are almost no human at all, as the frequently cited verses from the Qur'an on Friday sermons, testify about the Jews being "descendants of apes and pigs". Dehumanizing them, is the short way to making them disposable and "permissible" of murder, to be terrorized, tortured and eliminated

---

[135] For a comprehensive and authoritative summary of these aspects of Islam, see Majid Khadduri, *War and Peace in Islam,* Johns Hopkins University Press, Baltimore 1969.

from the face of the earth, as the leaders of Iran, Hizbullah, Hamas, Islamic Jihad and ISIS proclaim openly and repeatedly[136]. Thus rejecting the *dhimmis* and their "false" religions, *a priori* made them the target or murder, harassment, beating, humiliation and persecution, and their oppressors worthy Muslims who implemented the word of Allah, therefore not liable to any prosecution or punishment. When one watches today the shameful scenes in UNESCO, where Muslim countries tabled a resolution dislodging the Jews from their historical status in Jerusalem, just because Muslims refuse to recognize historical and archaeological facts that admit the rights and roots of any other people but the Muslims, instead of intelligently and tolerantly sharing those holy grounds between all historical claimants, one understands the depth of the intolerance built into Muslim faith.

According to Muslim rules, any attack by non-Muslims on Muslims is inherently illegal and immoral, and therefore it is incumbent upon all Muslims to assist their coreligionists, regardless of what they did to provoke the attack. Conversely, any Muslim attack on the West, for example, or on Israel, can always be justified as a defensive war against the Infidels, or as a defense against the spiritual invasion of the West, or as a battle to repulse the enemy from *Dar al-Islam* (for example, Palestine, Andalusia, Kashmir), is *eo ipso* a just war that all Muslims are called upon to support. In other words, once a war against the enemy has been entitled "Jihad", and any of the latter examples justifies a Jihad, the arena is wide open for war. Guerilla war, or *Islamikaze* terrorism and the like, are means of warfare that are allowed by Islam with all the attendant ideological and doctrinal rationalizations. The West has no standing in these definitions, and what it says, thinks or does, will not matter because the Islamic position is Allah- inspired and Shari'a-dictated,

---

[136] See Surat Muhammad 47:4; Surat al-'Imran 3:151; Surat al-Anfal 8: 12 and 8:60; Surat al-Baqarah 33:191 and 193; Surat al-Ahzab 33:26; Surat al-Hashr 59:2; Surat al-Nisa' 4::89; Surat al-Taubah: 9: 36, 73 111.

which means that it is beyond discussion, negotiation, debate, concession or compromise.

External wars in the West are considered quantitative issues (over territories, interests, assets), and when they are terminated, compromises are discussed until an agreement emerges; and when it does, it is binding on the parties who signed the concluding treaty or agreement, like a cease-fire, peace or other conventions. In Islam, wars are qualitative (over ideas, doctrines, "justice", redress of wrongs or simply in response to the Qur'anic injunctions to "battle the Infidel" until he submits or converts to Islam. Wars there are never terminated until the victory of Islam and the imposition of its rules, and if an agreement is signed under duress (for example following a military defeat), it always derives from the precedent of hudaibiyyah that had been established by the Prophet and therefore it became the eternal paradigm of how war should be terminated, if Muslims are obliged by necessity to arrest the war that turned against them. That agreement is therefore temporary (*hudna*), an armistice to gather strength and try again until victory is achieved, like in Muhammad's times; and it is to be violated at the first opportunity when Muslims feel confident enough to have regained superiority, or have found new styles of warfare that the enemy is unable to counter (such as the *Islamikaze* or other forms of asymmetrical war). *Sulh*, i.e. peace-cum-reconciliation, can be concluded only under the terms of a *Pax Islamica*, when the non-Muslims have accepted Islamic hegemony and submitted to its rule. This is the reason why Muslim authorities have justified the Camp David Accords of 1977 and the Oslo Accords of 1993 between the Arabs and Israel, in terms of a temporary hudaibiyyah-like truce which remains open-ended and reversible, when circumstances and the balance of forces so allow. Like during the Prophet's precedent, these agreements were only necessary to extort concessions from the enemy, but once they are made and cashed, they no longer necessarily bind, though Muslims would insist that their rivals adhere to the letter to their strict implementation. This eternal commitment of Islam to subjugate the enemy certainly helps us understand why Infidels under its rule do not justify any equal or advantageous treatment which may give them the idea that they are for ever exempted from the effort to better themselves through Islamization.

The utter contempt towards other faiths and the sense of superiority that Muslims sense toward the other, are well expressed in the next document, part of which was already cited above. It is from the Almohad Dynasty, dating ca 1198 and boasting that no church or synagogue was to be found in the entire realm of the Maghreb:

> Towards the end of his reign, Abū Yūsuf [the Almohad sovereign Abū YūsufYaʿqūb al-Mansūr, r. 1184–1198] ordered the [Muslims] of Jewish origin residing in the Maghreb to distinguish themselves from the rest of the population by wearing a particular attire. This consisted of a dark blue robe with sleeves that were so wide that they fell to their feet and, instead of a turban, a skull-cap (*qalansawa*) reaching past their ears and which was of such misshapen form that it could have been mistaken for a pack-saddle. This dress became that of all the Jews of the Maghreb and remained so right up until the end of the reign of the said prince and the early part of that of his son Abū ʿAbd Allah [the Just, r. 1224–1227]. Upon the multiple entreaties of the Jews who resorted to the intercession of anyone deemed useful to them, the latter sovereign consented to modify this attire. Abū ʿAbd Allah had them wear yellow robes and turbans and this is how they dress to the present day in the year 621 [1224].
>
> The reason why Abū Yūsuf compelled the [new Muslims] to resort to wear distinctive clothing was the doubt he harbored as to the sincerity of their belief: 'Were I sure

that they were true Muslims, he would say, I would allow them to merge with the Muslims through marriage or otherwise; if, however, I were sure that they were Infidels,I should have the men slain, their children enslaved and their belongings confiscated and distributed among the faithful. But I have swayed in their favour'. Ever since the Masmūda came to power we neither afford protection to Jews nor Christians and neither synagogue nor church is to be found throughout all the Muslim lands of the Maghreb. But the Jews in our parts externally profess to Islam; they pray in the mosques and teach the Qu'ran to their children complying with our religion and our law. God alone knows what is concealed in their hearts and what they harbor in their homes.[137]

So much for Islamic tolerance and for their boasting about the peace and harmony that reigned between them and their oppressed *dhimmis*, during the millennium and a half of Muslim dominion over Jews and Christians. In view of this *weltanschauung* of superiority and dominion of others, naturally the rules of war do not apply equally to all belligerents and clearly favor Muslims while only obligating their enemies, thus allowing Muslims to violate their agreements while constantly accusing their adversaries of disregarding their commitments. Thus, the Palestinians for example, committed themselves in Oslo (another hudaibiyyah in the words of their leader, Yasser Arafat), without reserve or qualification, to end terrorism and violence in general, not to introduce into the Palestinian territories any category of forbidden weapons, to maintain their armed forces at agreed levels and under one command, to put an

---

[137] Translation of 'Abd al-Wāhid b. 'Alī al-Marrākushī,20 *Kitāb al-mu'jib fi talkhīs akhbār ahl al-Maghrib* ('History of the Maghreb' written in 1224), ed. Reinhart Dozy (Leyden,1881), 223. *Reproduced as Document A-5 in Fenton and Littman,* p. 55.

end to incitement against Israel and the Jews, and to arrest terrorists and pursue them in justice or to extradite them to Israel. All that was a prerequisite to the progress of the peace process, but once they got to control their territories, they forgot about their obligations and fulfilled none of them; they only remembered Israel's duties under the agreement, which were not fulfilled either once the Palestinians dragged their feet on theirs.[138]. They had become accustomed to breaking their commitments, while Israeli governments were so afraid to "arrest the peace process" that they turned a blind eye and thereby gave the Palestinians the impression that they could get away with any violation. That unequal attitude toward implementing obligations, ultimately brought that peace process to its end. And when a new Israeli government came which made Israeli concessions in the peace accords contingent upon parallel Palestinian implementation, they cried:"foul play!", for they could not accept that they were obliged to do anything in return while Israeli concessions had become in their eyes a matter of course.

Intolerance is based on a concept of superiority, whereby the superior does not have to conform to the rules like the inferior, and this kind of attitude has guided the conduct of Muslims towards other religions. The world is aware of the many churches and synagogues that have been attacked and burned both in Islamdom and by Muslim minorities in the West, and that is considered normal in their eyes, as a continuation of the outrages that *dhimmis*' houses of prayer had suffered for over a millennium under Islam. Similarly, it is normal for them that while mosques must be erected throughout the western world, as of right, Saudi Arabia does not permit any non-Muslim institutions on its territory, and in other Islamic countries where there are any, they are constantly exposed to ravages. Likewise, Muslims can dwell in the entire world, including in the West and Israel, on whose doors they knock continuously for

---

[138] See R. Israeli, *The Oslo Process: the Euphoria of Failure,* Transaction NJ, 2012.

immigration, but several Muslim countries do not permit by law any member of those faiths in dwell in their midst, and certainly not to erect house of prayer, despite the fact that those faiths had pre-existed Islam on those lands before they were conquered and oppressed by Muslim expanding empires. This is hardly an act of tolerance.

No country in the West has seen its nationals follow the same shameful scenes current in the Muslim world, where US and Israeli flags, and the effigies of their leaders are burned ritually as a matter of routine, and even Muslim communities in the West have adopted the same despicable practice in their countries of refuge, amounting to the importation of the Arab-Israeli dispute into the lands which host them, often to their detriment and displeasure. These displays of outrage and contempt for others are not only important to notice for their own sake, but more for the symbols they evoke: they are a dramatic and repetitive expression of what psychologists may dub as "displaced aggression", namely when Muslims are unable to cause the damage they would like to whom they perceive as adversaries or enemies, they discharge their violent feelings and hateful attitudes to others via attacks on the contemptuous symbols of their targets, like symbols, flags, effigies and what have you, filling their own worlds of delusions and fantasies, where words, verbal abuse, demonstrations and destruction of the imagined other, are viewed as if they were attacks on the real targets. And that is often sufficient to calm their moods and to provide a surrogate and an outlet to unsatisfied desires and unrequited ambitions. In this regard, the pogroms, onslaughts on Jewish communities and attacks against Jewish individuals in the open in Islamdom, are of the same kind as the demonstrations of hatred, the manufacture of lies and false accusations, and the occasional attacks on Jewish worshippers or on their houses of worship that we observe today throughout the western world, and that we call "acts of terror".

The amazing phenomenon is that far from awakening Muslims

in the world today to their own intolerance, and prod them to repent and adapt to the international conduct between civilized nations, the moderate among them tend to align with the radicals, and continue to voice their condemnation against the West and Israel, who now substitute for the Christians and Jews of yesteryear, despite the visibly tolerant, "understanding" and forgiving attitudes of the West towards them. For example, when the western world, including Israel, recognized the Palestinian national aspirations, by accepting the PLO and signing agreements with it, the latter on the contrary hardened their position, by their continued attacks of the Jewish national movement (Zionism) which they call "racism", by denying any historical or spiritual link between Jews and their ancient patrimony, and by utterly refusing to recognize Israel as a Jewish state. For they see the concessions made towards them, when giving them international recognition, as a matter of course, and take as "proof" the fact that the world had yielded to their justified demands, while others must be denied the same rights, and be met in Arab and Muslim eyes with a negative response. For Western and Israeli tolerance towards them has confirmed, in their belief, the hegemony of the Muslim faith, patrimony and symbols which no one dares to challenge, while the claims to the same by others have been questioned and challenged by the corrupt UN institutions like UNESCO and the Human Rights Commission.

This has encouraged many Muslim communities in Islamdom and the West, including Israel, to demand the right to construct their mosques, or to perform the Friday rituals in the public square, even when this is known as a holy site to others. On Temple Mount in Jerusalem, for Jerusalem, they built their mosques on a site they knew was holy to the Jews, they transformed many churches (like the Hagia Sophia in Constantinople) and synagogues to mosques during their conquests of expansion, and turned every occupied land into *a waqf* (holy Muslim endowment) that cannot revert under any circumstances to non-Muslims (see repeated references to this in the Hamas Charter that was cited above). But woe to anyone who dares to turn a mosque into another house of prayer, or to occupy land that was, or is, Muslim territory, for that is intolerable and creates a *casus belli*. More recently, in the 1990s, new challenges arose when Muslims began illegally to build a mosque on the grounds and in defiance of, the Basilica of Annunciation in Nazareth; to kneel in prayer on Fridays before the main cathedral of Florence; and to deny the rights of Jews on Temple Mount, thereby declaring to Judaism and Christianity, in Lewis' memorable words: " Your time has passed. Now we are here. Move over"[139].

This is not exactly tolerance in the western sense, which accepts the other as it is, without value judgment, while in Islam the "tolerated", like the *dhimmis*, are considered inherently inferior, and only temporarily suffered, until such a time that they see the light and convert to Islam. In fact, one can see that kind of thinking in the verse from the Qur'an inscribed under the Dome of the Rock in Jerusalem: "He is God, He is One He does not beget, He is not begotten" which was meant to reject the basic dogma of Christianity about God and His Son, when the Muslims took over Jerusalem in the 7th century. That same verse was also inscribed on the temporary tent-mosque in front of the Basilica, which awaited the erection of the permanent mosque (that was ultimately aborted), and had obviously the same intention and meaning. Coupled with the denial of Jewish rights to statehood and on Temple Mount, this signifies in the eyes of Muslims that their creed has superseded both Judaism and Christianity. Hence the Muslim hatred of the construct "Judeo-Christian" tradition, which they regard as having been relegated to a passing episode in history, after the Seal of the Prophets (Muhammad) had dispensed to humanity the latest divine message. "Your time has passed, now we are here", is not only a statement of factual chronological sequence, but also a declaration

---

[139] Lewis B." How did the Infidels Win", *National Post*, 1 June, 2002.

of mastery, hegemony and exclusivity, backed by the will and the power to make it happen in the real world. For a creed that was designed by Allah to replace all others and to bring all humanity under its aegis, cannot be expected to tolerate and accept other faiths, let alone competitors for the same world constituency.

Returning to our main theme of the danger of the West to see its state and national structure dissipate, due to the incessant influx of Muslims to its borders, one should come to the following conclusions:

1. When Muslims predict the demise of the West and its replacement by Muslim rule, they are talking from their past experiences when they implemented that dream over the century, step by state;
2. Islamic political theory still stands firm on their world vision of converting the entire universe to *Dar al-Islam*;
3. Whenever Islam takeover political rule, and world powers allow it to radicalize, as was and likely will be back again ISIS, it has invariably attempted to enforce the laws of *dhimma* on Unbelievers, and there is no reson to assume that they won't do that again if and when they can;
4. Muslims take advantage of Western naivete and loss of fighting spirit, to press their expansionary momentum by exerting their pressure through force of the threat to use force, knowing that Europe and America have no stomach for their corpses returning home from fighting zones, to which Muslim youth have been flocking voluntarily in the thousands, defying martyr's death and rushing eagerly towards it as the highest achievement in their career;
5. Westerners must ask themselves whether the past Mulsim experiences described above are not deterrent enough to prevent them from opening themselves and their territorial sovereignty

to the persistent and unhindered Muslim takeover, whose ultimate goal is not hidden?

6. Cannot Westerners see for themselves that the past glorious Christian civilizations of Byzantine and the Levant have been gnawed to the finish by the Muslim conquests, until today hardly any vestige of them is still there to remind their past history, and even that has been constantly eroded?

7. In Asia too, conquering Islam has ravaged the great civilizations of India and Java and taken them over, an indication of their universal designs; they tore from the ancient and unique Hindu civilization the pieces which made up Pakistan and Bangladesh, into independent Islamic countries and turned the rest of India into a conflict –torn country beween the Hindu majority and the huge Muslim and restive minority of almost two hundred million, which cannot be satisfactorily made to reconcile to their reality; In China, Muslims in the North Western Xinjiang have also been nourishing a separatist movement which puts in permanent jeopardy that emerging great power's national security.

8. As all these trouble making local and regional restive and dissnenting Muslim movements of significant size gather momentum and will come to coordinate their moves, there is no telling what king of world power they can wield in their hands and the potential for rebellion and revolution that they can raise in a coorninated fashion.

9. The weakening of the Western states due to their inability to enforce national unity and one social contract linking between all parts of the citizenry, stemming from the diverging ideals and visions separating the divergent populations, will by necessity prompt the dissolution of the state framework, until a new Muslim Caliphal structure takes over.

Bibliography

Basic Documents

The Holy Qur'an

The Fez Cronicle (Depicting day to day life of the Jewish Community there

Outstanding Examples of Our Civilization for 11th Grade (Textbook in the Palestinian School System)

A Letter from a Gentleman of the Lord Ambassador Howard's Retinue to His Friend in London, dated at Fes, 1st November, 1669 (London: Moses Pitt, 1670). Pp. 152-3 in Fenton and Littman

Tuhfat al- Nazir, (a collection of fatwas, edited by Ali Chenoufi, 1966), A 8, pp. 57-59 in Fenton and Littman

Nawāzil azūna ('Collection of Legal Consultations') (Rabat: Bibliothèque Générale), Ms 521Q, fol.29b–30a., Cited in P. 58 in Fenton and Litman

Written and Electronic Media

AFP – Agence France Presse (French News Agency

Al-Ahram al-Arabi

Al-Ahrar, Egypt

American Thinker.com

Al-Arabi, Egypt

AP (Associated Press)

al-Ayyam (Yemen),
BBC News
Christian Science Monitor
Christian Voice
City Journal
Daily Telegraph,
Al Dustour, Jordan,
ExpressandStar
Front Page Magazine.com
Al-Hayat, London
.Al-Hayat, London
Jawa Report
Jerusalem Post
JoongAng Ilbo. South Korea
magazine@tikkun.org
MEMRI
Middle East Quarterly
Middle East Times
National Post
Neues Deutchland
The New York Sun
The New York Times Review of Books
The Times
Online Journalism Review
Le Point
Al Quds al-Arabi, (London*)*
Al Sharq al-Awsat, London
Terrorism and Political Violence
Al-Usbu', Egypt,
Al Usbu' al-Arabi, The Literary Weekly, Damascus
Wall Street Journal
The Weekly Standard
Die Welt

Books.

Baladhuri, Al-, *Kitab Futuh al-Buldan* (The Book of the Conquest of Countries), translated by Philip Hitti, Columbia, NY, 1916, cited by Bay Ye'or, *The Decline of Eastern Christianity Under Islam: From Islam to Dhimmitude*, Fairleigh Dickinson University Press, Madison, 1996, pp.272-3.

Bat Ye'or, *The Decline of Eastern Christianity Under Islam: From Islam to Dhimmitude*, Fairleigh Dickinson University Press, Madison, 1996.

Bat Ye'or, *Juifs et Chretiens sous l'Islam:Les Dhimmis face au defi Inegriste*, Paris, Berg International, 1994.

Bat Ye'or, *Islam and Dhimmitude*, Fairleigh Dickinson University Press, Madison, 2002.

Broder, Henryk, *Hurrah Wir Kapitulieren* (Hurrah, We Capitulate) München: Pantheon 2006.

Brenner, Emmanuel, *Les Territoires Perdus de la Republique*, 2002 (Editions Mille et une Nuits), Paris.

Bostom, Andy, *Islamic Antisemitism*, Prometheus Books, Amherst NY, 2008.

Bukay, David, *Islam and the Infidels: the Politics of Jihad, Da'wah and Hijrah,* Transaction NJ, 2016, p. 61.

Dhahabi, Muhammad al, *Ta'rikh al islam* (the History of Islam), Vol 50, Beirut, Dar al-Kitab al Arabi,, 1997 (Cited in Fenton and Littman).

Fenton, Paul and David Littman *Exile in the Maghreb*: Jews under Islam, Fairleigh Dickinson University Press, Madison, 2016.

Fernandez Morera, Dario, *The Myth of the Andalusian Paradise: Muslims, Christians, and Jews under Islamic Rule in Medieval Spain*, ISI Books, Wilmington, *2016.*

Houellebecq, Michel, *Soumission* (*Submission)* (Paris, 2015).

Ibn 'Aqnīn, Joseph, *Tibb al-nufūs* ('Hygiene of the Souls'), chap. 4, Ms Oxford, Bodl. Neubauer 1273, fols. 143–46. Cited in Pp. 52-55 in Fenton and Littman.

Israeli, Raphael, *Fundamentalist Islam and Israel:Essays in Interpretation,* University Press of America, Lanham, 1993.

Israeli —, *Muslims in China: a Study of Cultural Confrontation,* Curzon and Humanities Press, London and Atlantic Heights, 1980.

Israeli —, *Islam in China:Religion, Ethnicity, Culture and Politics,* Lexington Books, 2002.

Israeli —, *Back to Nowhere: Moroccan Jews in Dream and Reality,* Lampert Press, Germany, 2008.

Israeli —, *Muslim Minorities in Modern States: the Challenge of Assimilation,* Transaction, NJ, 2009, pp. 5-12.

Israeli —, *Islamikaze: Manifestations of Islamic Martyrology,* Frank Cass, London, 2003, the Introduction.

Israeli, Raphael, *Christianophobia: the Persecution of Christian Minorities under Islam,* WIPF and Stock, Oregon, 2016.

Israeli —, *Muslim Fundamentalism in Israel,,* Brassey's, London 1993.

Israeli —, *The Oslo Process: the Euphoria of Failure,* Transaction NJ, 2012.

Israeli —, *Retreating from the Mirage of Multi-Culturalism? The cases of Holland, Britain and Israel; Strategic Books TX. 2016.*

Israeli—The Internationalization of ISIS: The Islamic State in Iraq and Syria,Transaction, NJ, 2016, expcially, Ch. Three, The Islamic State in the Making.

Israeli —,*Misnomers and Cultural Choices: How Islam Tries to Impose its Norms on non-Muslims,* Strategic Books, TX, 2019.

Israeli, —, *Defeat, Trauma, Lesson,* Strategic Books, Texas, 2012.

Israeli —, *The Intractable Dispute: WHay Are Muslims and Arabs at Loggerheads with Jews and Israel.* Strategic Books, TX, 2019 .

Khadduri, Majid, *War and Peace in Islam,* Johns Hopkins University Press, Baltimore 1969.

Maghili, Sheikh al-, *Risala fil-Yahud* (Treatise Against the Jews) (ca 1495), ed. and published in Rabat, 2005, Cited in Fenton and Littman, Doc A-12, pp. 71-85.

Marrakushi, Abd al Wahid al, *Kitab al-Mu'jib fi takhlis akhbar al-Maghrib* (A summary of Maghribi History, 1224, edt. By R. Dozy, Leiden 1881. Document A 5 in Fenton and Littman, p. 55.

Nisan, Mordecai, *Minorities in the Middle East: A History of Struggle and Self-Expression*, McFarland & Company, Jefferson, NC. 2002.

Phillips, Melanie, *Londonistan: How Britain is Creating a Terror State Within,* Gibson Square, London. 2006.

Spencer, Robert, (ed), *The Myth Of Islamic Tolerance: How Islamic Law Treats Non-Muslims*, Prometheus books, 2005.

Yegar, Moshe, *Between Integration and Secession:the |Muslim Communities of Southeast Asia*, Lexington BOkks, Lanham, 2002.

Articles

Abu al-Hassan, Sheikh, (the Head of the fatwa Council), Cited by *MEMRI*, "Terror in America", No 28, 11 October, 2001.

Anderson, Andrew and Chris Hastings, "July 7 Bombs were a Demo, not Terrorism", *The Daily Telegraph*, 9 April 2006.

Barry, Colleen, "EU Proposes Monitoring Radical Mosques", *AP*, 12May, 2007.

Blair, Alexandra, "Teachers Demand End to State Cash for Faith Schools ", *The Times*, 12 April, 2006.

Darymple, Theodore, "An Update from France", *Wall Street Journal,* 11 February, 2006.

Demonpion, Denis, "Interview with Jean-Claude Marin", *Le Point*, 20 October, 2005, p. 25.

Dopfner, Matthias, "*Bush ist Dumm und Bose*" (Bush is Stupid and Evil), *Die Welt,* 21 April 2004.

"Dudley Mosque Refused Planning Permission", *Christian Voice*, 27 February, 2007.

Ehrenfeld, Rachel, "When in Rome…" *The New York Sun*, 19 April, 2006.

Farmawi, Doctor, Cited by *MEMRI*, "Terror in America", No 28, 11 October, 2001, Ibid.

Fatihi, Doctor, *AL-Ahram al-Arabi* of 20 October, 2001.

"Full Facts: Plea on Muslim Village", *Express and Star,* April, 2007.

Gabriel, Brigitte, "Muslims Muzzling Memphis", *American Thinker. com*, 10 April, 2006.

Gardham, Dancan "Tough Rules Expose Scale of Bogus Marriages", *The Daily Telegraph*, 16 May, 2005.

Glazov, Jamie, "Islamic Imperialism: Interview with Efraim Karsh", *Front Page Magazine.com*, 5 May, 2006.

Israeli,Raphael " The Charter of Allah: The Platform of the Islamic Resistence Movement", in *Fundamentalist Islam and Israel:Essays in Interpretation,* University Press of America, Lanham, 1993, p.123-170.

Israeli—"Islamikaze and their Significance", in *Terrorism and Political Violence,* 9:3, 1997, pp. 96-121.

Johnston.Philip," Rules to Stop Sham Marriages", THe *Daily Telegraph*, 24 May, 2007.

Kanfer, Stefan, ""France vs France: France's Muslim Prroblem will only get Worse", *City Journal*, Winter, 2006.

Kennedy Houck, David, "The Islamist Challenge to the US Constitution", *Middle East Quarterly*, Spring, 2006.

Knausgaard, Karl Ove, (Review of Hoellebecq) *The New Your Times Review of Books, November 8, 2015.*

Lagnado, Lucette. "Lawrence Durrell's Justine: Missing Alexandria", *Wall Street Journal*, October 19, 2019.

"Land Plan Becomes Raging Issue", ExpressandStar, 24 April, 2007.

Lewis, Bernard, "How did the Infidels Win?", *National Post,* 1 June, 2002.

Mat'ani, Doctor, Cited by *MEMRI*, "Terror in America", No 28,11 October, 2001.

Mawry, Munir al-, "Arab Intellectual s Receive Death Threats", *Al-Sharq al Awsat*, 10 April, 2006.

Paton, Graeme,"Academic: Extremism Debate is Being Stifled", *The Daily Telegraph*, 17 March 2007.

Petre, Jonathan, "Church Acts to Stem Sham Marriages", *The Daily Telegraph,* 23 April, 2007.

Pipes, Daniel, "Fighting Militant Islam, Without Bias", *City Journal*, Autumn, 2001.

Sabah, 'Atallah abu al- "A Letter to America", *al Risala,* 13 September, 2001, cited in *MEMRI*, "Terror in America", No 1.

Shahin, Doctor, *MEMRI*, "Terror in America", No 28, 16 October,2001.

Schwartz, Stephen, "Islam in the Big House: How Radical Muslims took over the American Prison System", *The Weekly Standard*, 24 April 2006.

Schwartz, Stephen, "Remarks in Domestic Security Preparedness Conference" on 12 April, 2006.

Underwood, Peter. "Multiculturalism in Korea". JoongAng Ilbo. South Korea 26 August 2010.

Shackelford, Rusty ("John Doe") "Islamists Post Hit-lists of Apostates", the *Jawa Report*, 11 April, 2006.

Simpson, Victor, "Europeans see Need for Power to Snoop", *AP*, 11 April, 2006.

"Spain Publishes Public School Primer on Islam", *AP*, cited by the *Jerusalem Post* .

Steele, John, "Freedom of Speech Row as talk on Islamic Extremists is Banned", *The Daily Telegraph*, 15 March, 2007.

Vidino, Lorenzo, "State Department Flirting with the Muslim Brotherhood",, 20 April, 2006. In the *Islamic Extremism in Europe Hearing,*before the Committee on Foreign Realtions, US Senate, 5 April 2006.

Zavis, Cat, "Prophet Jonah, Murder of Another Black Man by a White Police Officer, and the Limits of Forgiveness ", co-editor of Tikkun Magazine, magazine@tikkun.org, October, 2019.

Review Requested:
If you loved this book, would you please provide a review at
Amazon.com?